NEW DIMENSIONS OF CONNECTIVITY IN THE ASIA-PACIFIC

NEW DIMENSIONS OF CONNECTIVITY IN THE ASIA-PACIFIC

EDITED BY CHRISTOPHER FINDLAY
AND SOMKIAT TANGKITVANICH

Australian
National
University

PRESS

Pacific Trade and Development Conference Series
(PAFTAD)

ANU PRESS

Published by ANU Press
The Australian National University
Acton ACT 2601, Australia
Email: anupress@anu.edu.au

Available to download for free at press.anu.edu.au

ISBN (print): 9781760464745
ISBN (online): 9781760464752

WorldCat (print): 1277217753
WorldCat (online): 1277206715

DOI: 10.22459/NDCAP.2021

Cover design and layout by ANU Press

Contents

Abbreviations

4G	fourth generation
5G	fifth generation
ADB	Asian Development Bank
AI	artificial intelligence
AIIB	Asian Infrastructure Investment Bank
APEC	Asia-Pacific Economic Cooperation
ARCII	Asia-Pacific Regional Cooperation and Integration Index
ASEAN	Association of Southeast Asian Nations
AVOD	ad-based video-on-demand
B2B	business-to-business
B2C	business-to-consumer
BCIMEC	Bangladesh–China–India–Myanmar Economic Corridor
BRF	Belt and Road Forum
BRI	Belt and Road Initiative
BRICS countries	Brazil, Russia, India, China and South Africa
BRITCC	Belt and Road Initiative Tax Cooperation Conference
C2B	consumer-to-business
C2C	consumer-to-consumer
CCWAEC	China–Central Asia–West Asia Economic Corridor
CDB	China Development Bank
CELAC	Community of Latin American and Caribbean States

CGE	computable general equilibrium
Chinalco	Aluminium Corporation of China Limited
CIPEC	China–Indochina Peninsula Economic Corridor
CLM countries	Cambodia, Laos and Myanmar
CMREC	China–Mongolia–Russia Economic corridor
CPEC	China–Pakistan Economic Corridor
DAI	Digital Adoption Index
e-tailing	electronic retailing
ERS	extraregional sellers
EU	European Union
EWEC	East–West Economic Corridor
Exim Bank	Export–Import Bank of China
FDI	foreign direct investment
GDP	gross domestic product
GIS	geographic information system
GMM	generalised method of moments
GMS	Greater Mekong Subregion
GMV	gross merchandise value
GNI	gross national income
GPP	gross provincial product
GVC	global value chain
ICT	information and communication technology
ID	identity document
IoT	Internet of Things
JICA	Japan International Cooperation Agency
Lao PDR	Lao People's Democratic Republic
LPI	Logistics Performance Index
Mbps	megabits per second
MDB	multilateral development bank
MLEC	Model Law on Electronic Commerce (United Nations)
MPAC	Master Plan of ASEAN Connectivity

MSR	21st Century Maritime Silk Road
NCEI	US National Centers for Environmental Information
NDB	New Development Bank
NDBI	Normalized Difference Built-Up Index
NDRC	National Development and Reform Commission
NELB	New Eurasian Land Bridge
NIR	near-infrared
NSRI	New Silk Road Initiative
ODA	official development assistance
ODF	overseas development funding
OECD	Organisation for Economic Co-operation and Development
OFDI	outward foreign direct investment
P3	public–private partnership
PBC	People's Bank of China
PPP	purchasing power parity
PSR	Polar Silk Road
RMB	renminbi
SDG	Sustainable Development Goal
SEZ	special economic zone
SGE	static structural general equilibrium
Sinosure	China Export & Credit Insurance Corporation
SMEs	small and medium-sized enterprises
SOA	State Oceanic Administration
SREB	Silk Road Economic Belt
SRF	Silk Road Fund
SWIR	shortwave infrared
THB	Thai baht
UN	United Nations
UNESCAP	United Nations Economic and Social Commission for Asia and the Pacific

UPU	Universal Postal Union
US	United States
USGS	United States Geological Survey
WHO	World Health Organization
WTO	World Trade Organization

List of figures

List of boxes and tables

Contributors

Christopher Findlay is Honorary Professor in the Crawford School of Public Policy at The Australian National University.

Cyn-Young Park is Director of the Regional Cooperation and Integration Division in the Economic Research and Regional Cooperation Department, Asian Development Bank.

Natasha Beschorner is a senior digital development specialist in the Digital Development Department, World Bank.

Pelagia Karpathiotaki is a researcher in the Academy of China Open Economy Studies at the University of International Business and Economics, Beijing.

Racquel Claveria is a PhD student in economics at the University of Barcelona and a consultant at the Economic Research and Regional Cooperation Department, Asian Development Bank.

Santitarn Sathirathai is Group Chief Economist of Sea Group.

Somkiat Tangkitvanich is President of the Thailand Development Research Institute.

Yunhua Tian is a researcher in the School of Economics and Trade, Guangdong University of Foreign Studies.

Voraprapa Nakavachara is Assistant to the president for Global Engagement and a lecturer in the Faculty of Economics, Chulalongkorn University, Bangkok.

Wichsinee Wibulpolprasert is a research fellow at the Thailand Development Research Institute.

Winit Theanvanichpant is a researcher at the Thailand Development Research Institute.

Xiaohao Huang is a researcher in the School of Economics and Trade at Guangdong University of Foreign Studies.

Xun Wang is a research fellow in the National School of Development and the Institute of Digital Finance, Peking University.

Yanping Zhou is a researcher in the School of Economics and Trade at Guangdong University of Foreign Studies.

Yiping Huang is Professor and Deputy Director of the National School of Development and the Institute of Digital Finance at Peking University, and Chair of the China Finance 40 Forum Academic Committee.

Preface

The Pacific Trade and Development (PAFTAD) conference was held in Bangkok between 16 and 19 July 2019 with the theme 'New dimensions of connectivity in the Asia Pacific'. The conference was hosted by the Thailand Development Research Institute (TDRI) in conjunction with the International Institute for Trade and Development and the Mekong Institute. The papers presented at the conference are collected in this volume.

The 40th PAFTAD conference met to consider the policy and capacity gaps impeding greater connectivity in Asia and how to alleviate them. Significant economic gains are available from better connectivity. Regional connectivity is a key driver of trade integration and investment facilitation. Investment in the capacity to provide connectivity frees up the movement of goods and services, as well as the complementary flows of people and data. Improved access to and the provision of better quality infrastructure leads to falling trade costs and the creation of more efficient regional value chains. Second-round effects of enhanced connectivity include higher productivity and poverty reduction. Still, funding gaps persist that preclude the improvements in connectivity infrastructure offers, despite the benefits.

The chapters in this volume look at regional connectivity performance, China's Belt and Road Initiative (BRI), the impacts of connectivity—both physical and digital—and questions around investment in facilities to support connectivity. Close attention is paid to the impediments to infrastructure investment and how to overcome them. Preparing a commonly shared vision for infrastructure development in the region and developing a set of principles for the good governance of infrastructure projects could be the first steps to improving connectivity. The process emerging from sharing experiences in implementing these steps would benefit from consideration of how it links to other forms of regional cooperation. This can complement the role of multilateral development banks in deepening connectivity and actions to foster interactions between government and private sector investors.

A distinguished group of economists from East Asia and the Pacific met to discuss how regional cooperation and national government action can break the deadlocks related to policy and capacity gaps on connectivity. PAFTAD conferences have made an important contribution to policy thinking and policy development in the Asia-Pacific region for over 40 years. PAFTAD is famous for extensive discussion and debate around each chapter at the conference, followed by extensive revision for publication.

The PAFTAD team is grateful for the contributors to the book who collaborated enthusiastically to bring this research to publication. Our debt to the authors in the volume is obvious. Further, we are grateful for the invaluable and substantive contributions made by Peter Drysdale, Hugh Patrick, Mari Pangestu, Adam Triggs, Akira Kohsaka, Anna Strutt, Celia Reyes, Chia Siow Yue, Chul Chung, David Dollar, Edward Chen, Erik van der Marel, Francis Hutchinson, Gilberto Llanto, Il-Houng Lee, Jayant Menon, Jonathan Tsuen Yip Wong, Joseph Yap, Juan Palacios, Khalil Hamdani, Lin Chen, Lin Chien-Fu, Mia Mikic, Muhamad Chatib Basri, Narongchai Akrasanee, Robert Scollay, Shekhar Shah, Shiro Armstrong, Shujiro Urata, Siwage Dharma Negara, Somkiat Tangkitvanich, Souknilanh Keola, Stephen Howes, Tomoo Kikuchi, Vo Tri Thanh, Watcharas Leelawath, Wendy Dobson, Yiping Huang, Yves Tiberghien, Zaw Oo and Zhang Monan. They helped refine arguments and ideas at the conference and engage in thinking on connectivity issues facing Asian economies.

Narongchai Akrasanee, Twarath Sutabutr and Shujiro Urata participated in a stimulating panel discussion at the forum, which focused on how to connect the ASEAN Smart Cities Network. This was also Mari Pangestu's last conference as PAFTAD chair after many years of engagement with the group. Mari departed PAFTAD to take on a directorship at the World Bank. We are deeply grateful for her leadership of PAFTAD and regular presence at the conferences.

We are indebted to Sam Hardwick of ANU, and Wisarn Pupphavesa, Nuchanart Phumphruk and Jirakorn Yingpaiboonwong of the TDRI team, for all stages of the management of the PAFTAD conference that made it such a success. The book would not exist if it were not for the hard work of Dorothy Mason and later Brandon Harrington for managing PAFTAD, the publication process and the editors through to the finalisation of the book in 2021.

The PAFTAD International Steering Committee and the PAFTAD International Secretariat are grateful for the generous support of the donors whose continuing support make this important work possible. They include the Ford Foundation, the Canadian International Development Research Centre, the Korean Institute of International Economic Policy, the Asia Foundation of Toronto University, the National University of Singapore, the Taiwan Institute of International Economic Research, Colombia University, Sanaree Holdings and, last but not least, The Australian National University.

May we extend our sincere thanks to Emily Tinker, Teresa Prowse and ANU Press for working so patiently with us through the production process. We express our gratitude to Jan Borrie for her excellent copyediting work.

This is an important collection of essays at a critical point in time for the global economy where Asia can lead an effort to improve physical and digital connectivity. Infrastructure gaps threaten to prolong any recovery and perpetuate regional trade bottlenecks and stall deeper regional integration.

Christopher Findlay and Somkiat Tangkitvanich
September 2021

Introduction

Christopher Findlay and Somkiat Tangkitvanich

Introduction

A large body of research reports that significant gains are available from better connectivity. The consequences of investment in capacity to provide connectivity lead to significant changes in the full cost of movements of goods and services, as well as of the complementary flows of people and data.

With respect to goods, better connectivity has the most immediate effects in terms of trade flows, and thereby growth and equity (De 2006, 2009). In goods, infrastructure quality affects trade and port efficiency has the largest impact among all indicators (Nordås and Piermartini 2004). On the other hand, a deterioration in infrastructure raises trade costs (Limão and Venables 2001). Falls in trade costs facilitate the unbundling of production processes and the construction of value chains (Baldwin 2012). With respect to services, the World Trade Organization (WTO) has concluded that trade costs are higher than those for goods, but they have also fallen in the past two decades—one driver of which has been investment in infrastructure (WTO 2019b: Part D1).

There are second-round effects of these immediate consequences on productivity and growth. Work on the effects of participation in trade, at the firm level, highlights important effects of falling costs of engaging in trade (Bernard et al. 2018; Shu and Steinwender 2018). Participating in trade across borders involves significant setup costs and, if these costs are lowered (due to falling full costs of connectivity), more firms will participate. Those who do participate are likely to be the more productive firms, since they are the ones able to cover these setup costs. Falling costs of connectivity allow these firms to grow, likely also crowding out the less efficient, so productivity at an industry level improves. Furthermore, participation in trade can be a driver of productivity growth and innovation at the firm level.

Connectivity investments are linked to poverty reduction. They reduce the costs of participating in markets, which can have a substantial contribution to reductions in poverty. The incidence of transport costs is borne by farmers who sell into large markets where they are price-takers. Reductions in those costs can have a substantial impact on their labour income. With poverty concentrated in rural areas in developing countries, the consequences for its reduction can be important. For example, Menon and Warr (2008) model the effects of road investments in the Lao People's Democratic Republic (PDR), where they find interesting differences between types of road investment: far greater poverty reductions occur when areas with no roads are provided with dry-season access, compared with the extension to year-round access in areas with dry-weather roads.

This volume includes chapters on the consequences of changes in both physical and digital connectivity[1] for trade, for the location of economic activity, for forms of doing business (the growth of ecommerce in particular) and for the delivery of new services (especially in the financial sector). A study of China's Belt and Road Initiative (BRI) is also included. These studies are preceded by an assessment of the connectivity performance in the Asia-Pacific region and followed by a discussion of impediments to investment in projects that contribute to productivity. The collection as a whole provides the basis for a series of recommendations for regional cooperation, which are presented at the conclusion of this overview chapter.

Connectivity performance

In Chapter 1, Cyn-Young Park and Racquel Claveria provide a set of indicators of connectivity performance in the region, which they also combine into an overall index. They begin with an examination of recent indicators of infrastructure quality, which is relevant to

---

1   Other dimensions of connectivity regularly considered include those between people and between institutions. These, for example, are referred to along with physical connectivity in the master plans of ASEAN connectivity. The former are not included here (for a comprehensive discussion of migration, see World Bank 2018) and aspects of institutional connectivity are referred to in this collection in relation to regulatory alignment.

connectivity, including road infrastructure and the provision of rail, air and sea transport. They find that, compared with the world as a whole, performance indicators in Asia are generally higher, but there remains considerable variation within the region. South and Central Asia tend to perform less well than East and Southeast Asia.

The authors then link this performance in infrastructure to various indicators relevant to trade in goods. One of these is the trend in trade costs and another is a set of indicators of logistics performance. Generally, trade costs have fallen in the region and are now lowest in East Asia. What is alarming, however, are the relatively high costs of trade among Pacific Island economies. A similar pattern applies to logistics performance.

The authors also provide a measure of the regulatory environment that affects those movements. They find that, in 2019, Asia and the Pacific scored 15 percentage points below world's best practice in this respect. East and Southeast Asia are the best performers in the region. The European Union is taken as the benchmark for this assessment; however, there remains an interesting question, and a topic for further work, about the importance of the choice of institutions for integration (formal structures, as in the European Union, or market-led arrangements, as in East Asia) to create improvements in connectivity performance.

The authors extend their coverage of performance indicators of connectivity by considering the costs and time of moving goods across borders. They note the reduction in these items since 2014, especially in Central and South Asia, and also East and Southeast Asia. Gaps remain, however. Average border compliance time in South Asia is now about three days (down from five), but in East Asia, the time to complete export requirements is 18 hours (and 31 hours for imports). The consequences are significant: Hummels and Schaur (2013) find that the daily *ad valorem* tariff equivalent of time in transit is between 0.6 and 2.1 per cent. The assessment of Park and Claveria is that further reductions in these costs are possible, involving building more efficient infrastructure and changes in regulatory and other policy, including compliance with standards.

Park and Claveria examine linkages between infrastructure quality, regional integration and growth. They apply the Asia-Pacific Regional Cooperation and Integration Index (ARCII) of the Asian Development Bank (ADB), which refers to trade and investment, financial flows, regional value chains, infrastructure connectivity, movement of people and institutional integration. They observe that connectivity carries considerable weight in this measure and its contribution has increased over time. They also report the results of a study of the sources of growth in 156 countries over the decade to 2016 (noting that this period is relatively short for such studies). They find that changes in infrastructure connectivity make a significant contribution both to growth and to reductions in inequality, as well as to the extent of poverty in an economy. They stress, however, the important interactions, and two-way relationships, of infrastructure connectivity with other dimensions of the ARCII.

China's Belt and Road Initiative

The BRI is an important contributor to connectivity in the region. Pelagia Karpathiotaki, Yunhua Tian, Yanping Zhou and Xiaohao Huang examine in Chapter 2 the origins and consequences of the BRI, which consists of both land and sea corridors linking Europe and Asia. They present key elements of the BRI concept and their consistency with various elements of Chinese ways of thinking about development and the role of China in the world economy and with models of geopolitics. The governance model is also discussed, and forces leading to a more multilateral approach than originally proposed are identified.

This chapter also examines the contribution of the BRI to connectivity—first, in terms of reduced shipping times and the potential contribution to greater digital connectivity. The value of policy coordination across countries to improve performance is also noted. The conversion of these physical dimensions to economic effects is then explained, referring to significant falls in trade costs and also the positive consequences for trade flows, among the BRI members as well as between members and the rest of the world. In addition, there are positive spillovers from the BRI to trade costs among non-members. Other impacts examined include the shape of the trade network (showing China in a more central role), an increase in foreign direct investment (FDI) flows among, and from the rest of the world to, BRI members, and the reconstruction of global value chains among members with a greater focus on China.

Commentary on the BRI has identified a number of risks related to political and legal changes, the consequences for debt and environmental impacts. Efforts by China to respond to these issues are noted, including the application of frameworks for the assessment of debt sustainability and changes in governance arrangements. On procurement questions, the authors note three channels: national action, leadership by China in the design of processes and participation in multilateral structures such as those provided by the WTO.[2]

Impacts of connectivity: Physical

In Chapter 3, Wichsinee Wibulpolpresert, Winit Theanvanichpant and Somkiat Tangkitvanich provide a study of the consequences of investments in physical connectivity—in particular, the second (opened in 2011) and third (2013) Thai–Laos Friendship bridges across the Mekong River. They assess the three-way interaction of the infrastructure investment, local economic activity and urbanisation. The authors provide context for their case by reviewing studies of the consequences of improved connectivity. They refer to studies of the manner in which infrastructure investment reduces trade costs and to a number of studies of the situation in China, where high-speed rail connectivity improved dramatically. Common results in that work are that peripheral cities can decline as employment agglomerates in transport hubs. They stress, therefore, the chance that outcomes from improved connectivity will be uneven across localities. These distributional consequences are a factor in community responses to proposals for and the operation of new infrastructure facilities.

Wibulpolpresert et al. explain the differences in the context of the two bridges. The second bridge is linked to an existing special economic zone on the Laos side of the river, which had attracted FDI from Japan. The sequence of events they suggest was that industrialisation (via the zone) drove local urbanisation and the demand for connective infrastructure. The third bridge was built in the absence of local industrialisation and was designed to add to regional connectivity in general. In that case, the bridge might drive industrialisation and then, perhaps, urbanisation. The sequence of events is different in that case.

The authors explore these relationships using data on various economic variables measured at the regional level. Of special interest, however, is their use of satellite imagery, primarily to assess changes in urbanisation. The authors discuss the strengths and weaknesses of this novel data source.

---

2   China has provided a new proposal to join the WTO Government Procurement Agreement (see WTO 2019a).

Findings of the chapter include, first, evidence of the growth of cross-border trade as a result of the construction of the bridges. However, the authors find less-significant impacts in the local area of the bridges. Urbanisation did expand in the region, but the opening of the bridges did not shift its patterns significantly, which continued to be linked to existing highways and urban areas. There are echoes here of the outcomes of the studies of better connectivity in China, where direct proximity to new infrastructure has uneven effects.

The authors also stress that the consequences of connectivity depend on the context. They find that, in the case of the second bridge, where a special economic zone already existed, industrialisation was the driver of demand for connectivity. In the case of the third bridge, a special economic zone was built following its construction, so connectivity led rather than followed.

Impacts of connectivity: Digital

Moving from physical connectivity, the following three chapters of the collection examine the impacts of and issues with digital connectivity.

Natasha Beschorner begins, in Chapter 4, with a review of the growth of the application of digital technology and its implications, including the growth of e-commerce and digital services trade. However, the author observes the relatively low application (to 2018) of digital technology by individuals, business and government in the region, relative to world experience and according to a range of indicators relevant to each group. She also notes the prospects offered by further technological change, moving beyond the use of cloud computing to the application of 5G mobile networks and artificial intelligence.

Beschorner then seeks to understand the origins of the position of the region on the application of digital technology by reviewing the status of five elements—namely, connectivity, payments systems, skills in the workforce, complementary logistics, and digital policy and regulation. A number of indicators are compiled for each item. The policy measures include those relating to privacy, cybersecurity, consumer protection, digital entrepreneurship, and digital government and identification (ID). The author reports the variable performance across the region in all elements. She finds issues of commission and omission: some areas have excessive regulation or intervention but in others there are gaps to be filled. The author provides a list of priorities for action at the country level for each of the five elements.

The author notes that there are perceptions of new risks associated with the growth of the digital economy (such as the abuse of personal data or cyberattacks, as well as changes in labour markets) and calls for further work on the choice of the appropriate responses. The author also stresses the new opportunities for greater inclusiveness following the development of the digital economy.

Noting the interactions involved in the digital economy, the author makes the case for regional cooperation to support progress on raising the levels of performance in each of the five elements of its foundation, and provides examples of priorities for such cooperation—a theme of which is the focus on interoperability and regulatory alignment.

The focus in this chapter is generally on Association of Southeast Asian Nations (ASEAN) members. There is scope in further work to add to the analysis here by benchmarking ASEAN policy against others in the rest of the world including China. This work is facilitated by the release of new measures assessing policy applying to digital transactions (see, for example, Ferracane et al. 2018) and the consequences of the policy environment for various performance measures, such as the growth of digital transactions domestically and across borders, as well as the association between them. It is interesting to check, for example, whether regimes that are locally competitive but closed to cross-border transactions, and in which domestic transactions have also grown rapidly (see Chapter 6 by Huang and Wang for example), lead to the growth of international competitiveness.

There follow two chapters on specific elements of the digital economy: one on the consequences of the growth of e-commerce and the other on the payments systems in China.

Santitarn Sathirathai and Voraprapa Nakavachara review the impact of the growth of e-commerce on firms selling on the relevant platforms in Thailand in Chapter 5. They note the presence of many studies of the impacts on buyers who operate on e-commerce platforms but the lesser amount of work on the effects on sellers. They also note that much of the research literature examines the case of China, with less attention given to Southeast Asia. They then work with a relevant platform in Thailand to collect a large dataset of the experiences of nearly 7,000 merchants.

Sathirathai and Nakavachara begin by examining the effect of participation in e-commerce on the income of the participants' household, for participants who both did and did not previously operate a business offline. Both groups reported growth in household income, but the channels of effect differed. For new participants, the effect, not surprisingly, came via the additional or supplementary source of income. Of more interest are the results for the established firms, where the effects are more complex. These both lifted sales and improved efficiency. They were able to reach larger markets by lowering the effective cost of distance, which increased their extensive (number of clients) margin. They also increased sales outside their own region, adding to trade connectivity across the country. Of interest also is that the largest effects were found to be in the poorest regions.

Given these positive results, especially for inclusiveness, the authors propose a series of government actions to ameliorate impediments to participation in e-commerce, including infrastructure that provides access to the internet, building digital skills and regulatory reform to remove impediments to the growth of logistics and electronic payments.

In Chapter 6, Yiping Huang and Xun Wang discuss the development of mobile payment systems in China. They note the constraints on the development of and disincentives for the use of online payment systems that are common in other countries (card-reader machines and processing fees, respectively, as well as lack of trust among both buyers and sellers) and then, given the role of cash as a dominant medium of exchange, the scope for new payment systems to emerge. These were prompted in this context by the development of smartphone and QR-code technology. They report the rapid growth of mobile payment users since 2013 and provide a case study of the development of the largest provider, AliPay. The authors also outline the domestic regulatory reform that facilitated the growth of the system, including the recognition of electronic systems and the ability of nonfinancial institutions to participate in payment systems.

The authors note a number of additional consequences of the development of mobile payment systems, other than effects on the volume of transactions. One is that these systems lowered the cost of transfers, allowing families to share risk (migrant workers remitting income to their families, for instance, which previously might have been sent via travelling friends or bus drivers). The costs of entry into payment systems were reduced, which also facilitated the growth of new businesses or new areas of activity for existing business (as in the previous chapter on e-commerce in Thailand), which had the effect of supporting entrepreneurship development in China.

Huang and Wang discuss the internationalisation of the Chinese mobile payment system, given its domestic growth. A driver of its extension offshore was the rapid growth in tourists from China to international destinations. Another element of internationalisation is that the experience of development of the mobile payment systems supported the development of other capabilities related to financial transactions (or fintech, in other words), which added to the international competitiveness of the providers. There was an extension of mobile payments to loans, for example. In contrast, the authors note that members of the fintech sector in Southeast Asia remain focused on payment systems, and both regulatory and technological factors constrain their extension into new areas.

Other limiting factors to the growth of this sector are infrastructure and financial literacy. In response to these constraints, some countries have developed 'sandboxes' in which to experiment, while managing the risks involved, with new regulatory regimes.

Huang and Wang conclude by noting other issues that deserve attention, including the ownership and privacy of the data being collected. The application of artificial intelligence to the transaction data on file is in principle highly valuable, but its application leads to questions about who owns the relevant data and whether customers have made or are willing to make their data available. Another is the divide between communities with access to relevant infrastructure and those without. Rapid growth of this system then risks exacerbating inequalities. A third issue is a set of regulatory challenges as companies managing payment systems extend into wider sets of financial transactions and compete with banks, rather than, as originally occurred, being complementary to them. This potentially also leads to risks associated with contagion and when these businesses are internationally connected to balance-of-payments issues. The authors propose attention to options for both prudential supervision and consumer protection in this sector. A further issue could be the implications for competition of the 'winner takes all' aspect of these services, driven by the value of the network effects. This is a challenge for regional cooperation when market power gained in a large domestic market can be projected into performance in markets of trading partners.

Investment in connectivity

The final chapter, by Christopher Findlay, returns to the question of investment in facilities to support connectivity, either physical or digital. He observes that such projects are generally assessed as being highly prospective. He also points out that the benefits of infrastructure projects are even greater when the complementarity between projects is taken into account (for example, facilitating the capability of data flows to complement the movement of goods or service transactions) and when the benefits of networking across projects in different countries are realised. Governments have been the major funders of infrastructure, but constraints remain—both financial and human resources. Consideration is drawn, therefore, to private-sector engagement in funding, where significant pools of investible funds are evident.

Constraints arise, however, to private participation, including barriers to investment flows; but of more immediate interest in the context of the topics in this collection is the management of risks associated with infrastructure projects: their scale, longevity and specificity. Findlay notes bundles of issues associated with each of these elements, including those related to the recovery of costs sunk into projects that do not proceed, the impact of technological change that undermines business cases after project inception or political processes that shift over time and change government attitudes to projects.

Findlay observes that, given this set of issues and their significance, it is not surprising there are generally large gaps between estimates of the value of projects expected to be worthwhile from a social point of view (also considering the social view of the cost of funds) and those that are actually funded. In other words, the risk-adjusted rates of return fail to meet the hurdle rates of investors.

Findlay notes there is a global conversation under way with a focus on investment facilitation in general, but he proposes 10 'plus' measures that could cause the facilitation work to add greater value in the context of infrastructure projects. These include a focus on various aspects of good governance—for example, the application of cost-benefit analysis, efficient and competitive procurement procedures and access to human capital.

As Findlay also illustrates, issues of infrastructure have attracted considerable attention over time, and estimates of the 'gap' in investment are regularly reported, including by the multilateral agencies whose responsibilities sit in this field. Tools for assessing the sorts of risks he identifies have also been developed by multilateral agencies. Yet progress to narrow the gap is apparently difficult. There is plenty of 'talk' about the significance of the issue and the importance of resolving it, yet the problem remains.

Conclusion: A way forward

The editors' conclusion from these papers is that, if the economies of the region are serious about connectivity—that is, they have a genuine concern about infrastructure investment and are convinced of its benefits as laid out in the chapters here—then an action plan is valuable to resolve the matter of the insufficiency of investment.

At the national level, the main suggestion is to draw on the tools developed by multilateral agencies to identify serious impediments to infrastructure investment. This would be done in each economy so as to identify the two (or possibly three) most important items. A commitment would then be made to deal with those impediments.

This effort can be supported by regional cooperation in a number of ways.

First, a commonly shared vision for infrastructure development in the region could be prepared. This vision would not only refer to national ambitions, but also seek to capture the value of the spillovers between national plans—the additional value that can be captured by coordination. The specification of a vision supports the motivation to participate in the reform process just outlined and provides a reference point to set priorities. This vision should have a clear set of owners, such as a set of relevant ministers of East Asian economies. Some guidance could be taken from existing visions, such as that of the Master Plan of ASEAN Connectivity (MPAC), which seeks to achieve a 'seamlessly and comprehensively connected and integrated region'. However, while MPAC shows a high level of ambition, its implementation could be improved (see Box 1).

Box 1 Master Plan of ASEAN Connectivity

The Master Plan of ASEAN Connectivity (MPAC) was established in 2010. It began with 19 projects designed to contribute to narrowing the development gap among members and to ASEAN community-building. The original plan involved 125 initiatives. Evaluated by the World Bank (2016), 39 were completed, 34 removed and 52 remain uncompleted. The bank noted the lack of progress on a number of physical connectivity initiatives. In a study of the links to growth in the first three years of the original MPAC, Abeysinghe et al. (2019) find little impact (although the period of study is relatively short), as well as little potential consequence so far of the transmission of shocks from one economy to others in the group; the latter, however, is a consequence of connectivity, which is worthy of continuing attention. The World Bank (2016) examined issues in the design of the next phase of MPAC. It stressed the complementarity between strategies—for example, how institutional reform complements investment in physical capacity, how reform of cross-border processes adds value to infrastructure investments and how quality and efficiency improvements in existing infrastructure can be as important as investment in new facilities. It also stresses the possibility of divergent implications of projects at local and national levels. Following these observations, the latest version of the plan is MPAC 2025, which adopts the goal quoted above of a 'seamlessly and comprehensively connected and integrated region', places less focus on projects and more on programs and adopts better strategies for monitoring and review. Some of the uncompleted 2010 projects were also rolled into the latest plan. MPAC 2025 also includes a focus on digital innovation, regulatory cooperation and people movement. It stresses the importance of progress on infrastructure financing but does not offer a specific response. It highlights the role of logistics but does not specify an agenda for making progress.

Sources: Abeysinghe et al. (2019); Damuri (2019); World Bank (2016).

A parallel step to the work on a vision for connectivity is to develop a set of principles for the good governance of infrastructure projects. These might be developed in the context of the Asia Pacific Economic Cooperation (APEC) forum, for instance, to facilitate wider application and to also involve more investor economies. These principles can then become a reference point for national economic action, helping to identify not just constraints but also how to proceed. Managing this work in a multilateral setting also helps ameliorate concerns that a host country might have about dealing with a large investor country on bilateral terms. This includes arrangements for financial flows.

Following these two elements of the development of a shared vision and an action plan for reform, the next step is to record the plans and share the experiences of their implementation. There is already a long history of mutual-interest capacity-building in the region on which to draw for this step in the process. The design of this step could be informed by the MPAC experience to date (see Box 1).

Findlay also explains that the process emerging from these actions would benefit from consideration of how it links to other forms of cooperation, such as the BRI, MPAC and work by China and Japan to promote their cooperation in third countries and the Blue Dot Network.

Another element to consider is the role of multilateral banks. The purpose is certainly not to replace their role but to complement them. Findlay identifies a number of tasks. One is to assist with the perspective on the design of cross-country regional networks of linked infrastructure projects. Another is to support the process of fostering interactions between governments and private-sector investors, in the context of the vision, the commitments to reform and the network approach. A further contribution is an effort to introduce a degree of standardisation to projects in ways that facilitate the application of securitisation methods for funding.

To conclude, the gap in investment funding has been persistent, despite the apparent benefits from the improvements in connectivity that infrastructure offers. The risks that impede that investment can be traced to a series of policy and capacity gaps. National government action can break the deadlocks but is more likely to succeed in the context of regional cooperation. A ministerial-led process is valuable, involving the development of a vision for connectivity, principles for project governance, action plans for reform and reporting, capacity-building, collaboration with other regional initiatives and clarity around the roles of multilateral agencies.

References

Abeysinghe, T., Tan, K.G. and Nguyen, L.P.A. 2019. 'Master Plan on ASEAN Connectivity: Assessing growth impacts and interdependencies.' *International Journal of Logistics Economics and Globalisation* 8(1): 67–89. doi.org/10.1504/ IJLEG.2019.100210.

Baldwin, R. 2012. *Global supply chains: Why they emerged, why they matter, and where they are going*. Working Paper FGI-2012-1. Hong Kong: Fung Global Institute.

Bernard, A.B., Jensen, J.B, Redding, S.J. and Schott, P.K. 2018. 'Global firms.' *Journal of Economic Literature* 56(2): 565–619. doi.org/10.1257/jel.20160792.

Brooks, D.H. and Hummels, D. (eds). 2009. *Infrastructure's Role in Lowering Asia's Trade Costs: Building for trade*. Cheltenham, UK: Edward Elgar Publishing. doi.org/10.4337/9781781953273.

Damuri, J.R. 2019. 'Improving connectivity in the region.' Presentation to the Centre for Strategic and International Studies, Jakarta.

De, P. 2006. 'Trade, infrastructure and transaction costs: The imperatives for Asian economic cooperation.' *Journal of Economic Integration* 21(4): 708–35. doi.org/10.11130/jei.2006.21.4.708.

De, P. 2009. 'Empirical estimates of transportation costs: Options for enhancing Asia's trade.' In D.H. Brooks and D. Hummels (eds), *Infrastructure's Role in Lowering Asia's Trade Costs: Building for trade*, 73–112. Cheltenham, UK: Edward Elgar Publishing.

Ferracane, M.F., Lee-Makiyama, H. and van der Marel, E. 2018. *Digital Trade Restrictiveness Index*. Brussels: European Centre for International Political Economy.

Hummels, D.L. and Schaur, G. 2013. 'Time as a trade barrier.' *American Economic Review* 103(7): 2935–59. doi.org/10.1257/aer.103.7.2935.

Limão, N. and Venables, A.J. 2001. 'Infrastructure, geographical disadvantage, transport costs, and trade.' *The World Bank Economic Review* 15(3): 451–79. doi.org/10.1093/wber/15.3.451.

Menon, J. and Warr, P. 2008. 'Roads and poverty: A general equilibrium analysis for Lao PDR.' In D.H. Brooks and J. Menon (eds), *Infrastructure and Trade in Asia*, 115–42. Cheltenham, UK: Edward Elgar Publishing.

Nordås, H.K. and Piermartini, R. 2004. *Infrastructure and trade*. WTO Staff Working Paper No. ERSD-2004-04. Washington, DC: World Trade Organization. doi.org/10.2139/ssrn.923507.

Shu, P. and Steinwender, C. 2018. 'The impact of trade liberalization on firm productivity and innovation.' In J. Lerner and S. Stern (eds), *Innovation Policy and the Economy* 19: 39–68. Chicago: University of Chicago Press. doi.org/10.1086/699932.

World Bank. 2016. *Enhancing ASEAN connectivity monitoring and evaluation*. Report No. ACS17973. Washington, DC: The World Bank.

World Bank. 2018. *Moving for prosperity: Global migration and labor markets*. Policy Research Report. Washington, DC: The World Bank.

World Trade Organization (WTO). 2019a. 'China submits revised offer for joining government procurement pact.' *WTO News*, 23 October 2019. Geneva: WTO. Available from: www.wto.org/english/news_e/news19_e/gpro_23oct19_e.htm.

World Trade Organization (WTO). 2019b. *World Trade Report, 2019: The future of services trade*. Geneva: WTO.

1

Infrastructure connectivity and regional integration in Asia and the Pacific: Evidence from a new index of economic integration

Cyn-Young Park and Racquel Claveria

Introduction

Regional integration, especially through open trade and investment regimes, has been a prominent driver of economic growth that has lifted more than a billion people out of poverty in Asia and the Pacific. During the period 1990–2018, Asia's trade volume growth averaged 7.3 per cent annually—higher than the world average of 4.7 per cent. With that robust economic expansion, real per capita gross domestic product (GDP) (in constant 2010 dollar terms) more than doubled, from $2,807 to $6,557 over the same period.

In this process, the development of an export-oriented manufacturing industry helped attract foreign direct investment (FDI) and contributed to the creation and expansion of regional value chains across many economies in the region. Along with acceleration of trade and investment liberalisation, the private-sector-driven vertical integration of production systems across these economies has provided considerable impetus to deepen regional economic integration (ADB 2006). The intraregional share of Asia's total trade steadily increased from just under 50 per cent in 1990 to nearly 60 per cent in 2018. In addition, the intraregional share of total inward FDI to Asia increased from 41 per cent in 2001 to 48 per cent in 2018.

The remarkable success of the region's high-performing economies over the past several decades demonstrates how trade and participation in global value chains can drive industrialisation and economic growth. However, the level of regional integration varies widely across Asian economies, with geographically remote and low-income developing economies often struggling to access international markets and participate in global and regional value chains.

Many studies have investigated the trade openness and economic growth nexus for the economic benefits of regional integration. Earlier literature shows that cross-border trade and investment promote information flows and technology transfers, increasing the stock of knowledge capital and lifting both levels and growth rates of long-run outputs (Romer 1990; Grossman and Helpman 1990, 1991; Rivera-Batiz and Romer 1991). Later studies further extend the endogenous growth models to embody the scale economies and spillover effects of economic integration on productivity and growth through better competition, financial intermediation, labour mobility and human capital development, among others.

Recent research has highlighted the importance of infrastructure and seamless connectivity in promoting regional economic integration (UNESCAP 2017). This study suggested that regional economic cooperation and integration can support the attainment of the UN Sustainable Development Goals (SDGs), by ensuring that infrastructure projects have favourable social and environmental, as well as economic, impacts. Ensuring infrastructure projects connect small, low-income and geographically distant countries with the main markets of the region and placing a high priority on dealing with transboundary vulnerabilities and risks can help achieve the UN 2030 Agenda for Sustainable Development. An earlier ADB – Asian Development Bank Institute (2009) study estimated that the expected benefits of regional infrastructure projects for pan-Asian connectivity could be worth as much as US$13 trillion for developing countries in Asia during 2010–20 and beyond if the required investment was made.

In this context, many regional and subregional integration initiatives have placed strong emphasis on building and strengthening infrastructure connectivity to boost regional trade and economic integration (ADB 2017b). Indeed, it is often noted that geographic and institutional barriers significantly constrain the expansion of regional trade and access to international markets (ADB 2017a). Having extensive and efficient transportation networks can therefore help connect businesses and people and create business opportunities and jobs. Better transport and energy connectivity will also reduce the costs of doing business. Countries with geographical disadvantages, particularly those landlocked or sea-locked, have often found it difficult to engage in international trade due to poor connectivity. Moreover, small economies facing significant capacity constraints may not be able to design and implement the public investments and policy reforms that support regional trade and economic integration without support from neighbouring economies and donor communities.

This chapter aims to establish the link between various elements of regional integration—including infrastructure and connectivity—and economic growth, using rigorous empirical methodologies to show how different elements of regional integration contribute to economic growth and poverty reduction. In particular, the chapter looks at how infrastructure and connectivity, among other elements, can catalyse regional integration by facilitating regional trade and investment, strengthening regional value chains and promoting the movement of people.

Section two surveys the link between infrastructure connectivity and regional integration in Asia using both hard and soft infrastructure indicators. Section three employs a composite indicator approach, through the Asia-Pacific Regional Cooperation and Integration Index (ARCII), to gauge the contribution of infrastructure connectivity to regional integration. Section four empirically explores the impact of regional integration (as well as its components, including infrastructure connectivity) on economic growth, inequality and poverty reduction. Section five concludes and offers policy prescriptions.

Infrastructure connectivity and regional integration

Infrastructure connectivity is the backbone of trade and cross-border economic activities. Economic integration depends critically on the development of infrastructure that will strengthen connectivity both within and between countries and regions, freeing up the flow of goods and services, investment, people and ideas, as well as contributing to more efficient usage across borders of resources such as labour, land and energy (UNESCAP 2012).

Infrastructure covers a wide range of facilities and systems serving economic areas and functions, including both 'hard' and 'soft' infrastructure. Soft infrastructure includes legal, regulatory, procedural and other supporting policy frameworks, as well as human and institutional capacities; hard infrastructure relates to physical networks, such as roads, railways and ports. The extensiveness and quality of such hard infrastructure are essential for physical connectivity and reducing transport and trade costs. But its effective contribution to regional integration depends crucially on the efficiency of the associated soft infrastructure such as laws, policies, taxes and governance. For example, lengthy customs clearance times, inefficient administrative systems, high logistics costs and other barriers continue to hamper the free flow of goods and services in many developing countries in the region. The availability of information and communication technology and internet access has also emerged as an important enabling factor for digital connectivity, which has been particularly important for international businesses and trade in recent years.

Adequate quality infrastructure remains critical for regional economic integration. Despite many regional and subregional initiatives aimed at promoting seamless connectivity in Asia, the gap between supply and demand for high-quality infrastructure is significant and continues to widen. For example, between 2016 and 2030, Asia will need to invest more than US$1.7 trillion per year to maintain its strong growth momentum, continue to fight poverty and address climate change impacts, according to the Asian Development Bank (ADB 2017c). The ADB report also estimated the infrastructure financing gap would reach US$459 billion per year in 2016–20 (about 2.4 per cent of projected GDP for 25 developing countries).

Overall infrastructure quality

World	4.2
Asia	4.6
Southeast Asia	4.6
South Asia	3.8
East Asia	5.1
Central Asia	4.0

Quality of road infrastructure

World	4.1
Asia	4.5
Southeast Asia	4.5
South Asia	3.7
East Asia	5.1
Central Asia	4.0

Efficiency of air transport services

World	4.5
Asia	4.8
Southeast Asia	4.9
South Asia	4.0
East Asia	5.3
Central Asia	4.4

Efficiency of seaport services

World	4.0
Asia	4.1
Southeast Asia	4.3
South Asia	3.6
East Asia	4.7
Central Asia	2.9

Efficiency of train services

World	3.6
Asia	4.4
Southeast Asia	4.1
South Asia	3.8
East Asia	5.2
Central Asia	4.0

Reliability of water supply

World	4.8
Asia	5.1
Southeast Asia	5.1
South Asia	3.7
East Asia	5.6
Central Asia	4.7

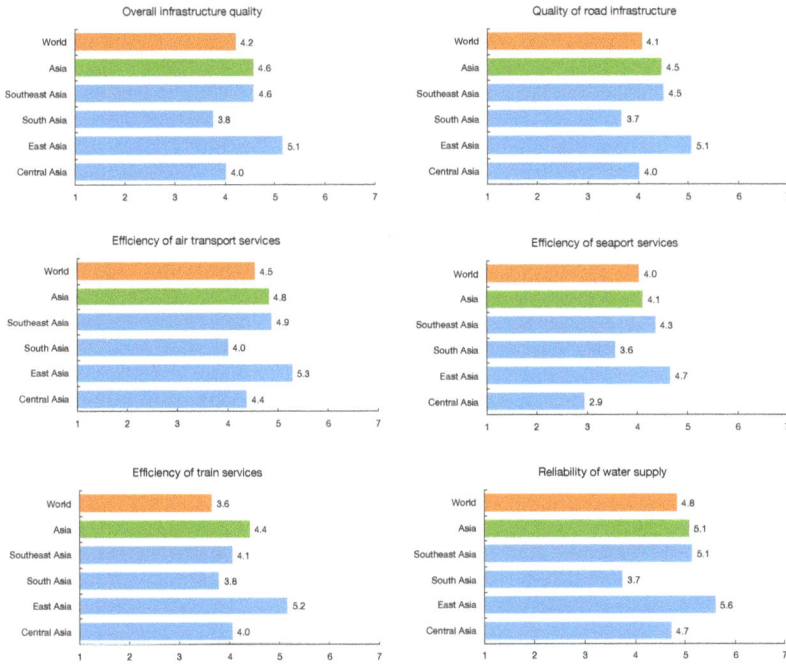

Figure 1.1 Quality of infrastructure in Asia, 2019

Notes: Scores range from 1 (extremely poor, inefficient and unreliable, among the worst in the world) to 7 (extremely good, efficient and reliable, among the best in the world). The *Global Competitiveness Report 2019* covered 141 economies.

Source: WEF (2019).

Despite rapid overall growth and significant improvements in transportation networks, electricity-generation capacity and water supply, the quality of infrastructure varies widely across countries and subregions in Asia (Figure 1.1). Remote, landlocked and mountainous countries are often at great disadvantage due to high trade and transport costs, with likely significant impacts on socioeconomic development.

The provision of a broad range of infrastructure services is also important for strengthening connectivity. Basic infrastructure services include business, financial and freight services, along with information and communication technology. These services indirectly benefit other economic sectors by making transactions more efficient.

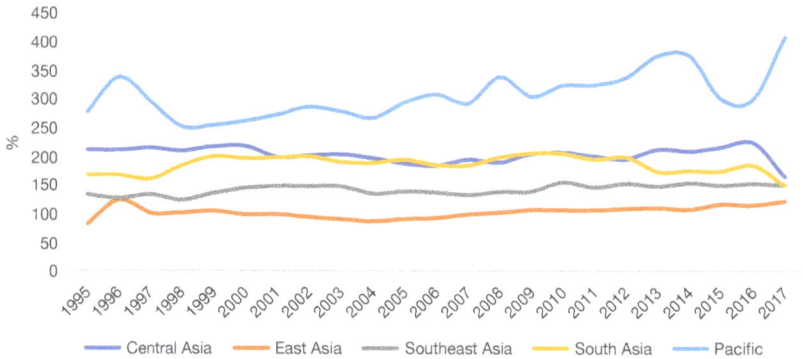

Figure 1.2 Trade costs of Asia and Pacific subregions with large developed economies, 1995–2017

Note: Trade costs shown are tariff equivalents, calculated as trade-weighted average trade costs of countries in each subregion compared with the three largest developed economies (Germany, Japan and the United States).

Source: UNESCAP (2019).

Strong regional infrastructure and seamless connectivity are essential for reducing trade costs, which is the key to accelerating the economic integration of developing countries into the global economy. While Asian and Pacific economies have made progress in reducing trade costs, significant room for improvement remains (ADB 2017a). Figure 1.2 presents the trend of trade costs across the Asia and Pacific subregions. While the levels have generally come down, they vary significantly by region. Trade costs are lowest in East Asia and highest among the Pacific Island developing economies, followed by the Central, West and South Asian economies.

Figure 1.3 shows the Logistics Performance Index (LPI) scores across subregions in Asia and the Pacific between 2007 and 2018. Across the subregions, LPI scores have climbed, and East Asia performs comparatively better than the other regions. Among the LPI subdimensions, timeliness is relatively higher (Figure 1.4).

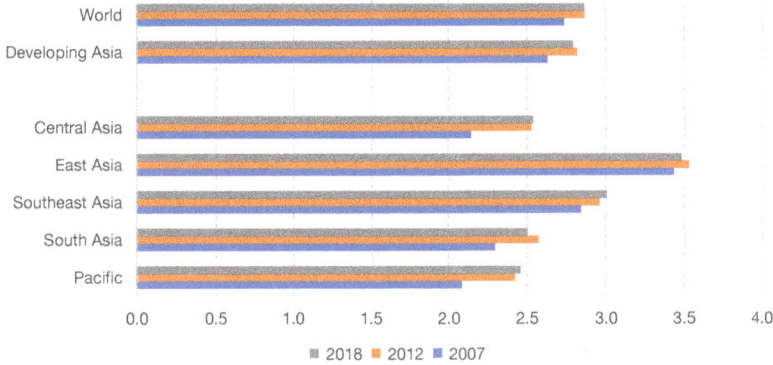

Figure 1.3 Logistics Performance Index, Asia's subregions, 2007, 2012, 2018

Notes: LPI scores are measured from 1 to 5, where 1 is rated as 'poorest performance' and 5 is 'best performance'. Countries are analysed in the following dimensions: efficiency of customs and border management clearance, quality of trade and transport infrastructure, ease of arranging competitively priced shipments, competence and quality of logistics services, ability to track and trace consignments, and frequency with which shipments reach consignees within scheduled or expected delivery times.

Source: Authors' calculations using data from World Bank (2015).

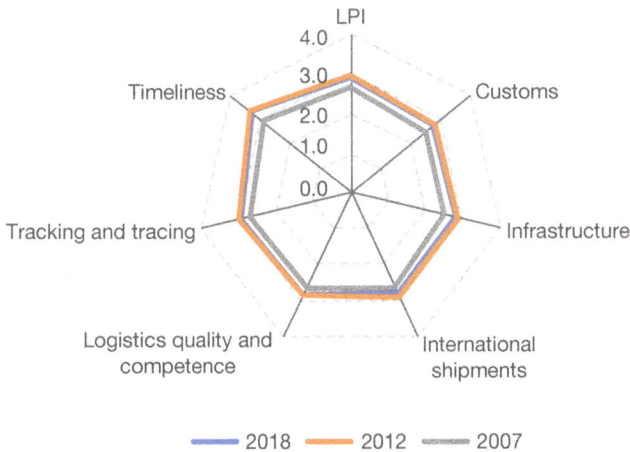

Figure 1.4 Logistics Performance Index dimensions: Asia, 2007, 2012, 2018

Notes: LPI scores are measured from 1 to 5, where 1 is rated as 'poorest performance' and 5 is 'best performance'. Countries are analysed in the following dimensions: efficiency of customs and border management clearance, quality of trade and transport infrastructure, ease of arranging competitively priced shipments, competence and quality of logistics services, ability to track and trace consignments, and frequency with which shipments reach consignees within scheduled or expected delivery times.

Source: World Bank (2015).

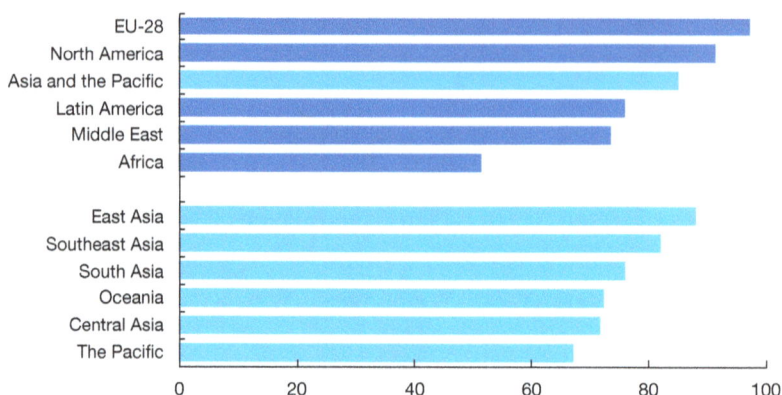

Figure 1.5 Distance to 'best-performer frontier' in trading across borders by region, 2019

EU-28 = European Union member countries

Notes: 100 represents the 'best-practice' frontier. For example, a score of 75 means an economy is 25 percentage points away from the frontier constructed from the global best performance. The figure may change from year to year.

Source: ADB calculations using data from World Bank (2020).

Figure 1.5 presents the distance to best-performer frontier in trading across borders. The distance-to-frontier scores show improved regulatory environments for cross-border trade, especially by reducing the overall cost and complexity of compliance with border and documentary requirements. In 2019, Asia and the Pacific were 15 per cent of the way to the global 'best-practice frontier' and surpassed the performance of Latin America and the Middle East.[1] The European Union (EU) and North America remain the best performance 'frontiers' in trading across borders. East and Southeast Asia are the best regional performers.

The time and cost associated with exporting and importing goods (that is, the trading across borders indicators) have generally improved over time (Figure 1.6). The time to trade decreased across Asia and the Pacific—most notably, in South Asia—through improvements in border and documentary compliance time, but it was still more than 20 times as long as in North America in 2019. The average border compliance time in South Asia remains about three days for exports and imports, but this subregion improved the most, with an average reduction of almost

---

1   The distance-to-frontier score measures how far, on average, an economy is at a point in time from the best performance (the 'frontier') and assesses the absolute change in the economy's regulatory environment over time (World Bank 2020).

five days from 2014 to 2019. East Asia recorded the shortest border compliance time to trade among subregions, at 18 hours to export and 31 hours to import (Figure 1.6).

The cost to trade fell from US$355 in 2014 to US$258 in 2019, as measured by the average cost for border compliance to export. The average cost was highest in the Pacific economies (US$657), followed by Central Asia (US$365), Southeast Asia (US$275), South Asia (US$240) and East Asia (US$224). The highest export cost was in Samoa, at US$1,400. The cost associated with border compliance to import rose in the Pacific, from US$574 in 2014 to US$622 in 2019—the highest among the subregions. The cost declined substantially both in East Asia (from US$508 to US$273) and in South Asia (from US$565 to US$333) and remained almost unchanged in Central and Southeast Asia.

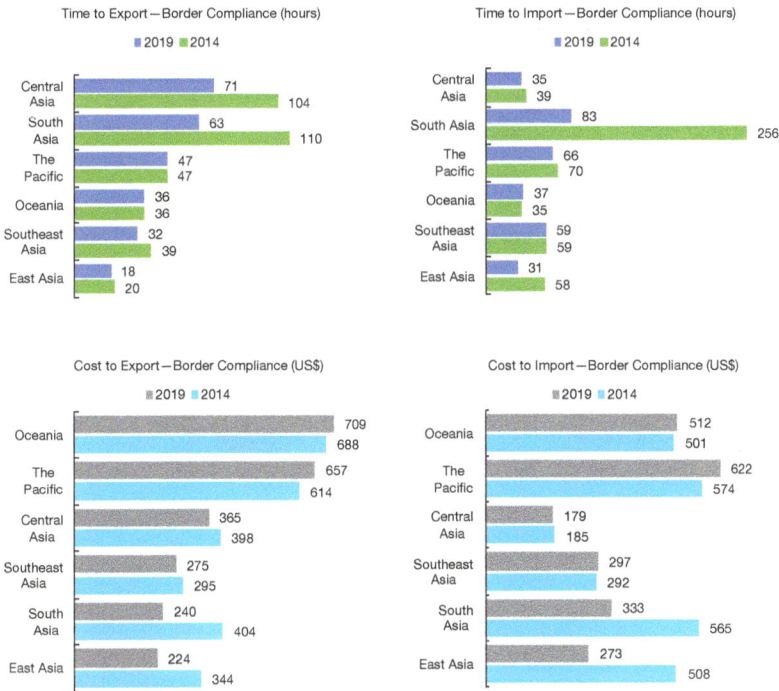

Time to Export — Border Compliance (hours)

■ 2019 ■ 2014

Subregion	2019	2014
Central Asia	71	104
South Asia	63	110
The Pacific	47	47
Oceania	36	36
Southeast Asia	32	39
East Asia	18	20

Time to Import — Border Compliance (hours)

■ 2019 ■ 2014

Subregion	2019	2014
Central Asia	35	39
South Asia	83	256
The Pacific	66	70
Oceania	37	35
Southeast Asia	59	59
East Asia	31	58

Cost to Export — Border Compliance (US$)

■ 2019 ■ 2014

Subregion	2019	2014
Oceania	709	688
The Pacific	657	614
Central Asia	365	398
Southeast Asia	275	295
South Asia	240	404
East Asia	224	344

Cost to Import — Border Compliance (US$)

■ 2019 ■ 2014

Subregion	2019	2014
Oceania	512	501
The Pacific	622	574
Central Asia	179	185
Southeast Asia	297	292
South Asia	333	565
East Asia	273	508

Figure 1.6 Time and cost to export and import, Asia's subregions, 2014 and 2019

Note: Aggregates are weighted averages based on total exports or imports.

Source: ADB calculations using data from World Bank (2020).

Reforms for better regulatory and institutional systems have been key to reducing the complexities of cross-border trade and related trade costs. Innovations in trade facilitation such as electronic submission and processing of documentation play a crucial role in reducing trade costs. In Georgia, for example, the introduction of electronic submission and processing in 2005 has since reduced the processing time for export documents from 48 hours to two hours. A customs union or trade agreement among major trading partners can also cut time and costs to trade. For instance, the Kyrgyz Republic reduced export time by 10 hours and cost by $85 after joining the Eurasian Economic Union in 2015. Domestic reforms to reduce trade documentation requirements also reduce administrative burdens and trade costs. In Kazakhstan, for example, the time for export documentation compliance fell substantially when the country removed two documentation requirements for customs clearance.

However, room still exists to lower trade costs. For example, policy measures can support the building of more efficient trade infrastructure, enhance trade facilitation, lower or streamline nontariff barriers, accelerate regulatory reforms to meet international standards and harmonisation, open up services trade and expand trade capacity. Improving the business climate to enhance competition and maximising the complementarity between trade and investment can also boost trade and trade integration in the region.

A multidimensional index of regional economic integration

Empirical evidence of the growth impact of regional integration has been elusive (Park and Claveria 2018b). Some studies look at participation in trading blocs, the share of intraregional trade in total trade and the reduction or elimination of tariffs as measures of regional integration to establish the statistical link between regional integration and growth. Yet, while some findings point to significantly positive relationships, others are inconclusive.

In addition, past studies often employed trade-focused measures of regional integration, which were often criticised for their limited scope of regional integration. Indeed, regional integration is a multidimensional process extending beyond efforts to liberalise trade. Appropriate measures should cover various facets, such as promoting trade and investment, facilitating the movement of capital across borders, building and developing regional value chains, enhancing infrastructure and connectivity, improving people's mobility, and providing the legal and institutional bases for international policy cooperation. In this context, the ADB (2017b) introduced the Asia-Pacific Regional Cooperation and Integration Index (ARCII) as a comprehensive measure of regional integration, which departs from the typical trade-focused metrics. This chapter uses the ARCII to gauge the progress of regional integration, assess its main drivers and determine its impact on economic growth and poverty reduction.

The ARCII combines 26 indicators, categorised into six regional cooperation and integration dimensions: 1) trade and investment, 2) money and finance, 3) regional value chains, 4) infrastructure connectivity, 5) movement of people, and 6) institutional and social integration.[2] The latest ARCII estimates indicate that the pace of regional integration in Asia was broadly steady during 2006–17 (Figure 1.7).

Key regional integration trends

Across subregions, East and Southeast Asia appear to be the most integrated with Asia. Central and South Asia scored below the average for regional integration (Figure 1.7).

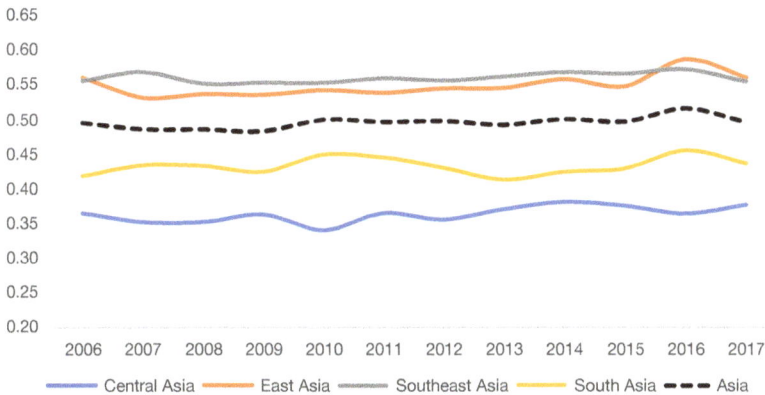

Figure 1.7 Asia-Pacific Regional Cooperation and Integration Index: Asia and Asia's subregions, 2006–17

Sources: Authors' calculations using the methodologies of Huh and Park (2018) and Park and Claveria (2018a).

---

2   Appendix Table 1.1 lists the ARCII dimensions and indicators. See Huh and Park (2018) and Park and Claveria (2018a) for detailed discussion of ARCII, and Asia Regional Integration Center (2015) for the ARCII database, methodology and other related resources.

Across dimensions, the performance of Asian subregions varies (Figure 1.8). For example, East Asia scored highest in the dimensions of money and finance, infrastructure and connectivity, regional value chains, and institutional and social integration. Southeast Asia outperformed other subregions in trade and investment and the movement of people. South and Central Asia trailed the other subregions on most dimensions.

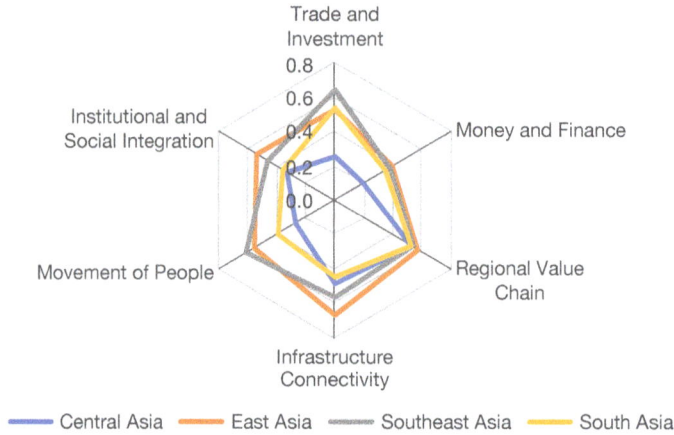

Figure 1.8 Dimensional subindexes to the Asia-Pacific Regional Cooperation and Integration Index: Asia's subregions, 2017

Sources: Authors' calculations using the methodologies of Huh and Park (2018) and Park and Claveria (2018a).

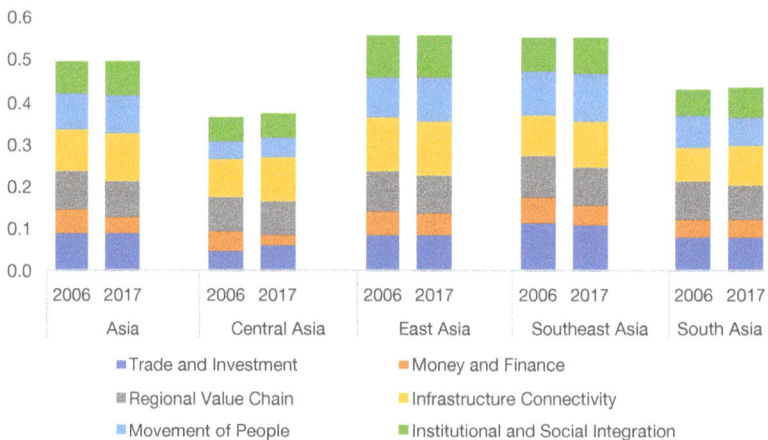

Figure 1.9 Dimensional contributions to the Asia-Pacific Regional Cooperation and Integration Index: Asia and Asia's subregions, 2006 versus 2017

Source: Authors' calculations.

Meanwhile, among the six dimensions, infrastructure connectivity contributes the most to the overall integration index (Figure 1.9). Hence, it appears to be the most forceful and stable foundation for regional integration in Asia. Moreover, the contribution of infrastructure connectivity to regional integration has increased over the years across Asia's subregions.

Regional integration and inclusive growth: An empirical exercise

From the perspective of multilateral organisations (such as the ADB and the United Nations), regional integration is not only an end in itself, but also a means to achieve the overarching objectives of economic growth and poverty reduction. To gauge the impact of regional integration and its components in promoting growth and reducing poverty, Park and Claveria (2018b) utilised the ARCII to estimate the growth, inequality and poverty impacts of regional integration.

Park and Claveria (2018b) constructed an unbalanced panel dataset for 156 countries for 2006–16 to run separate regressions for growth, inequality and poverty that included the regional integration index as another explanatory variable, in addition to other control variables.[3] In all regressions, indicators for both trade and financial openness were included to control the country-specific economic openness regardless of regional preference.[4]

---

3   Corresponding regional integration indexes (similar to the composition of ARCII) were constructed for the European Union, Latin America and Africa. Meanwhile, Appendix Table 1.2 presents the variables employed in the growth, inequality and poverty regressions. The control variables are listed in Appendix Table 1.3.

4   It is important to recall that ARCII measures a regional bias in economic integration relative to integration with the world. That is, the index may be higher for some countries that have just begun regional rather than global economic integration, while it may be lower for some countries that are very open and integrated with the world but not necessarily inclined towards integration—that is, only regionally oriented. Hence, to control for such an open-integration component in the regional integration index, financial and trade openness variables are included in all the equations. See Park and Claveria (2018b) for full discussion of the theoretical bases and specifications of the regression equations.

Correlation analysis for the full sample indicates significantly positive associations among the dimensional indexes (Table 1.1). Indeed, this reaffirms mutually reinforcing and interrelated components of regional integration across dimensional indexes. For instance, infrastructure helps to link markets and resources. This sets the stage for corresponding benefits in terms of economies of scale and greater competition. However, benefits from improved physical connectivity may be constrained if the volume of trade and investment flow is small. Therefore, integration of trade and investment is important in maximising the benefits of cross-border and physical connectivity. Moreover, as more economies are physically connected, there is greater cross-border trade and investment. Labour mobility across borders grows. Monetary and financial transactions increase through formal and informal channels. However, stronger monetary and financial links mean that a country's financial instability may be transmitted to its neighbours. Greater monetary and financial cooperation and integration are therefore essential in maintaining macroeconomic and financial stability and preventing financial crises (ADB 2006).

Park and Claveria (2018b) employed the generalised method of moments (GMM) estimation and found that infrastructure connectivity was significantly and robustly associated with higher growth and lower inequality and poverty.[5] In particular, infrastructure connectivity—along with dimensions of the regional value chain and institutional and social integration—is a significant driver of economic growth (Table 1.2). Throughout a series of robustness tests, infrastructure and connectivity and institutional and social integration continue to show significant and positive impacts on growth. The results also indicate that infrastructure and connectivity lead to improved income distribution through an inequality-reducing effect that is stronger at low-income levels (Table 1.3).

---

5   As is typical in the empirical literature, GMM was utilised as the estimation procedure to address the econometric issues inherent in growth, inequality and poverty regressions. These include the observed heterogeneity across countries, persistence of the dependent variable, potential endogeneity and long lagged effects of the regressors on the dependent variable (particularly in the case of economic growth). Full GMM estimation results are available on request.

Table 1.1 Pairwise Pearson correlation coefficients of ARCII dimensional indexes, 2006–16

	Trade and investment	Money and finance	Regional value chain	Infrastructure connectivity	Movement of people	Institutional and social integration
Trade and investment	1					
Money and finance	0.520***	1				
Regional value chain	0.110***	0.406***	1			
Infrastructure connectivity	0.189***	0.265***	0.323***	1		
Movement of people	0.485***	0.497***	0.276***	0.287***	1	
Institutional and social integration	0.237***	0.528***	0.756***	0.474***	0.431***	1

*** significant at the 1 per cent level

Note: Figures indicate Pearson correlation coefficients.

Source: Authors' calculations.

Table 1.2 Generalised method of moments estimation results: Growth regressions

Dependent variable: Log(real GDP per capita)	Baseline	Baseline with financial openness	Baseline with financial and trade openness
Log(infrastructure connectivity)	1.079**	1.274**	1.640***
	(0.468)	(0.509)	(0.549)
Log(institutional and social integration)	0.501***	0.576***	0.642***
	(0.139)	(0.153)	(0.169)
With control variables	Yes	Yes	Yes

*** significant at the 1 per cent level

** significant at the 5 per cent level

Notes: Table indicates summary of results when the dimensional subindexes enter the growth regressions separately. For brevity, dimensional subindexes with significant coefficients are shown. Windmeijer robust standard errors are in parentheses.

Source: Authors' calculations using revised estimations in Park and Claveria (2018b).

Table 1.3 Generalised method of moments estimation results: Inequality regressions

Dependent variable: Log(Gini index)	Baseline	Baseline with financial openness	Baseline with financial and trade openness
Log(infrastructure connectivity)	−3.230**	−2.567*	−2.763**
	(0.943)	(1.422)	(1.361)
Log(infrastructure connectivity) x log(real GDP per capita)	0.348***	0.272*	0.294*
	(0.103)	(0.159)	(0.151)
Log(real GDP per capita)	2.095***	2.024**	2.019**
	(0.638)	(0.837)	(0.866)
Log^2(real GDP per capita)	−0.0999***	−0.0989**	−0.0981**
	(0.0328)	(0.0415)	(0.0440)
With control variables	Yes	Yes	Yes

*** significant at the 1 per cent level

** significant at the 5 per cent level

* significant at the 10 per cent level

Notes: Table indicates summary of results when the dimensional subindexes enter the growth regressions separately. For brevity, dimensional subindexes with significant coefficients are shown. Windmeijer robust standard errors are in parentheses.

Source: Authors' calculations using revised estimations in Park and Claveria (2018b).

The empirical findings are generally consistent with the development insight that better infrastructure will help economies grow faster. Investment in infrastructure not only increases an economy's capital stock, but also broadens the reach of economic activities and trade, creating opportunities for the realisation of economies of scale. This, in turn, lowers production and distribution costs, which allows more goods to reach more people across greater geographic areas. Moreover, infrastructure creates jobs and boosts business opportunities and helps narrow the development gap nationally and subregionally, promoting inclusive and sustainable growth.

Moreover, infrastructure connectivity tends to exert a significant and negative impact on poverty (Table 1.4). Overall integration as well as that of trade and investment, money and finance, and institutional and social integration are significant and robust drivers of poverty reduction. Their impact in curbing poverty is even more pronounced for lower-income countries.

Table 1.4 Generalised method of moments estimation results: Poverty regressions

Dependent variable: Log(Poverty headcount ratio)	Baseline	Baseline with financial openness	Baseline with financial and trade openness
Log(overall RII)	−16.56***	−13.29***	−20.35
	(3.518)	(4.658)	(14.30)
Log(overall RII) x log(real GDP per capita)	1.813***	1.441***	2.241
	(0.361)	(0.459)	(1.613)
Log(trade and investment)	−2.730***	−3.069**	−5.598***
	(0.907)	(1.374)	(2.075)
Log(trade and investment) x log(real GDP per capita)	0.296***	0.332**	0.648**
	(0.0999)	(0.153)	(0.255)
Log(money and finance)	−9.582***	−8.439***	−8.656***
	(1.853)	(1.909)	(2.009)
Log(money and finance) x log(real GDP per capita)	1.208***	0.881***	0.897***
	(0.193)	(0.221)	(0.235)
Log(infrastructure and connectivity)	−6.353***	−11.42*	−26.93**
	(2.319)	(5.839)	(10.70)
Log(infrastructure and connectivity) x log(real GDP per capita)	−3.682	−1.422**	−3.298***
	(5.401)	(0.615)	(1.061)
Log(institutional and social integration)	0.469	−7.275	−18.44*
	(0.573)	(5.445)	(11.00)
Log(institutional and social integration) x log(real GDP per capita)	0.722***	0.791	2.016*
	(0.254)	(0.560)	(1.121)
With control variables	Yes	Yes	Yes

*** significant at the 1 per cent level

** significant at the 5 per cent level

* significant at the 10 per cent level

Notes: Table indicates summary of results when the dimensional subindexes enter the growth regressions separately. For brevity, dimensional subindexes with significant coefficients are shown. Windmeijer robust standard errors are in parentheses.

Source: Authors' calculations using revised estimations in Park and Claveria (2018b).

Improved infrastructure can help reduce poverty by providing the poor with greater opportunity to participate in market activities. Cross-border infrastructure projects—for example, in transport, energy and telecommunications—are essential for the movement of goods, services, people and information across countries. They enlarge market access, reduce economic distance, facilitate trade, and increase investment and labour flows. The resulting intensification of cross-border economic activities can create employment, particularly in the labour-intensive sectors of developing economies, thus contributing to poverty reduction (ADB 2006).

Concluding remarks

The Asia-Pacific has made remarkable progress in regional economic integration, which has been anchored in the region's strong trade and investment linkages and the associated expansion of regional value chains. Together with market-driven actions, government-led policies have promoted regional economic integration. In the process of regional economic integration, regional economies have removed barriers to trade and the transfer of capital (both physical and human) and technology. Strong regional dynamics, driven by intraregional trade and financial flows, have also encouraged the participation of low-income countries in the fast-growing regional and global value chains and boosted their economic performance.

Nevertheless, the progress of economic integration has not been even across subregions and countries in Asia and the Pacific, leading to unequal economic and social outcomes. Infrastructure connectivity and easier access to markets are often critical factors that divide high-performance countries from low-performance ones. Therefore, providing adequate quality infrastructure remains critical for regional integration and how individual countries can leverage regional integration for inclusive growth.

The United Nations Economic and Social Commission for Asia and the Pacific (UNESCAP 2017) also recognises the significant potential of regional economic integration and interconnectivity to support implementation of the 2030 Agenda for Sustainable Development at regional and subregional levels. Substantially increasing investment in transport, energy and information and communication technology infrastructure can contribute directly to some SDGs, especially by ensuring access to affordable, reliable and modern forms of energy for all (Goal 7) and building resilient infrastructure, promoting inclusive and sustainable industrialisation and fostering innovation (Goal 9). Such infrastructure projects should also help connect small, low-income and geographically distant countries with the main regional markets. In addition, strengthening regional cooperation and integration can generate opportunities for increasing employment and incomes across the region.

In reviewing the progress of regional integration, with particular focus on infrastructure connectivity, this chapter finds empirical evidence for the positive impacts of regional integration and infrastructure connectivity on economic growth that are inclusive and reduce poverty. However, there remains considerable room for further policy efforts to enhance regional integration and boost regional connectivity. Effective investment in regional infrastructure and connectivity will turn the region into an attractive place for business, investment and living. Further integration efforts should pay greater attention to ensuring impacts on regional economies are more inclusive, with broader economic participation and socially equitable results. Prioritisation of development strategies should focus on connecting the poor, remote and disadvantaged to regional centres.

Appendix Table 1.1 ARCII dimensions and indicators

Trade and investment integration	Proportion of intraregional goods exports to total goods exports
	Proportion of intraregional goods imports to total goods imports
	Intraregional trade intensity index
	Proportion of intraregional foreign direct investment (FDI) inflows to total FDI inflows
	Proportion of intraregional FDI inflows plus outflows to total FDI inflows plus outflows
Money and finance integration	Proportion of intraregional cross-border equity liabilities to total cross-border equity liabilities
	Proportion of intraregional cross-border bond liabilities to total cross-border bond liabilities
	Pairwise dispersion of deposit rates averaged regionally relative to that averaged globally
	Pairwise correlation of equity returns averaged regionally minus that averaged globally

Regional value chain	Ratio between average trade complementarity index over regional trading partners and average trade complementarity index over all trading partners
	Ratio between average trade concentration index over regional trading partners and average trade concentration index over all trading partners
	Proportion of intraregional intermediate goods exports to total intraregional goods exports
	Proportion of intraregional intermediate goods imports to total intraregional goods imports
Infrastructure and connectivity	Ratio between average trade cost over regional trading partners and average trade cost over all trading partners
	Ratio between average liner shipping connectivity index over regional trading partners and average liner shipping connectivity index over all trading partners
	Logistics performance index (overall)
	Doing Business Index (overall)
Movement of people	Proportion of intraregional outbound migration to total outbound migration
	Proportion of intraregional tourists to total tourists (inbound plus outbound)
	Proportion of intraregional remittances to total remittances
	Proportion of other Asian countries that do not require an entry visa
Institutional and social integration	Proportion of other Asian countries with which free-trade agreements have been signed
	Proportion of other Asian countries that have an embassy
	Proportion of other Asian countries that have signed business investment treaties
	Proportion of other Asian countries that have signed double taxation treaties
	Cultural proximity with other Asian countries relative to that with all other countries

Sources: Huh and Park (2018); Park and Claveria (2018a).

Appendix Table 1.2 Variables in growth, inequality and poverty regressions: Description and sources

Variable	Description	Source
Real GDP per capita	GDP per capita based on purchasing power parity (PPP), constant 2011 international $	World Bank (2021)
Secondary school enrolment	School enrolment, secondary (% gross)	World Bank (2021)
Investment (% of GDP)	Gross capital formation (% of GDP)	World Bank (2021)
Inflation rate	Inflation, consumer prices (annual %)	World Bank (2021)
Control of corruption	Control of corruption, estimate	World Bank (2021)
Financial openness	Sum of foreign assets (monetary, Other Depository Corporations Survey, net foreign assets, liabilities to nonresidents) and foreign liabilities (monetary, Other Depository Corporations Survey, net foreign assets, claims on nonresidents) divided by GDP (all in domestic currency)	International Monetary Fund International Financial Statistics (IMF n.d.)
Log(M2/GDP)	Logarithm of money supply (M2) divided by nominal GDP (both $ million)	CEIC (Available from: insights.ceicdata.com)
Trade openness	Exports plus imports (% of GDP)	World Bank (2021)
Social benefit incidence	Benefit incidence of social insurance programs to poorest quintile (% of total social insurance benefits)	World Bank (2021)
Gini	Gini index (World Bank estimate)	World Bank (2021)
Poverty gap	Poverty gap at $1.90 a day (2011 PPP) (%)	World Bank (2021)
Poverty headcount ratio	Poverty headcount ratio at $1.90 a day (2011 PPP) (% of population)	World Bank (2021)

Source: Park and Claveria (2018b).

Appendix Table 1.3 Control variables in growth, poverty and inequality regressions

Growth regression	Inequality regression	Poverty regression
Secondary school enrolment Investment Government consumption Inflation rate Control of corruption index	Log(real GDP per capita) Log^2(real GDP per capita) Secondary school enrolment Social transfers Population growth Inflation rate	Log(real GDP per capita) Log(Gini index)

Source: Park and Claveria (2018b).

References

Asian Development Bank (ADB). 2006. *Regional Cooperation and Integration Strategy*. Manila: ADB.

Asian Development Bank (ADB). 2017a. *Aid for Trade in Asia and the Pacific: Promoting connectivity for inclusive development*. Manila: ADB.

Asian Development Bank (ADB). 2017b. *Asian Economic Integration Report 2017: The era of financial interconnectedness—How can Asia strengthen financial resilience?* Manila: ADB.

Asian Development Bank (ADB). 2017c. *Meeting Asia's Infrastructure Needs*. Manila: ADB.

Asian Development Bank (ADB) and Asian Development Bank Institute. 2009. *Infrastructure for a Seamless Asia*. Tokyo: ADBI. Available from: www.adb.org/sites/default/files/publication/159348/adbi-infrastructure-seamless-asia.pdf.

Asia Regional Integration Center. 2015. *Asia-Pacific Regional Cooperation and Integration Index*. Manila: ADB. Available from: aric.adb.org/database/arcii.

Grossman, G.M. and Helpman, E. 1990. 'Comparative advantage and long-run growth.' *American Economic Review* 80(4): 796–815.

Grossman, G.M. and Helpman, E. 1991. 'Trade, knowledge spillovers, and growth.' *European Economic Review* 35(2–3): 517–26. doi.org/10.1016/0014-2921(91)90153-A.

Huh, H.-S. and Park, C.-Y. 2018. 'Asia-Pacific Regional Integration Index: Construction, interpretation, and comparison.' *Journal of Asian Economics* 54(February): 22–38. doi.org/10.1016/j.asieco.2017.12.001.

International Monetary Fund (IMF). n.d. *IMF Data: Access to macroeconomic & financial data*. Washington, DC: IMF. Available from: data.imf.org.

Park, C.-Y. and Claveria, R. 2018a. *Constructing the Asia-Pacific Regional Cooperation and Integration Index: A panel approach*. ADB Economics Working Paper Series No. 544. Manila: ADB. doi.org/10.22617/WPS189334-2.

Park, C.-Y. and Claveria, R. 2018b. *Does regional integration matter for inclusive growth? Evidence from the multidimensional regional integration index*. ADB Economics Working Paper Series No. 559. Manila: ADB. doi.org/10.22617/WPS189608-2.

Rivera-Batiz, L.A. and Romer, P.M. 1991. 'International trade with endogenous technological change.' *European Economic Review* 35(4): 971–1001. doi.org/10.1016/0014-2921(91)90048-N.

Romer, P. 1990. 'Endogenous technological change.' *Journal of Political Economy* 98(5): S71–102. doi.org/10.1086/261725.

United Nations Economic and Social Commission for Asia and the Pacific (UNESCAP). 2012. *Growing Together: Economic integration for an inclusive and sustainable Asia-Pacific century.* Bangkok: UNESCAP.

United Nations Economic and Social Commission for Asia and the Pacific (UNESCAP). 2017. *Enhancing Regional Economic Cooperation and Integration in Asia and the Pacific.* Bangkok: UNESCAP.

United Nations Economic and Social Commission for Asia and the Pacific (UNESCAP). 2019. *ESCAP-World Bank Trade Costs Database.* Bangkok: ESCAP Trade, Investment and Innovation Division. Available from: www.unescap.org/resources/escap-world-bank-trade-cost-database.

World Bank. 2015. *Logistics Performance Index Database.* Washington, DC: World Bank Group. Available from: lpi.worldbank.org.

World Bank. 2020. *Doing Business.* [Database]. Washington, DC: World Bank Group. Available from: www.doingbusiness.org.

World Bank. 2021. *DataBank.* Washington, DC: World Bank Group. Available from: databank.worldbank.org.

World Economic Forum (WEF). 2019. *Global Competitiveness Report 2019: How to end a lost decade of productivity growth.* Geneva: WEF. Available from: www.weforum.org/reports/how-to-end-a-decade-of-lost-productivity-growth.

2

China's Belt and Road Initiative: Contributions to connectivity

Pelagia Karpathiotaki, Yunhua Tian, Yanping Zhou
and Xiaohao Huang

Introduction

The first signs of China's desire to go abroad in a coordinated manner can be found in the first speech of Xi Jinping on 15 November 2012 in Beijing, when he emerged as general secretary of the Chinese Communist Party and, among others, highlighted the priority of national rejuvenation and China's role in world affairs:

> Our responsibility is to unite and lead people of the entire party and of all ethnic groups around the country while accepting the baton of history and continuing to work for realizing the great revival of the Chinese nation in order to let the Chinese nation stand more firmly and powerfully among all nations around the world and make a greater contribution to mankind. (BBC News 2012)

That day marked a turning point, as it changed the way China viewed the rest of the world and upgraded its role as a global player.

About a year later, in September 2013, during a visit to Kazakhstan, President Xi made a speech titled 'Promote People-to-People Friendship and Create a Better Future' and introduced the Silk Road Economic

Belt (SREB) (an overland route), which, along with the 21st Century Maritime Silk Road (MSR) (a maritime route), announced a month later in Indonesia, came to be collectively known today as the Belt and Road Initiative (BRI). The first geographical presentation of the BRI was made in a map published by Xinhua News Agency on 8 May 2014. According to this map, the SREB would begin in Xi'an, whereas the MSR would start in Quanzhou's harbour in Fujian Province.

The political significance of the BRI initially was demonstrated in the 'Decision of the Central Committee of the Communist Party of China on Some Major Issues Concerning Comprehensively Deepening the Reform', adopted on 12 November 2013, according to which:

> We will set up development-oriented financial institutions, accelerate the construction of infrastructure connecting China with neighbouring countries and regions, and work hard to build a Silk Road Economic Belt and a Maritime Silk Road, so as to form a new pattern of all-round opening. (Article 26, Section VII)

The BRI has become so integral to China's foreign policy strategy that it was adopted into the Chinese Communist Party's constitution on 24 October 2017:

> The Party shall constantly work to develop good neighbourly relations between China and its surrounding countries and work to strengthen unity and cooperation between China and other developing countries. It shall follow the principle of achieving shared growth through discussion and collaboration, and pursue the Belt and Road Initiative. (CPC 2017)

Since 2013, many official documents and white papers have been published that clarify the principles, priorities and thematic specialisations of the BRI. Undoubtedly, the first official and probably one of the most important documents on the BRI was the 'Vision and Actions on Jointly Building the Silk Road Economic Belt and 21st Century Maritime Silk Road', jointly issued by the National Development and Reform Commission (NDRC), the Ministry of Foreign Affairs and the Ministry of Commerce at the Boao Forum on 28 March 2015. It is an action plan on the principles, framework and cooperation priorities and mechanisms of the BRI.

According to this document, the BRI is:

- open to all countries, and international and regional organisations for engagement
- advocates peace and cooperation, openness and inclusiveness, mutual learning and mutual benefit
- promotes practical cooperation in all fields, and works to build a community of shared interests, destiny, and responsibility featuring mutual political trust, economic integration and cultural inclusiveness.

In 2016, the State Council published the Thirteenth Five-Year Plan for National Informatisation, devoting a section to the construction of an 'online Silk Road' and encouraging the full participation of Chinese internet companies. In May 2017, speaking at the first BRI forum in Beijing, President Xi reiterated the critical role of the digital Silk Road in the overall initiative. He called for further integration into the BRI of next-generation network technologies—including artificial intelligence, nanotechnology, quantum computing, big data, cloud computing and the concept of smart cities—to enable innovation-driven development (Xinhuanet 2017).

In January 2017, China and the World Health Organization (WHO) agreed to jointly implement a BRI project focused on health. In August that year, China hosted an international conference on health related to the Silk Road. On 16 March 2020, during the COVID-19 pandemic and while Italy was facing perhaps the greatest humanitarian crisis in its modern history, President Xi, during a phone conversation with then Italian Prime Minister Giuseppe Conte, raised the notion of working closer with Italy to build a 'Health Silk Road'.

Today, the BRI's overland route comprises six land corridors:

1. The China–Mongolia–Russia Economic corridor (CMREC).
2. The New Eurasian Land Bridge (NELB).
3. The China–Central Asia–West Asia Economic Corridor (CCWAEC).
4. The China–Indochina Peninsula Economic Corridor (CIPEC).
5. The China–Pakistan Economic Corridor (CPEC).
6. The Bangladesh–China–India–Myanmar Economic Corridor (BCIMEC).

In addition, the maritime route of the BRI proposes more direct linkage of Chinese ports with emerging countries and economic regions such as the Association of Southeast Asian Nations (ASEAN). According to another official document, the 'Vision for Maritime Cooperation under the BRI', released on 20 June 2017 by the NDRC and the State Oceanic Administration (SOA), the BRI comprises three sea routes, or blue economic passages:

7. The China–Indian Ocean–Africa–Mediterranean Sea Blue Economic Passage, linking the CIPEC, CPEC and CCIMEC.
8. The China–Oceania–South Pacific Blue Economic Passage.
9. The China–Northern Europe Blue Economic Passage, through the Arctic Ocean.

On 28 January 2018, China's State Council Information Office released a white paper titled 'China's Arctic Policy', detailing the country's plan to develop shipping lanes opened up by climate change.

The original name of the BRI was coined in 2013 by President Xi, who drew inspiration from the concept of the Silk Road, which was established during the Han Dynasty 2,000 years ago and was an ancient network of trade routes that had for centuries connected China to the Mediterranean via Eurasia. The term 'Silk Road' was coined by German geographer Ferdinand von Richthofen in 1877. In China, the ancient trading routes across Eurasia were more prosaically called the northern and southern routes. The reference to the ancient Silk Road was not chosen by chance. It conjures up images of peaceful and diverse exchanges from one prosperous end of the Eurasian continent to the other and is easily identifiable in countries outside China as a shared heritage defying civilisational differences.

Chinese sources never refer to the BRI as the New Silk Road Initiative (NSRI) because this term was first envisioned in 2011 by the United States as a means for Afghanistan to integrate further into the region by resuming traditional trading routes and reconstructing significant infrastructure links broken by decades of conflict. The NSRI shares a focus on energy and transportation infrastructure with China's SREB.

In the 'Vision and Actions' document, the BRI is described as 倡议 ('a call for action'), translated into English as 'initiative'. In August 2015, China's NDRC, together with the Ministry of Foreign Affairs and Ministry of Commerce, clarified that the BRI is the official English translation and words such as 'strategy', 'program', 'agenda' and 'project' are inaccurate

(Xie 2015). According to the official documents, the BRI is a unilateral concept that requires willing cooperation from others who also have a stake in the provision of public goods, which is why Chinese officials will not use the term 'strategy', which requires close association or alliances among those who share its specific goals. Because the initiative relies on voluntary participation, it faces a collective action problem.

The BRI is not just a development plan; it is also an important element of Chinese foreign policy in the twenty-first century, and therefore the definition of what constitutes a BRI project is broad. For the purposes of this chapter, BRI projects are any that originated in China (that have direct Chinese participation at a consultant, owner, contractor and financer level) and are focused on Asia, Europe and Africa, but open to all partners and fulfil the scope of the two Chinese policy documents that outline the BRI: the 'Vision and Actions on Jointly Building the Silk Road Economic Belt and 21st Century Maritime Silk Road' and the 'Vision for Maritime Cooperation under the Belt and Road Initiative'. In 2019, the NDRC compiled an official list of participating BRI nations and approved projects. Many of the BRI-branded projects began before 2013 but gained momentum under the initiative.

In this chapter, we focus on the contributions of the BRI to connectivity, and its consequences, but first, we examine some of its philosophical and geopolitical features, including its governance. These are the topics of the following two sections. We then identify the BRI's contributions to connectivity. We examine the economic effects of connectivity on trade, foreign investment and global value chains. Subsequently, we examine some risks in the BRI, including political and legal, debt sustainability questions, governance risks and those associated with the environment. The final section of the chapter provides a conclusion.

BRI foundations

Philosophy

The BRI is a unique megaproject in global economic history, which is in line with President Xi's 'Thoughts' on China as a global power and globalisation in the twenty-first century, and which contributes to his mission of national rejuvenation. At its core, the initiative incorporates elements of Chinese and Western philosophy.

In contrast with Western philosophy, the BRI is not a project 'based on models', which means it does not have a clearly defined framework, clearly measurable goals or defined action steps or a timetable, but will gradually evolve and adapt to the dynamics of the international environment. The BRI generates strategic flexibility, seeks relative advantage for China and preaches avoidance of direct conflict. According to Chinese philosophy, a Chinese general does not set goals or make plans; he tries to detect and exploit the internal dynamics of the 'environment' and adapts his decisions to the natural course of things, to make the conditions work in his favour.

Another element of Chinese philosophy that also characterises the BRI is 'transformation'—mainly as an ideological concept. According to Engels and Marx, only in the final analysis is the economy the driving force of history, but people are becoming aware of the conflicts that are taking place in the economic world, in the ideological field. 'Transformation' is a process that causes gradual changes that often are not visible in the short term, reducing the chance of friction, in contrast with the term 'action' (as in Western philosophy), in which friction is usually inevitable. Through the BRI, China seeks to 'transform' the international environment and promote an alternative model of globalisation and world order adapted to the twenty-first century with a moral advantage to create a fairer world based on globally accepted values (not Western or Eastern) and without any discrimination regarding different political or social systems (Karpathiotaki 2016).

On the other hand, the official geographical presentation of the BRI and its basic principles incorporate elements of Western philosophy and culture. The BRI's 'roads', 'corridors' and 'passages' give shape to the project, creating geometric 'ideal models', which in fact are not absolutely and immediately applicable but they contribute to a better understanding of the project by the Western world. In addition, the principles and values that officially are promoted by the BRI are in line with the principles of the UN Charter, and especially Article 26 of the Charter of Economic Rights and Duties of States adopted by the UN General Assembly in 1974:

> All States have the duty to coexist in tolerance and live together in peace, irrespective of differences in political, economic, social and cultural systems, and to facilitate trade between States having different economic and social systems. International trade should be conducted without prejudice to generalized non-discriminatory

and non-reciprocal preferences in favour of developing countries, on the basis of mutual advantage, equitable benefits and the exchange of most-favoured-nation treatment. (UN 1974)

The BRI is China's attempt to balance the Western-centric perception of the world and propose a new world order that resembles the one determined in 1648 by the Peace of Westphalia treaties. China, through the BRI, seeks to redefine the role of the 'state' in the twenty-first century as the basic political unit of the international system, which can interact with other states in the global market but at the same time maintains control of its economic future, its political system and its foreign policy. This is in contrast to the perception of the 'flat world', without 'borders', which in some degree described globalisation until recently.

The success of the BRI is not easily or immediately measurable but it will be judged largely at the ideological level and, in future, it could be measured by the impact it has on the global community and the acceptance of the BRI's values.

Geopolitics

China is the largest nation in Eurasia, with an extensive coastline stretching from the tropical zone to the temperate zone. It has one of the most advantageous geographical positions on the planet, while from a geopolitical point of view, it faces challenges through its proximity to other potential world powers (Russia, India, Japan). In this environment, China's strategic decision to 'go out' by land and sea through the BRI could be seen as an expected and realistic political decision, with its main goals, on the one hand, to achieve its key national interests of economic survival and growth and, on the other, to increase its political capital at the international level to settle key issues of its national security. The BRI does not take a missionary approach to international relations, as was the case with the United States after World War II, because China does not seem to propagate any particular ideology or system of governance.

The BRI is an effort to create a network of infrastructure on the southern Eurasian coast ('Rimland') and in Central Asia ('Heartland'), but also in the Arctic north, with final destinations in Europe that could lead to the unification of Eurasia and provide autonomy from the oceanic communications network dominated by the United States.

This infrastructure could shape a new anthropogeographic reality in Eurasia that could affect the international system and have extremely important geopolitical implications for the world (Costas 2019).

The BRI could be seen as China's 'anti-containment' strategy because it contributes to the 'unification' of Eurasia—an attempt to counter the United States' 'containment' strategy that traditionally seeks the 'division' of Eurasia and the prevention of the emergence of a dominant power in the region. The United States' containment strategy incorporates theoretical elements of different geopolitical theories (Mackinder, Spykman and Mahan), emphasises control of Rimland (Asia Minor, Arabia, Iran, Afghanistan, Southeast Asia, China, Korea and eastern Siberia excluding Russia), and combines Mackinder–Spykman's theory with Mahan's argument, which considered naval power and control of the ocean as the key elements for world domination.

The melting of the Arctic ice sheet 'liberates' Russia from the north, with Rimland no longer a semicircle formed by the inaccessibility of the Arctic, and now more of a ring. The melting of the Arctic ice not only adds more sea routes to the existing maritime transportation network but also contributes to the 'unification' of the Eurasian maritime region into a single and indivisible web of maritime routes that allow the Eurasian east to communicate with the west without crossing the open ocean dominated by the United States. The MSR and the Polar Silk Road (PSR) are key elements of China's strategy and contribute to the shaping of a single maritime transportation web around the Eurasian continent, which geopolitically is much more important than the simple sum of its various sea routes (Costas 2019).

In conclusion, the BRI is a key element of a new geopolitical mechanism that, seeking to protect China's national and security interests, incorporates historical experience (the Cold War), is a response to US efforts to contain China's emergence and contributes to the transfer of the balance of power from the Western hemisphere to the Eastern, which could facilitate the emergence of a new bipolar global system to succeed the current unstable multipolar one. Even if the international system does not become bipolar in the near future, a multipolar system based on a more equal balance of power could create greater stability in the international system than what we are experiencing today.

Development

China's BRI is the largest such initiative in global history. Investing in infrastructure is a crucial aspect of a successful growth strategy. Woetzel et al. (2017) find that in all countries there is a significant gap between what they are spending and their infrastructure requirements if they are to continue to grow well until 2035. The BRI initiative is generally popular in the developing world, where almost all countries face infrastructure deficiencies and are not willing to attract private investment, which generally requires a very high rate of return, making it expensive. Therefore, developing countries that want to establish infrastructure quickly often have little alternative than to participate in the BRI.

China lends money to developing countries to construct infrastructure for transport, power and water supply and other sectors. In his opening remarks at the Belt and Road Forum in Beijing in May 2017, President Xi noted: 'Infrastructure connectivity is the foundation of development through cooperation … We should improve transregional logistics networks and promote connectivity of policies, rules and standards so as to provide institutional safeguards for enhancing connectivity' (Xinhuanet 2017).

The World Bank and other development banks were originally set up for this core function, but now only about 30 per cent of World Bank lending is for infrastructure and its procedures are extraordinarily bureaucratic and time-consuming (Jones 2019). On the other hand, China is offering to finance infrastructure at what could be called commercial terms. Most of its loans are in dollars on commercial terms that are more generous than developing countries can get from private investors, but much more costly than funds from Western donors or the concessional windows of the multilateral development banks (Dollar 2020). In addition, many BRI projects would be unbankable by Western standards. Even so, they can still be important to the countries involved and they 'make sense' to China.

To illustrate, ASEAN countries traditionally could rely on Western support—through bilateral financing and the multilateral development banks—to finance some of their infrastructure investment. However, that is no longer the case. Japan is the only remaining significant financier of infrastructure. During 2015–17, Japan committed US$13 billion to transport and energy infrastructure in ASEAN countries. No other Western donor reached $1 billion per year. The total from the six major Western sources—Australia, Japan, the Asian Development Bank (ADB), World Bank, United States and South Korea—amounted to about 2 per cent of the infrastructure financing needs of the ASEAN countries. There are two main reasons for this: first, the overall amount of Western aid is not keeping up with demand and, second, the donors are generally turning away from infrastructure. Another aspect of declining Western support is the ideological view that infrastructure can be left to private investment, which has proved hard to achieve.

BRI governance

The BRI has typically been described as a cooperative arrangement among likeminded states interested in advancing infrastructure and connectivity projects around the world. The initiative is not yet a formal institutionalised body and is still highly centralised and coordinated from the top by the Chinese political leadership. As the breadth and depth of the BRI have grown in terms of the projects undertaken, the actors involved and the objectives being pursued, the need for a more formalised institutional architecture has become clear.

Institutional evolution

On 4 November 2014, the eighth meeting of the Central Leading Group for Financial and Economic Affairs, chaired by President Xi, focused on the BRI. On 9–11 December 2014, the BRI was identified at the Central Economic Work Conference as a key strategy for 2015 for the promotion of regional economic development. At the end of March 2015, the Chinese Government issued its 'Vision and Actions' document defining the BRI's guiding principles, routes and cooperation priorities and identifying the NDRC as the lead organisation for coordinating BRI efforts, with some shared responsibility from the ministries of commerce and foreign affairs. At the same time, two task forces were established under the State Council's guidance to supervise all BRI-related activities: the Leading Small Group on Advancing the Construction of the Belt and Road, and the Office of the Leading Small Group on Advancing the Construction of the Belt and Road, located within the NDRC, which manages the day-to-day central oversight and coordination work with relevant ministries and entities. In addition, in 2017, the Belt and Road Promotion Centre within the NDRC was created. Moreover, nearly 32 Chinese provinces are also participating.

At the top of the chain, President Xi gives guidance during regular study sessions specifically dedicated to the BRI. Following the Thirteenth National People's Congress in March 2018, Vice-Premier and Politburo Standing Committee member Han Zheng became chairman of the Leading Small Group, while State Counsellor and former minister of foreign affairs Yang Jiechi, Vice-Premier Hu Chunhua, Secretary-General of the State Council Xiao Jie and NDRC Director He Lifeng assumed responsibility as vice-chairmen.

BRI leading small groups have also been created in relevant Chinese ministries and in each province. Similar to the central one, ministerial and provincial groups meet on a regular basis and include representatives from a variety of relevant government entities whose responsibilities pertain to the advancement of the BRI. Since 2013, several white papers have been released to inform global audiences of the BRI's new priorities.

China has vowed to provide financial support for the BRI. In its initial stages, the Chinese Government extended the scope of its financial backing to US$90 billion for the Silk Road Fund (SRF), which was established in 2014 to foster development along the BRI route. Its major stakeholders are the State Administration of Foreign Exchange, the Export–Import Bank of China (Exim Bank), China Investment Corporation and China Development Bank. Moreover, China has built very large banking institutions to support its outward investments and its credit, lending and aid activities, such as the China Development Bank (CDB) and the Exim Bank.

BRI takes a more multilateral approach

To date, China has organised two Belt and Road Forums (BRFs) for International Cooperation in Beijing, in 2017 and 2019, with the participation of state leaders from around the world. The purpose of the BRF is to build a more open and efficient international cooperation platform, a closer, stronger partnership network and to push for a more just, reasonable and balanced international governance system. Key terms supporting multilateralism—such as 'inclusive', 'voluntary participation' and 'being open to all and respectful of national and international commitments'—have been prominent in the forum's rhetoric. President Xi called for the BRF to become a regular event, suggesting it would be used to implement a multilateral institutional architecture for the BRI.

In addition to the BRF, China has initiated two international development–oriented banks, the Asian Infrastructure Investment Bank (AIIB) and the New Development Bank (NDB). The AIIB began operations in January 2016 and has evolved into a high-profile multilateral institution that now has 102 approved members worldwide, while the NDB was established in 2014 and remains largely restricted to the five BRICS countries (Brazil, Russia, India, China and South Africa).

Another aspect of the BRI related to global governance is collaboration with multilateral development banks (MDBs)—in particular, the World Bank Group, the European Bank for Reconstruction and Development, the ADB, the AIIB, the NDB and the European Investment Bank. These six MDBs signed a joint memorandum of understanding with China on 14 May 2017 to support the BRI. In terms of overall finances and institutions, however, the MDBs are only one piece of a larger picture.

In recent years and especially since the first BRF, Beijing has taken a range of steps to exert more control over the BRI, including a more muted publicity drive, clearer rules for state-owned enterprises, restricting the use of the BRI brand and building overseas auditing and anticorruption mechanisms. It is also stepping up efforts to get developed nations to join in to spread the risk of building projects in poorer nations and to counter allegations the BRI is an attempt to build China's political influence. However, to fully engage with other stakeholders, China would have to invent a bureaucratic framework with reasonable consistency, setting up clear criteria for selecting potential projects that are credit-worthy. This consistency would have to be spelt out clearly, and practised diligently, to reassure international partners.

In May 2017, during the first BRF for International Cooperation, the BRF Advisory Council was created to give multilateral intellectual support to the forum. The council is an international policy advisory body with 11 members from international organisations, research and politics. Two members are from China and the remainder are from Asia, Europe and Africa. The council is led by Shamshar Akhtar, former executive secretary of the UN Economic and Social Commission for Asia and the Pacific, and Justin Yifu Lin, former senior vice-president of the World Bank and Honorary Dean of the National School of Development at Peking University.

The BRF and its advisory council could emerge as the major multilateral platform for BRI cooperation. They may also benefit from the models of some existing multilateral platforms on how to institute an architecture of supporting mechanisms. The principles of extensive consultation, joint efforts and shared benefits call intrinsically for a multilateral approach to working together. Becoming more multilateral could also broaden the support base of BRI cooperation and enhance the sense of ownership of all partners.

Indicative of this orientation are the findings and recommendations of the first report issued by the BRF Advisory Council. It proposed to promote an open world economy by fostering a global, broad-based partnership built on connectivity, to focus on building high-quality BRI cooperation by galvanising a shared commitment to multilateralism, to build a 'clean Silk Road' with 'zero tolerance for corruption' and to use green finance to accelerate achieving the ambitions of the BRI. According to the report, the development of cooperative financing and sectoral multilateral mechanisms would also be essential for sustaining further development of cooperation in the long term.

The BRF Advisory Council has also suggested that BRI cooperation stay committed to upholding multilateralism, safeguarding the rules-based multilateral trading system centred on the World Trade Organization (WTO), promoting free and open trade and investment and opposing all forms of protectionism. However, in this regard, greater synergy needs to be tapped between the BRI and various national, regional and global development strategies, including, among others, the UN 2030 Agenda for Sustainable Development (which aims to improve global development along 17 Sustainable Development Goals), the African Union's Agenda 2063, the development plan of the Eurasian Economic Union, the Master Plan on ASEAN Connectivity, the Asia Pacific Economic Cooperation (APEC) Connectivity Blueprint, the Community of Latin American and Caribbean States (CELAC) and the EU Strategy on Connecting Europe and Asia.

The move to create a multilateral architecture for the BRI is inevitable. To date, most formal arrangements exist in the form of bilateral treaties or contracts on specific projects. Since its 2013 launch, the BRI has not been described as a formal organisational setup; rather, the BRI has been used as a descriptive label for a range of projects being undertaken around the world that involve China in some way.

The advisory council's report directly addressed the issue of enhancing the BRI's institutional architecture. It suggested the BRF become formalised and meet every two to three years to discuss and set the broad parameters of the BRI. From this, there can also be 'satellite events' on a regional or sectoral basis to examine particular issues. The BRF Advisory Council further recommended expanding and leveraging diversified sources of finance for BRI projects—in particular, to fill the funding gap for sustainable infrastructure.

Formalising the BRI's activities through a multilateral architecture will also bring more effectiveness to the connectivity and infrastructure projects through more organised planning that in turn increases the effectiveness of the projects. And, as the advisory council explains, 'going more multilateral could broaden the supporter base of the Belt and Road cooperation and enhance the sense of ownership of all partners' (Yang 2019). The advisory council's suggestions must be acted on to transform the BRI into a formal international institution.

The BRI's impacts on connectivity

In this section, we review the consequences of the BRI for both transport and digital connectivity. We then discuss the importance of policy coordination across economies to capture these benefits.

Infrastructure connectivity

Transport connectivity

BRI-related transport infrastructure projects—such as railways, highways and ports—will build on existing transportation networks, creating new links and making the connectivity of networks denser. Reed and Trubetskoy (2019) compiled the first geocoded database of BRI transport infrastructure projects in Eurasia (see Figure 2.1).[1] The status of these projects differs widely: some are already operational, such as Highway AH-3 and Highway AH-4 connecting Russia, Mongolia and China; other projects are under construction, like the Juba–Mombasa Railway connecting Kenya and South Sudan; still others are uncertain, such as the Dushanbe–Afghanistan rail upgrade in Tajikistan. In Figure 2.1, the improvement in railway construction is remarkable. For example, while in 2011 there were only 17 trains travelling between Europe and China, carrying goods worth just US$600 million, by 2018, there were more than 6,000 train trips between Europe and China carrying goods worth US$16 billion (see Figure 2.2). The China–Europe Railway Express connects 108 cities in 16 countries across Eurasia, with the main destinations in Germany, Russia, Kazakhstan, Tajikistan, Poland, Belarus, Netherlands and Uzbekistan.

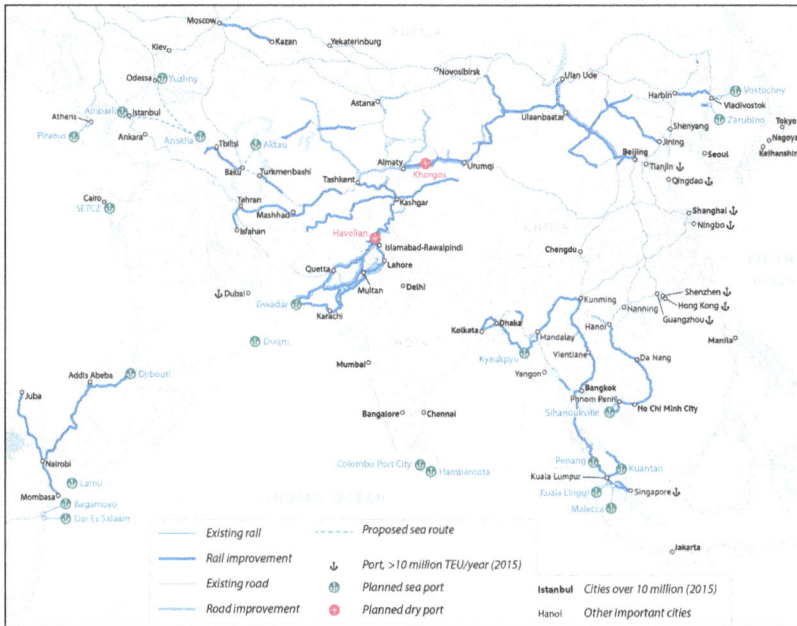

Figure 2.1 BRI-related transport projects by 2018

TEU = 20-foot equivalent unit

Sources: Reed and Trubetskoy (2019); World Bank (2019).

---

1   The full list of BRI-related transport projects is provided in Appendix A of Reed and Trubetskoy (2019). It is worth noting that there is no official list and no uniform definition of BRI-related transport projects.

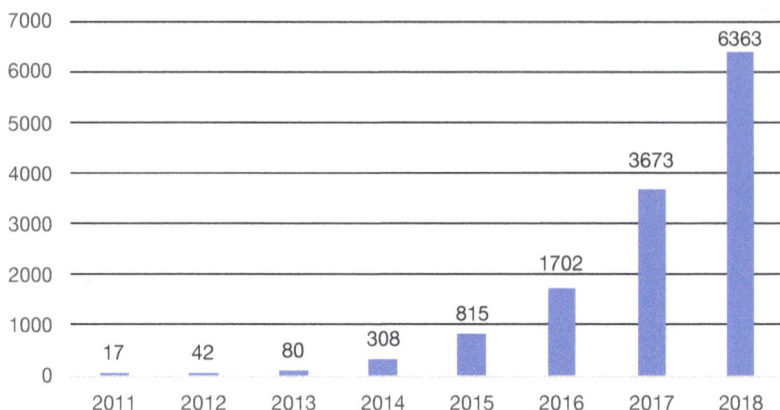

Figure 2.2 Number of China–Europe Railway Express trains, 2011–18

Source: Silk Road Guoxin Big Data Technology Co. Ltd (n.d.).

Based on the list of BRI-related transport projects compiled by Reed and Trubetskoy (2019), de Soyres et al. (2018) obtained information on rail and maritime infrastructure linked to the BRI, allowing a comparison of the pre-BRI and post-BRI scenarios.[2] They exploit geographic information system (GIS) analysis to calculate the reduction in shipping times between cities.[3] As a starting point, the transportation network in 2013 was used to estimate the pre-BRI shipping time. The post-BRI travel time is computed in accordance with the 'improved scenario', including all planned BRI-related rail and maritime projects by 2018.

Before the implementation of the BRI, shipping between some BRI locations was slow as there was little access to quality transport infrastructure and services (see Table 2.1). For instance, the average shipping time within East Asia and the Pacific was longer than within other regions, taking 19.6 days. It takes, on average, 26.8 days to ship goods between East Asia and the Pacific and Central and Eastern Europe, and the average shipping time between East Asia and the Pacific and Central and Western Asia is also long, at 22.5 days.

---

2   The majority of BRI-related transport projects comprise rail and maritime infrastructure. Note that there is a slight difference between the list in de Soyres et al. (2018: Annex 2) and that in Reed and Trubetskoy (2019).

3   The global database in de Soyres et al. (2018) includes 1,000 cities in 191 countries.

Table 2.1 Average pre-BRI shipping time within and between regions, 2013

Average shipping time (days)	Central and Eastern Europe	Central and Western Asia	East Asia and the Pacific	Middle East and North Africa	South Asia	Sub-Saharan Africa
Central and Eastern Europe	3.3					
Central and Western Asia	13.4	13.0				
East Asia and the Pacific	26.8	22.5	7.1			
Middle East and North Africa	12.8	15.4	20.4	9.0		
South Asia	22.4	20.3	15.5	15.2	11.8	
Sub-Saharan Africa	19.8	23.2	20.6	14.4	17.6	4.0
Regional	13.9	16.6	19.6	14.0	17.8	18.5

Note: Averaged over all country pairs in each regional pair.

Sources: de Soyres et al. (2018); World Bank (2019).

The implementation of BRI-related transport projects can reduce shipping times for the BRI corridor economies (see Figures 2.3 and 2.4). The findings of de Soyres et al. (2018) show that average shipping time between the BRI economies can decrease by 1.7 per cent (for the lower bound) and 3.2 per cent (for the upper bound).[4] In particular, the decline in travel time is larger along the BRI economic corridors. The smallest improvement in shipping time is for the China–Mongolia–Russia Economic Corridor, for which the reduction in shipping time ranges between 3.6 per cent and 3.8 per cent on average. The largest improvement is for the China–Central Asia–West Asia Economic Corridor, which will experience a simple average decrease in travel time ranging between 10.3 per cent and 11.9 per cent.

---

4   In the lower-bound scenario, there is no mode switching between the pre-BRI and the post-BRI shipping routes; in the upper-bound scenario, mode switching is allowed, so that routes can be moved from maritime lanes to railway lines for larger gains in shipping times.

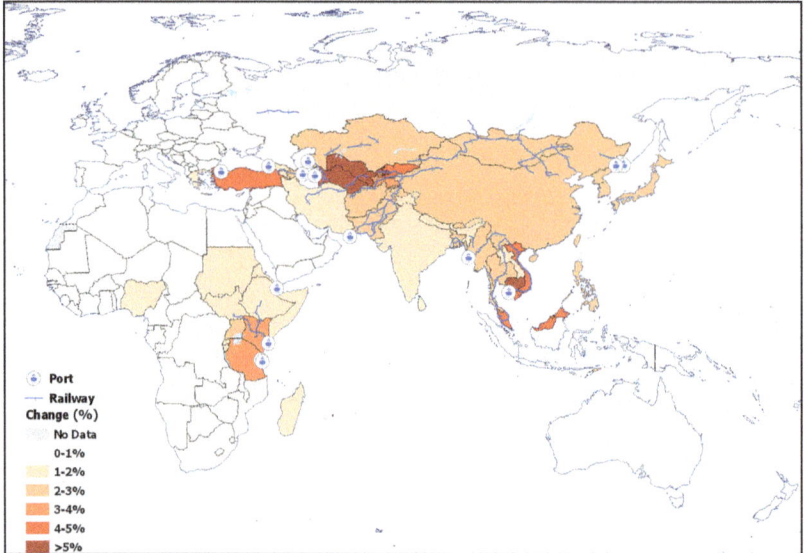

Figure 2.3 Average decline in shipping time by economy: Lower bound

Note: For each economy, the aggregate proportional reduction is calculated as the average proportional shipping time reduction with all other economies in the world.

Source: de Soyres et al. (2018).

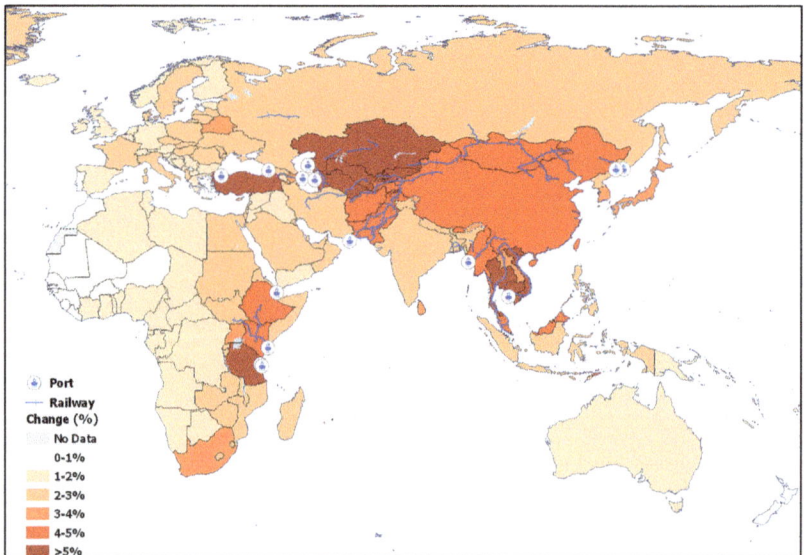

Figure 2.4 Average decline in shipping time by economy: Upper bound

Note: For each economy, the aggregate proportional reduction is calculated as the average proportional shipping time reduction with all other economies in the world.

Source: de Soyres et al. (2018).

Interestingly, the BRI can induce a positive spillover effect on shipping times for the non-BRI economies, which will also benefit from the improved transportation network when their transport routes pass through the new or upgraded ports or railways. As an example, the construction of Tanzania's Bagamoyo Port is anticipated to benefit not only Tanzania but also surrounding countries. Consequently, when all BRI-related transport projects are implemented, the proportional decrease in travel time from Rwanda to Australia is predicted to be 0.5 per cent. Likewise, the improvement for Djibouti's port will see a reduction of 1.2 per cent in the shipping time between Ethiopia and Australia. In general, shipping times across all country pairs in the world can come down, on average, by 1.2 per cent (for the lower bound) and 2.5 per cent (for the upper bound).

Digital connectivity

The level of digital connectivity within and between the BRI economies varies widely. The World Bank (2016b) suggests the digital gap within economies can be as large as that between economies. Many people remain untouched by the modern digital revolution. As shown in Figure 2.5a, apart from Singapore, Malaysia, Kazakhstan and economies in the Arabian Peninsula, the proportion of the population using the internet was less than 55 per cent in most Asian economies in 2018, even in China, which had the largest number of internet users. Mobile broadband networks provide a significant channel for digital connectivity, but there are also two extremes to the coverage of fourth-generation (4G) mobile signals among the BRI economies. As shown in Figure 2.5b, 4G coverage is high in China, Thailand, Eastern Europe and the Arabian Peninsula, but low in the rest of Asia, particularly the landlocked countries.

Efforts are being made to address the digital divide among the BRI economies. According to the China Academy of Information and Communication Technology, China is considering establishing several cross-border overland fibre-optic cable systems and supplying international internet transmission services. Therefore, countries bordering China will have greater access to global submarine cables. So far, remarkable progress has been made in the construction of China–Kyrgyzstan, China–Myanmar, China–Pakistan and China–Russia cross-border fibre-optic cables, which will effectively facilitate communication connectivity within the BRI region. In addition, the China–Nepal cross-border fibre-optic cable, which launched in 2018, provides China and East Asian countries with the shortest internet path to Africa and the Middle East.

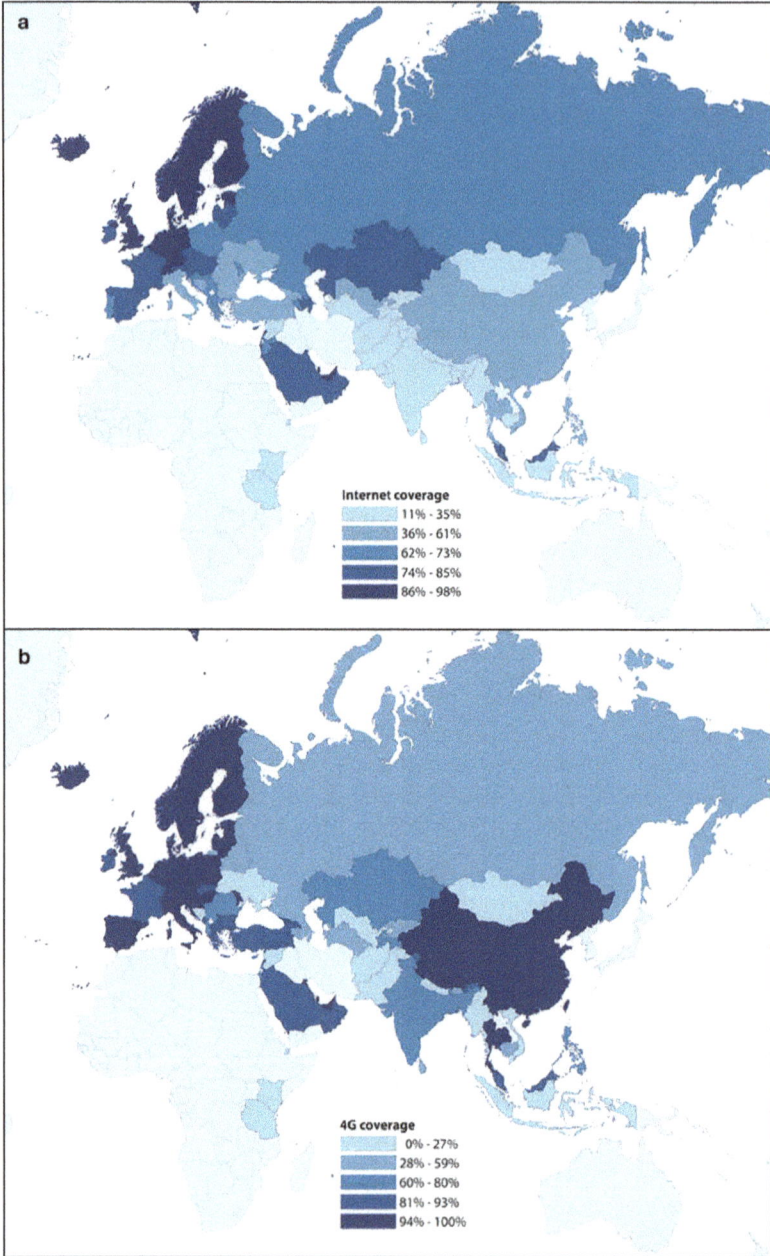

Figure 2.5 Internet users and access to mobile broadband, 2018

a. Internet users (percentage of population) b. 4G coverage (percentage of population)

Note: Western European economies are included as comparators since most BRI-related infrastructure projects are in Eurasia, and a network is only as good as its weakest link.

Source: World Bank (2019).

Policy coordination

Policy coordination has played a significant role in shortening shipping times—for instance, by reducing border delays and the frequency of cargo transhipment. As an example, although there are roads linking the two non-bordering countries China and Uzbekistan, vehicles from one country were not allowed to enter the other for a long time, so their goods needed to transit through Kyrgyzstan for eight to 10 days. In the wake of the implementation of the 'China–Uzbekistan Intergovernmental Agreement on International Road Transport', the transit period between the two countries has been reduced to two days, and the cost of freight per tonne has been cut by US$300–500 (Wu 2018). More and more countries and international organisations have signed intergovernmental BRI cooperation agreements over the years. By the end of January 2020, the Chinese Government had signed 200 cooperation agreements with 138 countries and 30 international organisations. In addition, the BRI has expanded from Eurasia to Africa, Latin America and the South Pacific.

Great importance is attached to the continued integration of the various development strategies, plans, platforms and projects among the BRI economies, achieving complementary advantages and producing effects according to the theory that 'one plus one is greater than two'. So far, the BRI has been dovetailed with Kazakhstan's Bright Road Initiative, Vietnam's Two Corridors and One Economic Circle Plan, Indonesia's Global Maritime Fulcrum Doctrine, Poland's Amber Road Framework, Mongolia's Development Road Program, Saudi Vision 2030 and so on, effectively promoting common prosperity and development.

There are other examples of efforts on policy coordination. First, the Digital Silk Road has been an important part of the BRI. In December 2017, China, Egypt, Laos, Saudi Arabia, Serbia, Thailand, Turkey and the United Arab Emirates jointly launched the Belt and Road Digital Economy International Cooperation Initiative. Sixteen countries have signed a memorandum of understanding with China for the construction of the Digital Silk Road. Second, China published the 'Action Plan on Belt and Road Standard Connectivity (2018–2020)' in December 2017, under which it has signed 85 standardisation cooperation agreements with 49 economies. Third, the BRI's long-term tax cooperation mechanism is maturing. In May 2018, China coorganised the Belt and Road Initiative Tax Cooperation Conference (BRITCC) and issued the 'Astana Proposal by BRITCC Participating Jurisdictions for Enhancing Cooperation in Tax Matters', expanding the tax cooperation network to 111 countries and regions. Fourth, in terms of legal operations, China published the 'Statement of the Co-Chairs of the Forum on the Belt and Road Legal Cooperation' in July 2018. Moreover, China has carried out cooperation on intellectual property, issuing the 'Joint Statement on Pragmatic Cooperation in the Field of Intellectual Property Among Countries Along the Belt and Road' with 49 BRI economies in August 2018.

Economic effects of BRI connectivity

Better infrastructure connectivity and greater policy coordination under the BRI framework can inject strong impetus into the economies of the BRI countries and regions, making the trade network between them more intensive, leading to more foreign direct investment (FDI) flows and improving their positions in global value chains (GVCs).

Impacts on trade

Trade costs

Declines in shipping times can be transformed into decreases in trade costs by estimating the 'value of time' by sector (Hummels and Schaur 2013). De Soyres et al. (2018) investigated the BRI's effect on trade costs based on their research on shipping time reductions mentioned above (see Figures 2.6 and 2.7). Their findings show that implementing all BRI-related transport projects will result in a reduction of average trade costs for the BRI economies ranging between 1.5 per cent and 2.8 per cent, and for the world ranging between 1.1 per cent and 2.2 per cent. Similar to the changes in shipping times, trade costs will decrease along the BRI economic corridors, ranging from 2.4 per cent for the China–Mongolia–Russia Economic Corridor to 10.2 per cent for the China–Central Asia–West Asia Economic Corridor in the upper-bound scenario.

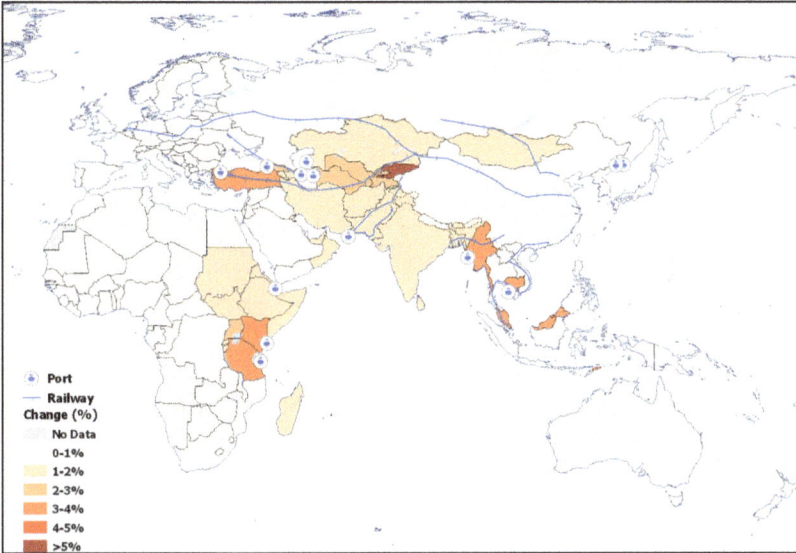

Figure 2.6 Average decline in trade costs by economy: Lower bound
Note: For each economy, all destinations are weighted by import flows.
Source: de Soyres et al. (2018).

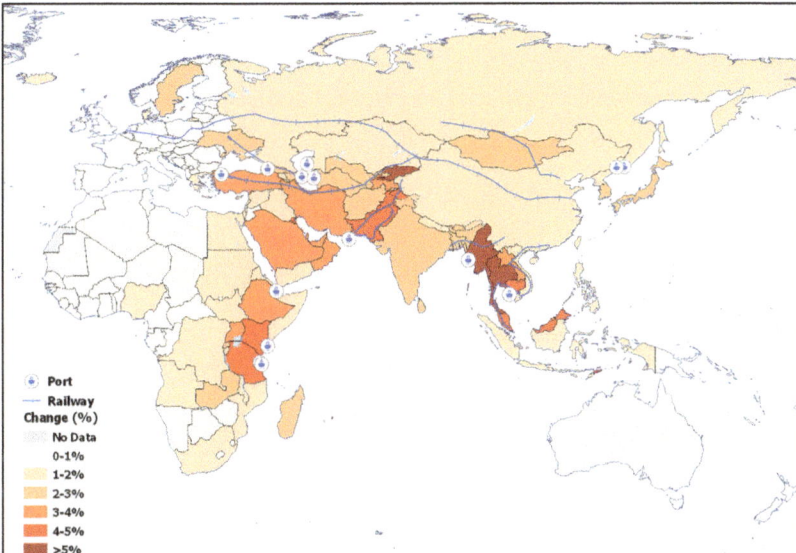

Figure 2.7 Average decline in trade costs by economy: Upper bound
Note: For each economy, all destinations are weighted by import flows.
Source: de Soyres et al. (2018).

Overall trade flows

Based on the results for trade cost reductions from de Soyres et. al. (2018), Maliszewska and van der Mensbrugghe (2019) and de Soyres et al. (2019) use a dynamic computable general equilibrium (CGE) model and a static structural general equilibrium (SGE) model, respectively, to study the impacts of BRI infrastructure improvements on trade (see Figure 2.8).[5]

According to the results from the CGE model, the exports of the BRI economies increase by 2.8 per cent (in 2030 relative to the baseline) and global exports increase by 1.7 per cent. The BRI countries that will experience the largest trade growth are Thailand (14.9 per cent), Malaysia (12.4 per cent), Pakistan (9.8 per cent) and Bangladesh (8.7 per cent). Non-BRI economies can also benefit from the denser transport network generated by BRI-related transport projects, experiencing an increase in export volume of 0.7 per cent in aggregate. Among the non-BRI economies, Ethiopia will obtain the largest trade gains by taking advantage of the new ports in East Africa, with an increase in exports of 3.9 per cent. The United States and the remaining high-income economies will also benefit greatly, with their export volumes increasing by 3.4 per cent and 1.4 per cent, respectively.[6] However, not all non-BRI economies will benefit from the BRI's improved transportation network. The non-BRI economies in Latin America and the rest of Western Europe will experience a slight decrease in trade (by –0.5 per cent and –0.3 per cent, respectively) due to trade diversion.[7]

The trade effects of the BRI infrastructure improvements projected by the SGE model are similar to those predicted by the CGE model but tend to be much larger. The BRI economies are projected to increase exports by up to 9.7 per cent, while global export volumes will go up by 6.3 per cent. The proportional increase in the non-BRI economies' exports is predicted

---

5   The CGE model in Maliszewska and van der Mensbrugghe (2019) is the ENVISAGE model developed by the World Bank, incorporating five production factors, 28 sectors and 34 countries and regions. The SGE model in de Soyres et al. (2019) is based on the Ricardian model in Caliendo and Parro (2015), which includes sectoral linkages, trade in intermediate goods and sectoral heterogeneity, comprising 107 countries and regions. The CGE model has a more detailed structure of the economy than the SGE model, which comes at the expense of a higher level of aggregation of countries into large regions.

6   The remaining high-income economies include Australia, New Zealand, Hong Kong, Japan, South Korea, Taiwan and Canada.

7   The rest of Western Europe includes Austria, Belgium, Cyprus, Denmark, Finland, France, Germany, Greece, Ireland, Italy, Luxembourg, Malta, Netherlands, Portugal, Spain, Sweden, the United Kingdom, Switzerland and Norway.

to be 4.1 per cent. The results from the two models are complementary and should be viewed as providing a range for the potential trade-promoting effects of the BRI transport infrastructure improvements. Unlike the CGE analysis, the SGE model stresses the connections through GVCs because it supposes that there are strong complementarities between the foreign and domestic inputs in production. As trade costs fall due to the denser transportation network, the SGE model projects that firms will increase their use of imported input products, with larger promotion effects on their productivity and export volumes.

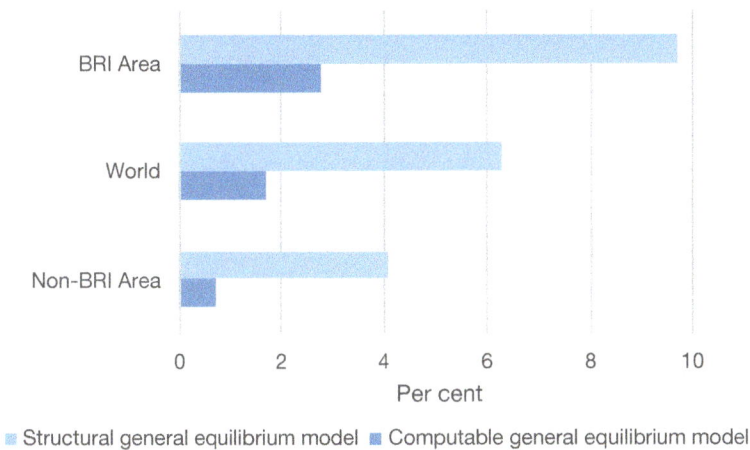

■ Structural general equilibrium model ■ Computable general equilibrium model

Figure 2.8 Export-promoting effects of BRI infrastructure improvements: Upper bound

Sources: de Soyres et al. (2019); Maliszewska and van der Mensbrugghe (2019); World Bank (2019).

Bilateral trade flows

The BRI is anticipated to reshape trade relationships for participating economies with each other and with the rest of the world. Long trading times before the implementation of the BRI led to the downturn in intra–BRI country trade (see Table 2.1). The SGE model predicts that implementing all BRI-related transport projects will induce growth of 7.2 per cent in intra–BRI country trade.

Changes in trade flows will differ by region, depending on the extent to which new or improved infrastructure affects trade costs and the countries' economic structures. Table 2.2 reports that all BRI regions, except the Middle East and North Africa, will expand their exports to East Asia and the Pacific, reflecting a surge in imports for economies like China,

Thailand and Malaysia. The BRI transport infrastructure improvements will also lead to an increase in exports from East Asian and Pacific economies to other BRI regions—most remarkably, to the Middle East and North Africa (10.98 per cent), Europe and Central Asia (8.63 per cent)—and among themselves (5.88 per cent). Regional value chains will be intensified. Other significant changes in bilateral trade flows are the increase in exports from the Middle East and North Africa to Europe and Central Asia (37.87 per cent) and South Asia (25.90 per cent). This can be interpreted by firms' access to cheaper inputs from other BRI regions, which enhances their competitiveness in overseas markets. Such channels are of particular importance for firms in Europe and Central Asia, whose exports to non-BRI areas will increase by 18.35 per cent.

Table 2.2 Changes in BRI regional trade flows

	From BRI to BRI	East Asia and Pacific	Europe and Central Asia	Middle East and North Africa	South Asia	Sub-Saharan Africa	Non-BRI area
Exporters	East Asia and Pacific	5.88	8.63	10.98	0.75	−4.05	9.86
	Europe and Central Asia	0.27	9.59	13.69	0.29	23.82	18.35
	Middle East and North Africa	−1.76	37.87	3.76	25.90	8.21	8.59
	South Asia	5.98	13.86	8.52	1.12	−1.45	5.65
	Sub-Saharan Africa	16.95	22.37	11.00	17.43	−0.28	15.03

Source: de Soyres et al. (2019).

In terms of the trade effects of BRI digital connectivity, Zhang (2018) uses the gravity model to investigate the impact of telecommunications infrastructure construction on bilateral trade flows among the BRI countries in Asia, which shows that each 1 per cent increase in the level of telecommunications infrastructure will lead to a 1.56 per cent rise in import volumes. Compared with transport infrastructure, the improvement in telecommunications infrastructure can not only raise trade efficiency, but also reduce information asymmetry, which helps the price mechanism come into play.

Impact of BRI policy coordination on trade

Policy coordination in the BRI framework plays a non-negligible role in achieving unimpeded trade. Based on the quadratic assignment procedure, Chong and Qin (2017) compare the trade networks before and after the implementation of the BRI and find that intergovernmental trade agreements have a significant and positive impact on trade in the BRI economies. Tao and Qiao (2020) achieved a similar result by using the gravity model. Tian and Liu (2019) examine the validity of the BRI and suggest it has boosted bilateral trade among the participating economies, helping avoid the trend of reverse globalisation. Zheng and Zhou (2019) further classify the BRI corridor economies into those that have reached intergovernmental trade agreements and those that have not, noting that trade agreements have a greater potential trade-promoting effect on the BRI economies without agreements. This can be explained by the fact that the BRI economies without trade agreements mostly adopt protectionist policies and set higher trade barriers for their relatively backward economies. Once a trade agreement is reached to lower trade barriers, it will create a lot of trade.

Policy coordination can magnify the trade gains from infrastructure improvements. De Soyres et al. (2019) simulate two scenarios of complementary policy reform for the BRI economies: 1) a 50 per cent decline in border delays, and 2) a 50 per cent decline in preferential tariffs. As shown in Figure 2.9a, a decrease in border delays and tariffs will amplify the promotion effects of BRI-related transport projects by a factor of about four on global trade, and even five on trade among the BRI economies. In terms of border delays, if, in addition to the transportation network improvements, border delays are reduced by half, exports from the BRI economies will increase by 28.1 per cent. This is not surprising given the long delays at the borders of many BRI economies. It can be verified in Figures 2.9b and 2.9c: the largest trade-promoting effect of BRI infrastructure improvements and border delay reductions will be for low-income economies and the Middle East and North Africa, which tend to have longer border delays. In terms of tariffs, a 50 per cent decline in tariffs among all the BRI economies will amplify the trade-promoting effect of BRI-related infrastructure projects more than the 50 per cent decline in border delays. Not surprisingly, regions with higher tariffs, such as sub-Saharan Africa, will obtain the largest trade gains under this policy scenario.

a

- Infrastructure
- Infrastructure and reduced border delays
- Infrastructure and reduced preferential tariffs
- Infrastructure, borders, and tariffs

b

- Infrastructure
- Infrastructure and reduced border delays
- Infrastructure and reduced preferential tariffs
- Infrastructure, borders, and tariffs

c

- Infrastructure
- Infrastructure and reduced border delays
- Infrastructure and reduced preferential tariffs
- Infrastructure, borders, and tariffs

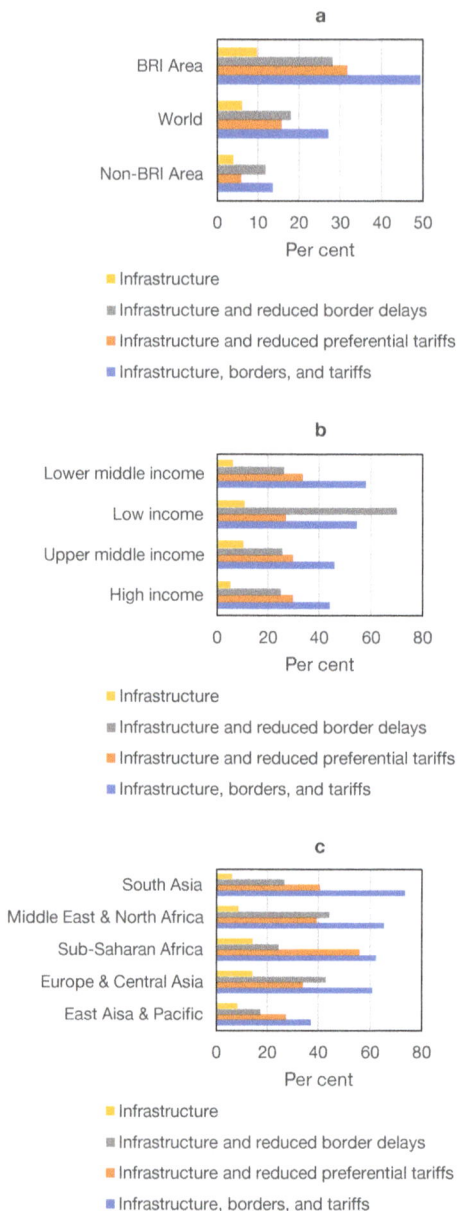

Figure 2.9 Trade-promoting effects of BRI infrastructure improvements and policy coordination

a) Gains by area

b) Gains by income group

c) Gains by region

Source: de Soyres et al. (2019).

Enhancement of trade facilitation

Both infrastructure connectivity and policy coordination can promote trade through enhancing trade facilitation. Feng and Zhang (2019) identify a core of 23 countries along the six BRI corridors by sifting through the data in the *Global Enabling Trade Report 2016*, the *Global Competitiveness Report 2019* and the World Bank's *World Development Indicators* (WEF 2016, 2019; World Bank 2021a). Based on this, they compute changes in the levels of trade facilitation in the six BRI corridors from 2013 to 2018. Their trade facilitation index is weighted by four first-level indicators—namely, 'government capacity and policy environment', 'customs and border management', 'logistics and infrastructure' and 'financial and communication capability'—which are subdivided into 11 second-level indicators and 27 third-level indicators.

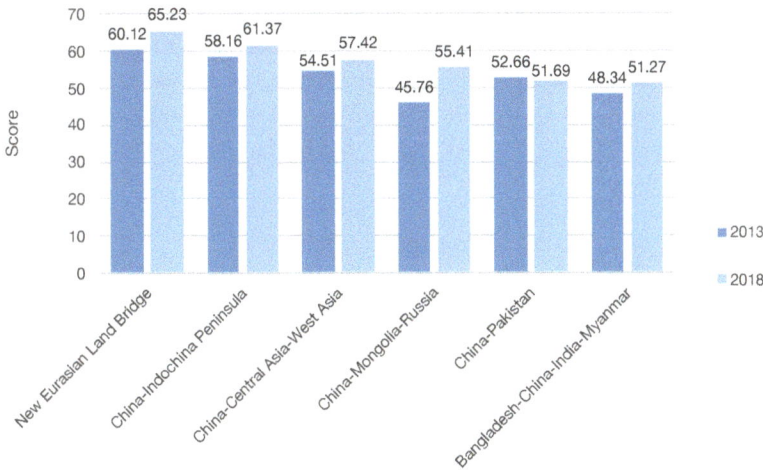

Figure 2.10 Trade facilitation scores for the BRI economic corridors, 2013 and 2018

Source: Feng and Zhang (2019).

Since 2013, with the exception of the China–Pakistan Economic Corridor, trade facilitation in the BRI economic corridors has improved significantly but the degree of development varies with each corridor (see Figure 2.10). Among them, the New Eurasian Land Bridge (65.23 points) had the best performance in 2018, while the Bangladesh–China–India–Myanmar Economic Corridor (51.27 points) had the worst, with its weakest areas in 'financial and communication capability' and 'logistics and infrastructure' (Feng and Zhang 2019). The China–Mongolia–Russia Economic

Corridor has experienced the largest improvement in trade facilitation, particularly in 'financial and communication capability' and 'customs and border management' (Feng and Zhang 2019).

Impact on the structure of trade networks

The BRI has brought the trade network between the corridor economies closer and changed its structure from a multicore pattern to one with China as its single core. Zhao and Sun (2019) map the simplified BRI trade network for 2003 and 2017, which retains only the largest trade flows between the 66 BRI countries and regions (see Figures 2.11 and 2.12). Before the launch of the BRI, China had become one of the central nodes of the regional trade network, in 2003, directly connecting economies including Thailand, India, Vietnam, Saudi Arabia, Egypt, Israel and so on. Meanwhile, Russia was also a core node of this regional trade network, linking economies such as Turkey, Romania, Greece and the other members of the Commonwealth of Independent States. Hence, there was a multicore BRI trade network in 2003. However, some BRI economies remained independent from this network, such as Slovakia, Czech Republic, Slovenia, Croatia and North Macedonia, which indicates the network was relatively loose in 2003.

The structure of the BRI trade network changed in 2017. China's central role has been significantly enhanced: more economies have direct trade linkages with China. There were many economies indirectly connecting with China through 'brokers' (like India, Thailand and Israel) in 2003, but in 2017, China became their largest trading partner. Zhao and Sun (2019) indicate the sustained development of China's economy and trade is the most important reason for this transformation. On the other hand, the density of the Commonwealth of Independent States' trade network, with Russia as its core, has decreased. The scope of the isolated local trade network has also declined: only the largest trade flows of Slovenia, Croatia and Bosnia and Herzegovina were not directly connected to the core BRI trade network in 2017. This reflects the fact the BRI has reduced the decentralisation of regional trade in the area and gradually deepened regional trade integration.

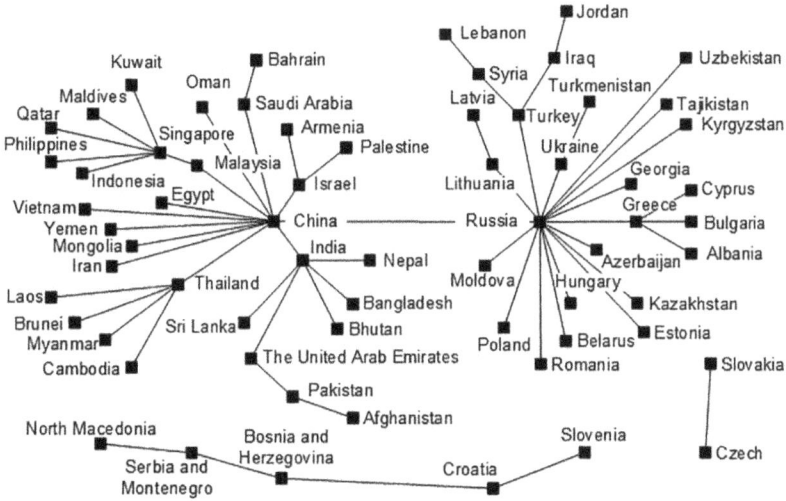

Figure 2.11 Structure of BRI corridor economies' trade networks, 2003

Source: Zhao and Sun (2019).

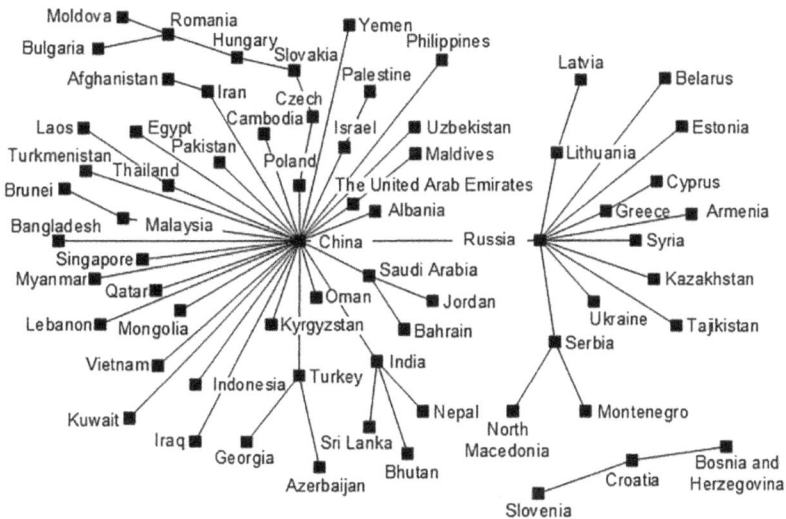

Figure 2.12 Structure of BRI corridor economies' trade networks, 2017

Source: Zhao and Sun (2019).

Impacts on foreign direct investment

Longer travel time is a barrier to FDI flows. Based on the estimates in de Soyres et al. (2018), Chen and Lin (2018) studied the impact of the proposed BRI transportation network on FDI flows to the BRI economies. They find the proposed infrastructure improvements are projected to induce a 4.97 per cent increase in total FDI flows to the BRI economies. Specifically, there will be a 4.36 per cent increase in FDI flows within the BRI area, a 4.63 per cent increase in FDI flows from the Organisation for Economic Co-operation and Development (OECD) economies and a 5.75 per cent increase in FDI flows from the non-BRI area.

Across regions, the proposed BRI transportation network will lead to the largest increase in FDI flows to BRI economies in sub-Saharan Africa (7.5 per cent), followed by Central Asia (7.3 per cent), East Asia and the Pacific (6.3 per cent), South Asia (5.2 per cent), Europe (3.7 per cent) and the Middle East and North Africa (3.4 per cent) (see Figure 2.13).

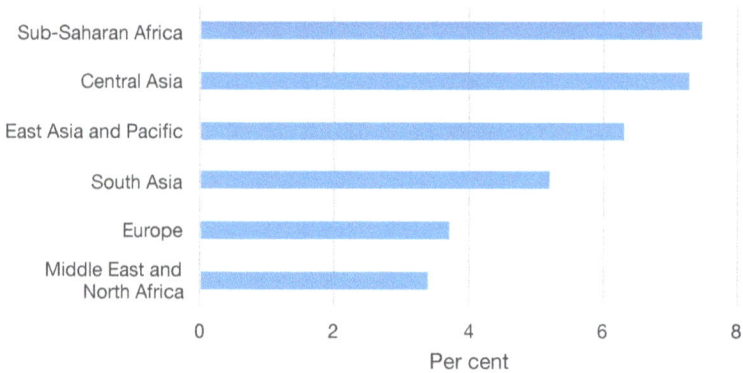

Figure 2.13 Promotion effects on FDI of BRI infrastructure improvements
Sources: Chen and Lin (2018); World Bank (2019).

Impacts on global value chains

Based on value added in trade, Dai and Song (2019) measure the changes in correlations among GVCs from 2010 to 2017, finding that there has been a significant overall trend of enhancement and considerable adjustment. They further explore whether the reconstruction of GVCs is related to China's BRI. Their results show the industrial relevance of the BRI area to GVCs has been significantly reinforced, while that in the non-BRI area has been significantly weakened. It is worth noting that the relevance between the BRI and non-BRI areas has also shown a strengthening trend. From these results, a preliminary judgement can be reached that the implementation of the BRI has promoted the reconstruction of GVCs to a certain extent.

In fact, the economies along the BRI economic corridor have comparative advantages such as cheap labour and abundant natural resources, which make them important destinations for a new round of international industrial gradient transfers and considerable partners with which China can carry out cooperation on production capacity. Therefore, there are two possible reasons for the aforementioned GVC change. On the one hand, with the rising prices of production factors in China, especially labour costs, multinational companies in developed economies will relocate more of their industries and production links to BRI economies. On the other hand, in the BRI framework, China has actively transferred its industries that have gradually lost their comparative advantages to other BRI economies, and even carried out cooperation in high-end industries such as environmental protection, thus promoting the integration of the BRI economies into GVCs. If the former factor dominates, the reconstruction of GVCs may not be caused by China's BRI. To figure out this problem, Dai and Song (2019) first measure the changes in the upstream dependence of the BRI economies on North America, Western Europe and China.

The results in Table 2.3 show that the BRI economies in most regions have intensified their upstream dependence on North America, Western Europe and China, which verifies that the BRI economies are indeed important destinations for a new round of international industrial transfers. However, it should be noted that the upstream dependence of the BRI economies on China has increased the most.

Table 2.3 Changes in upstream dependence of the BRI economies on North America, Western Europe and China, 2010–17 (per cent)

	East Asia	ASEAN	Eastern Europe	South Asia	Central Asia	Others
North America	0.25	0.47	0.61	−0.27	−0.19	0.46
Western Europe	0.46	0.75	4.76	−0.29	−0.71	1.31
China	1.26	1.49	0.92	0.45	−0.12	1.35

Source: Dai and Song (2019).

Dai and Song (2019) also compute the changes in the downstream influence of North America, Western Europe and China on the BRI economies. As shown in Table 2.4, China's downstream influence on the BRI economies has increased more than that of North America. Compared with Western Europe, China also has a greater upward trend in its downstream influence on the BRI economies—except for those in Eastern Europe, because they have close relations with Western Europe. Therefore, in terms of both upstream dependence and downstream influence, it can be inferred that the implementation of China's BRI has significantly promoted the reconstruction of GVCs.

Table 2.4 Changes in the downstream influence of North America, Western Europe and China on the BRI economies, 2010–17 (per cent)

	North America	Western Europe	China
East Asia	0.16	0.15	1.11
ASEAN	0.19	0.12	0.88
Eastern Europe	0.11	0.76	0.30
South Asia	–0.06	–0.04	0.06
Central Asia	0.00	–0.01	0.00
Others	0.45	0.73	1.47

Source: Dai and Song (2019).

Based on data from 2004 to 2014, Peng and Li (2018) find that China's outward foreign direct investment (OFDI) in the BRI economies can improve its position in GVCs through the industrial separation effect. This is because, after transferring certain industries to the BRI economies, Chinese firms can make room for higher-tech production links or industries that retain comparative advantages. At the same time, China's OFDI in the BRI economies can improve the host country's position in GVCs through positive technology spillovers and demand-pull effects. In the case of industrial separation, on the one hand, Chinese firms may transfer some advanced technologies to the BRI economies to ensure the quality of imported intermediate products; on the other, when firms can spare more energy to improve product quality, consumer demands for products will increase, which will further strengthen the existing production mode and gradually improve the host country's position in GVCs.

Risks along the Belt and Road

BRI-related projects involve various inherent risks, which are exacerbated by weak risk-prevention and control mechanisms and poor economic foundations in many participating economies. How to identify and manage these risks appropriately and efficiently becomes increasingly worthy of attention.

Political and legal risks

The complexity and impact of political and legal risks are difficult to assess. Political changes and differences in legal systems may lead to changes in the way foreign loans or direct investment are made and pose more challenges to the implementation of cross-border projects.

A political risk may be distinguished from others by defining it as one that causes losses due to certain political incidents, such as a change in national government or the deterioration of relationships between countries. Political risks can be categorised as geopolitical risks, risks of political power change, sovereign credit risks, as well as risks of nationalisation. Since most of the BRI economies are in geopolitically fragmented regions, and the development of the BRI entails the interests and strategic goals of some world powers, geopolitical risks become a major component of political risk. Most of the time, the risk of a change in political power will affect OFDI through evoking turbulence in society and increasing uncertainties about the executive effectiveness of contracts. Sovereign credit risks exist as the host countries or regions may default during the projects. According to the *Handbook of Country Risk* issued by the China Export & Credit Insurance Corporation (Sinosure 2017, 2018), the overall sovereign credit level of the BRI economies is far below the world average. In addition, to protect domestic industries, the host government may issue policies to restrict the effective control of local assets by foreign-invested enterprises, which is actually an expropriation of those enterprises.

One typical case of political risk is the Myanmar Myitsone Hydropower Project initiated by the Myanmar Government with the China Power Investment Corporation in 2006. There have been many twists in the development of the project over the past decade or so, and it is still on hold. This is mainly due to the political conflicts between the central government and the Kachin Independence Army, the National League for Democracy and various Western nongovernmental organisations in Myanmar, which is in a geopolitically fragmented region and faces risks created by games among the great powers.

Legal risks comprise changes to or uncertainties in systems of foreign investment, intellectual property protection, labour rights protection, environmental regulation, taxation, foreign exchange management and so on. There are significant differences between the laws and regulations of the BRI economies and, in many, they are incomplete.

In 2012, the Aluminium Corporation of China Limited (Chinalco) announced its intention to make a bid for a proportional takeover of up to 60 per cent of the common shares of Ivanhoe Mines' subsidiary coalminer SouthGobi Resources, which eventually failed. To stop Chinalco's acquisition of SouthGobi Resources, the Mongolian Government hastily introduced new foreign investment supervision laws. Mongolia lacks a complete legal system and a stable legal environment for investment. Overall, the legal factors played an influential role in the failure of this acquisition.

According to Guo (2020), there are a number of options to reduce the risks mentioned above. The governments of BRI corridor economies could actively undertake political diplomacy with one another and sign more high-quality bilateral or regional trade and investment agreements so their economies can build and rely on multilateral, pluralistic and multilevel cooperation mechanisms to provide policy and institutional guarantees. More specifically, the BRI economies could establish a joint meeting mechanism for their leaders to coordinate and resolve issues associated with trade and investment cooperation and provide a normalised platform for healthy, orderly and sustainable development of cooperation.

Debt sustainability risks

As described in a report called *Harmonizing Investment and Financing Standards Towards Sustainable Development Along the Belt and Road* by the China Development Bank (CDB 2019), the debt sustainability of countries along the BRI economic corridor has become a focus regionally and has also drawn attention from the international community. It is necessary to balance the relationship between financing development needs and debt sustainability.

Table 2.5 Sovereign credit risk ratings of the BRI countries and regions, 2017–18

Region	Country	2017	2018	Region	Country	2017	2018
Northeast Asia	Russia	BB	BBB	South Asia	India	BBB	BBB
	Mongolia	CC	CCC		Pakistan	B	B
Southeast Asia	Singapore	A	AA		Bangladesh	BB	BB
	Malaysia	A	A		Sri Lanka	CCC	CCC
	Indonesia	BBB	BBB		Maldives	CC	CC
	Myanmar	B	B		Bhutan	CCC	CCC
	Thailand	BBB	BBB		Nepal	CCC	CCC
	Laos	CCC	CCC	Central Asia	Kazakhstan	BBB	BBB
	Cambodia	B	B		Uzbekistan	B	B
	Vietnam	BB	BB		Tajikistan	CCC	CCC
	Brunei	BBB	BBB		Turkmenistan	BBB	BBB
	Philippines	BBB	BBB		Kyrgyzstan	CC	CC
	Timor-Leste	CC	CC	Central and Eastern Europe	Moldova	B	B
West Asia and North Africa	Yemen	CCC	CC		Belarus	BB	BB
	Iraq	BB	BB		Ukraine	CCC	CCC
	Iran	BB	BB		Albania	CCC	B
	Israel	AA	AA		Estonia	A	A
	United Arab Emirates	A	A		Bulgaria	BB	BB
	Oman	BB	BB		Bosnia and Herzegovina	CCC	CCC
	Turkey	BBB	BB		Poland	AA	AA
	Syria	C	C		Montenegro	CCC	B
	Jordan	BB	BB		Czech Republic	AAA	AAA
	Lebanon	BB	BB		Croatia	BBB	BBB
	Saudi Arabia	A	A		Latvia	BBB	BBB
	Qatar	A	A		Lithuania	A	A
	Kuwait	BBB	BBB		Romania	BBB	BBB
	Bahrain	BB	BB		North Macedonia	BB	BB
	Egypt	CCC	CCC		Hungary	A	A
	Afghanistan	CC	CC		Serbia	B	B
	Azerbaijan	BB	BB		Slovakia	AA	AA
	Georgia	B	B		Slovenia	A	A
	Armenia	CCC	CCC				

Sources: Sinosure (2017, 2018).

Debt sustainability risks come from a country's present and future ability to fulfil its debt servicing obligations, which are affected by its current debt level and prospective borrowings. In general, a key factor for achieving external and public debt sustainability is macroeconomic stability. Large infrastructure investments involving debt financing in the BRI economies entail risks to debt sustainability. There is a need for systematic understanding, management and alleviation of debt sustainability risk by taking into account its historical and systematic causes from the perspective of national and global development. The level of sovereign credit risk is an indicator with which to analyse the sustainability of sovereign debt. Sinosure grades this risk into nine levels, from low to high: AAA, AA, A, BBB, BB, B, CCC, CC and C. As shown in Table 2.5, the overall level of debt sustainability risk in the BRI economies is high, but shows a slight downward trend.

According to the World Bank (2019), in economies where there is low scrutiny or low risk of debt distress, if indebtedness is not substantially increased as a result of the BRI, they will generally have the fiscal space to increase investment. However, it is necessary that projects are selected and implemented well to maximise the gains and that financial terms are appropriate and transparent. In addition, evaluating the BRI's impact on the BRI economies' debt sustainability outlook and fiscal risks is also an important procedure. Economies with limited or no fiscal space for expansion would need to limit the number of debt-financed projects, rely on grants or highly concessional financing, favour FDI over debt financing and, if possible, increase public savings to finance additional investments.

When it comes to a concrete method for analysing debt sustainability risks, a framework is provided by China's Ministry of Finance. Specifying the scope of debt is the first step. China's framework clarifies the scope of debt as the general public sector debt on which the principal and/ or interest must be paid to creditors, including bonds, loans and other accounts payable. Dividing economies into groups and predicting their macroeconomic trends are critical methods to make the analysis clearer and more accurate. After these procedures, stress testing is performed on different scenarios to measure the sensitivity of the expected debt burden index to changes in given situations. Following the test, we could judge the risk signals, modify the model result and obtain a risk rating report.

It is worth noting that accurate and timely information is the premise of reliable analysis. Governments should actively participate in the construction of the BRI risk-monitoring system and jointly build a comprehensive early warning system for project risk.

Governance risks

Governance risks vary across corridor economies and correlate closely with the quality of domestic institutions.

Large infrastructure projects can induce corruption—a common governance risk that is reflected in the abuse of public office for private gain. Infrastructure sector corruption can include improper influence over budgeting, the selection of projects and rent extraction in return for a carriage permit, construction contracts, leases or concessions (World Bank 2007). The World Bank indicates that corruption risks correlate closely with a country's development level, since less-developed countries lack a strong rule of law and combating corruption is fundamentally about addressing poor governance. There is, indeed, a positive correlation between the Corruption Perception Index and the Rule of Law Index (see Figure 2.14). Countries or regions with high levels of corruption tend to have weak rule of law. This may be because the weak rule of law promotes and reduces the possibility of detecting corruption. According to the World Bank's *Worldwide Governance Indicators* database (2021b), the average score for corruption control in 64 major BRI economies was –0.26 in 2018 (ranging from –2.5 to 2.5) (see Figure 2.15). There were 40 BRI economies (that is, more than half of the major BRI economies) with a Control of Corruption ranking in the bottom 50 per cent of the world. Consequently, the efficiency and transparency of BRI government work will be affected, which means FDI is likely to suffer corruption risks in the BRI economies.

Procurement in the BRI projects should be open, transparent and executed by the best-placed firms, regardless of their ownership or nationality, to avoid risk. For host borrowing economies, following international best practice is necessary to maximise value for money, which is also important for China and the financial institutions that finance BRI projects as it can help ensure the integrity and financial performance of projects.

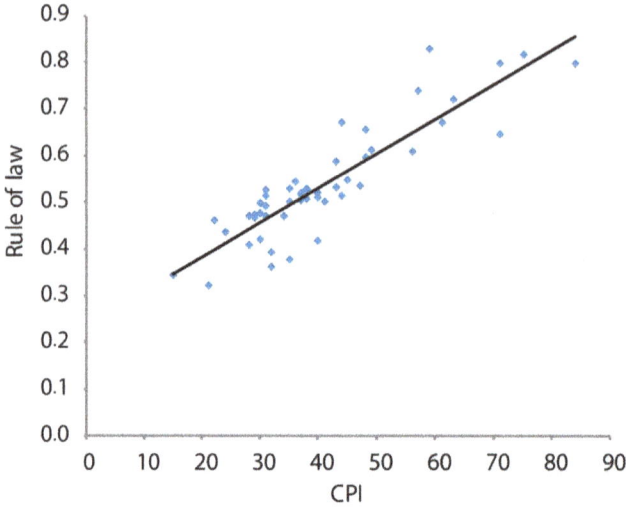

Figure 2.14 Relationship between Corruption Perception Index and Rule of Law Index for BRI economies, 2017

Note: Rule of Law Index scores range from 0 to 1, with 0 indicating weak perceived rule of law and 1 indicating strong perceived rule of law.

Source: World Bank (2019).

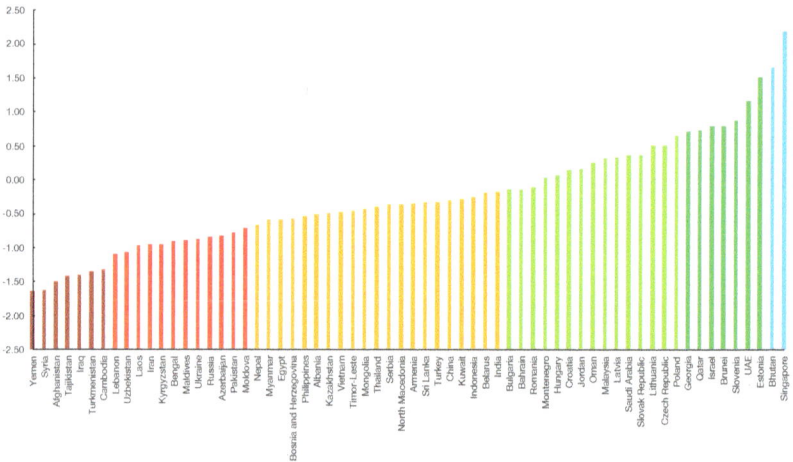

Figure 2.15 Control of Corruption scores for the BRI economies, 2018

Notes: The Control of Corruption scores range from –2.5 (weak control, high corruption) to 2.5 (strong control, low corruption). Blue bars indicate countries with governance scores in the top 10 per cent of 215 countries in the world; dark-green bars indicate countries in the top 10–25 per cent; light-green bars indicate countries in the top 25–50 per cent; orange bars indicate countries in the top 50–75 per cent; light-red bars indicate countries in the top 75–90 per cent; and dark-red bars indicate countries in the bottom 10 per cent.

Source: World Bank (2021a).

Studies by the World Bank (2019) suggest that corruption mitigation can be divided into supply-side measures and demand-side measures. On the supply side, developing common auditing standards and enhancing audit and related institutions are critical. The multistakeholder Construction Sector Transparency Initiative can help economies obtain greater benefits from public infrastructure investment by improving transparency and accountability. Using a set of indicators called red flags that can alert officials to potential corruption during the infrastructure construction period is essential. Implementing integrity pacts and applying information and communications technology can also enhance transparency and reduce corruption risks. Social responsibility is the starting point for demand-side measures. Community monitoring and citizen report cards that strengthen public accountability can be implemented to effectively combat corruption and improve governance of projects.

Studies by the World Bank emphasise three tracks to improve procurement practices by the BRI host economies, China and multilateral international agreements. For the BRI hosts, a first step could be to use diagnostics related to the readiness of the national procurement system with pre-tendering due diligence before determining which procurement rules to apply. Mobilising resources to document the awarding of projects across economies could be an effective approach to increase transparency and generate more information. Two similar paths for China to enhance competition and transparency are associated with international best practice and establish a threshold for BRI projects. One is to introduce international competitive bidding and the other is to include foreign-invested enterprises and organise public national competition once the threshold is exceeded. In addition, multilateral cooperation, such as the WTO Government Procurement Agreement, can promote the use of transparent and competitive procurement practices.

Environmental and social risks

Many BRI projects are large-scale transportation projects that expose local communities to environmental and social risks.

Environmental risks refer to environmental pollution, natural resource destruction and other problems created during project construction that result in the risk of projects being shelved or huge fines for foreign-invested enterprises. Many BRI economies already have resource and environmental problems and, thus, numerous conservation areas have been constructed (see Figure 2.16). However, many still lack strong environmental supervision and protection systems (Guo 2020). In addition, environmental risks are also affected by political, economic and legal factors. For example, the host country may approve an engineering project for the sake of economic development, but it may also adopt strict environmental protection measures in the construction process under pressure from the public and domestic environmental nongovernmental organisations, or due to regime change or legal revision. Therefore, environmental risks need to be taken seriously.

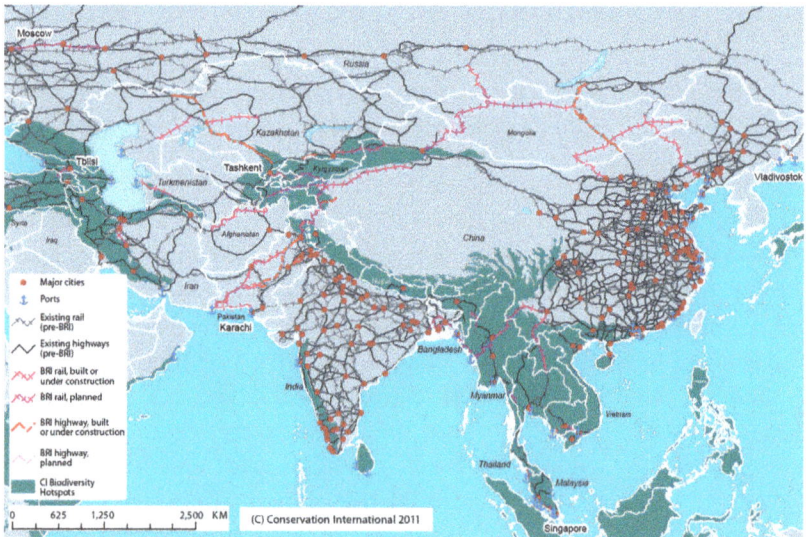

Figure 2.16 BRI road and railway projects in relation to biodiversity risks

CI = Conservation International

Source: World Bank (2019).

According to Losos et al. (2018), the impacts of environmental risks include both the direct impacts of infrastructure construction and the indirect impacts caused by firms' response to new routes. Direct BRI environmental impacts include pollution from increased traffic, topographical and hydrological damage and the alteration of habitats at the expense of biodiversity. BRI projects tend to follow existing transport routes and substitute them with rail, which can reduce pollution compared with road and air travel. Indirect BRI environmental impacts could be both positive and negative. The positive impacts could include densification of settlement and production and a switch to off-farm activities that support rural land consolidation and restoration (Kaczan 2016). However, the negative effects are more pronounced, including increased emissions and opening up border locations to development. Environmental problems can develop by the creation not just of new settlements, but also of particularly high-cost activities such as logging and illegal wildlife trade.

Social risks are closely related to environmental risks, because communities and their environment are directly or indirectly affected by large-scale infrastructure projects. According to the World Bank (2019), the impacts that should be considered include:

- threats to human security
- disproportionate risks to vulnerable people
- discrimination against individuals or groups in the provision of development resources and project benefits
- involuntary requisition of land or restrictions on land use
- tenure and use of land and natural resources
- health, safety and wellbeing of workers and communities affected by projects
- cultural heritage.

In particular, the BRI projects pose a unique challenge of rapid migration to meet the need for labour. Rapid migration has negative impacts on local public infrastructure, utilities, housing, sustainable resource management and social dynamics (World Bank 2016a). More specifically, it leads to increased demand and competition for local goods and services, resulting in rising prices, the crowding out of local consumers and increased demand on resources, thus causing social conflict, increased rates of illegal activity and crime and even increased risks of the spread of infectious diseases.

There are four aspects to the policies to mitigate environmental risks that will be discussed in this section: avoid, reduce, restore and offset (World Bank 2019). Transport routes need to be arranged to *avoid* vulnerable environments—that is, to remove risks at the source. As a result, identification and analysis of alternative routes are essential. Integrating environmental consciousness into projects will *reduce* adverse impacts on the environment. Engineering and complementary policies include wildlife crossings, tunnel and bridge engineering, regulation and enforcement of forest and vulnerable species protection and social cost-benefit analyses in selecting transport options. Remedial measures for repairing damage created by the construction process are necessary to *restore* the environment. Meanwhile, *offset* can include investments in offsite locations to compensate for environmental damage that cannot be avoided, reduced or restored, so as to ensure neutral or positive environmental outcomes overall.

For social risks, the World Bank (2016a) has a framework for screening investments to identify the risk profile for labour influxes and determine the necessary mitigation measures—such as encouraging the local recruitment of workers, affirmative action measures during the recruitment process to give women employment opportunities and ensuring that sufficient background checks are conducted on workers. Trafficking of women and children for prostitution as well as of drugs are issues that deserve attention. The spread of sexually transmitted diseases along traffic corridors should also be taken seriously by governments, which requires corresponding policies to limit their spread and raise people's awareness of prevention.

China has in fact made some efforts to reduce the environmental and social risks of the BRI. On 25 April 2019, 19 international financial institutions signed the 'Green Investment Principle of the Belt and Road Initiative' at the second BRF for International Cooperation. This principle aims to improve the BRI investment environment and social risk management level and promote green investment. It covers strategy formulation, corporate governance, project management, information disclosure and communication and the use of green financial tools.

Conclusion

China's BRI is a unique megaproject in global economic history, which is in line with President Xi Jinping's 'Thoughts' on China as a global power and on globalisation in the twenty-first century and contributes to fulfilling his mission of national rejuvenation. The project at its core incorporates elements of Chinese and Western philosophy, generates strategic flexibility and seeks relative economic advantage. The BRI is a key element of a new geopolitical mechanism that is seeking to protect China's national and security interests, incorporates historical experience (the Cold War) and could be seen as China's 'anti-containment' strategy because it contributes to the 'unification' of the Eurasian mainland (Heartland and Rimland) and seeks autonomy from the oceanic transportation network that is dominated by the United States.

China's BRI has brought the connectivity between the BRI countries closer in terms of infrastructure and policy. As a result, it has shortened shipping times, lowered trade costs and injected strong impetus into the economies of the BRI countries, making the trade network between them more intensive, leading to greater FDI flows into them and improving their positions in GVCs.

The BRI projects involve various inherent risks, such as political and legal, debt sustainability, governance and environmental and social. Although Chinese companies have a wealth of experience, they may encounter many problems due to the wide range of BRI projects. With numerous opportunities for development presented by the BRI, these potential risks and the necessary countermeasures have become issues for attention.

References

BBC News. 2012. 'Full text: China's new party chief Xi Jinping's speech.' *BBC News*, 15 November. Available from: www.bbc.com/news/world-asia-china-20338586.

Caliendo, L. and Parro, F. 2015. 'Estimates of the trade and welfare effects of NAFTA.' *The Review of Economic Studies* 82(1): 1–44.

Chen, M. and Lin, C. 2018. *Foreign investment across the Belt and Road: Patterns, determinants, and effects.* Policy Research Working Paper 8607. Washington, DC: World Bank Group. doi.org/10.1596/1813-9450-8607.

China Development Bank (CDB). 2019. *Harmonizing Investment and Financing Standards Towards Sustainable Development Along the Belt and Road: Economic development along the Belt and Road.* Beijing: CDB and United Nations Development Programme.

China Export & Credit Insurance Corporation (Sinosure). 2017. *The Handbook of Country Risk 2017.* Beijing: China Financial Publishing House.

China Export & Credit Insurance Corporation (Sinosure). 2018. *The Handbook of Country Risk 2018.* Beijing: China Financial Publishing House.

Chong, Z. and Qin, C. 2017. 'The trade network structure of "One Belt One Road" and its influence factors: A study based on analytic network process.' *International Economics and Trade Research* 33(5): 16–28.

Communist Party of China (CPC). 2017. *Constitution of the Communist Party of China: Revised and Adopted at the 19th National Congress of the Communist Party of China on October 24, 2017*. Available from: www.xinhuanet.com/english/download/constitution_of_the_communist_party_of_china.pdf.

Costas, G. 2019. 'The visit of President Xi Jinping: The "Silk Road" and Greece.' [In Greek], *SL Press*, 11 November. Available from: slpress.gr/ethnika/h-episkepsi-toy-proedroy-si-tzinpingk-o-quot-dromos-toy-metaxioy-quot-kai-i-ellada.

Dai, X. and Song, J. 2019. 'Will "One Belt One Road" help China restructure GVC?' *World Economy Studies* 11: 108–21, 136.

de Soyres, F., Mulabdic, A. and Ruta, M. 2019. *Common transport infrastructure: A quantitative model and estimates from the Belt and Road Initiative*. Policy Research Working Paper WPS8801. Washington, DC: World Bank Group. doi.org/10.1596/1813-9450-8801.

de Soyres, F., Mulabdic, A., Murray, S., Rocha, N. and Ruta, M. 2018. *How much will the Belt and Road Initiative reduce trade costs?* Policy Research Working Paper WPS8614. Washington, DC: World Bank Group. doi.org/10.1596/1813-9450-8614.

Dollar, D. 2020. 'Order from chaos: Seven years into China's Belt and Road.' *Brookings Blog*, 1 October. Washington, DC: Brookings Institution. Available from: www.brookings.edu/blog/order-from-chaos/2020/10/01/seven-years-into-chinas-belt-and-road.

Feng, Y. and Zhang, Q. 2019. 'Evaluation report on trade facilitation of the six economic corridors under the Belt and Road Initiative.' *Frontiers* 19: 64–91.

Guo, Z. 2020. *Risks and Prevention & Control Mechanisms of Chinese Enterprises' OFDI: A perspective of the 'Belt and Road'*. Beijing: China Centre for International Economic Exchanges.

Hummels, D. and Schaur, G. 2013. 'Time as a trade barrier.' *American Economic Review* 103(7): 2935–59. doi.org/10.1257/aer.103.7.2935.

Jones, B. (interviewer). 2019. *China's Belt and Road: The new geopolitics of global infrastructure development. A Brookings Interview*. April. Washington, DC: Brookings Institution. Available from: www.brookings.edu/wp-content/uploads/2019/04/FP_20190419_bri_interview.pdf.

Kaczan, D.J. 2016. Can roads contribute to forest transitions? PhD Thesis, Sanford School of Public Policy and Nicholas School of the Environment, Duke University, Durham, NC.

Karpathiotaki, P. 2016. One Belt, One Road: The new type of globalization. PhD thesis, University of International Business and Economics, Beijing.

Li, X., Fan, Y. and Wu, L. 2017. 'CO$_2$ emissions and expansion of railway, road, airline and inland waterway networks over the 1985–2013 period in China: A time series analysis.' *Transportation Research Part D: Transport and Environment* 57: 130–40. doi.org/10.1016/j.trd.2017.09.008.

Losos, E., Pfaff, A., Olander, L., Mason, S. and Morgan, S. 2018. *Reducing environmental risks from Belt and Road Initiative investments in transportation infrastructure*. Policy Research Working Paper 8718. Washington, DC: World Bank Group. doi.org/10.1596/1813-9450-8718.

Luo, Y., Xue, Q. and Han, B. 2010. 'How emerging market governments promote outward FDI: Experience from China.' *Journal of World Business* 45(1): 68–79. doi.org/10.1016/j.jwb.2009.04.003.

Maliszewska, M. and van der Mensbrugghe, D. 2019. *The Belt and Road Initiative: Macro and sectoral impacts*. Policy Research Working Paper WPS8814. Washington, DC: World Bank Group.

Ministry of Finance of the People's Republic of China (MOF). 2019. *Debt Sustainability Framework for Participating Countries of the Belt and Road Initiative*. Beijing: MOF.

Peng, P. and Li, J. 2018. 'OFDI and bilateral moving up in the global value chain: An empirical study on the Belt and Road Initiative.' *Industrial Economics Research* 6: 75–88.

Reed, T. and Trubetskoy, A. 2019. *Assessing the value of market access from Belt and Road projects*. Policy Research Working Paper WPS8815. Washington, DC: World Bank Group. doi.org/10.1596/1813-9450-8815.

Silk Road Guoxin Big Data Technology Co. Ltd. n.d. *Belt and Road Portal*. Beijing. Available from: www.yidaiyilu.gov.cn/xwzx/gnxw/102792.htm.

Tao, Z. and Qiao, S. 2020. 'Research on the influencing factors of the "Belt and Road" international trade: An empirical test based on trade agreements and logistics performance.' *Journal of Social Sciences* 1: 63–71.

Tian, J. and Liu, X. 2019. 'Validity test of regional trade agreements in the context of "reverse globalization": A case study of the Belt and Road Initiative.' *Macroeconomics* 7: 71–83.

United Nations (UN). 1974. *Charter of Economic Rights and Duties*. Article 26, GA Res. 3281(xxix), UN GAOR, 29th Sess., Supp. No. 31 (1974) 50. New York: UN General Assembly.

Witt, M.A. and Lewin, A.Y. 2007. 'Outward foreign direct investment as escape response to home country institutional constraints.' *Journal of International Business Studies* 38(4): 579–94. doi.org/10.1057/palgrave.jibs.8400285.

Woetzel, J., Garemo, N., Mischke, J., Kamra, P. and Palter, R. 2017. *Bridging infrastructure gaps: Has the world made progress?* McKinsey Global Institute Executive Briefing. New York: McKinsey & Company. Available from: www.mckinsey.com/business-functions/operations/our-insights/bridging-infrastructure-gaps-has-the-world-made-progress.

World Bank. 2007. *The Many Faces of Corruption: Tracking vulnerabilities at sector level*. Washington, DC: World Bank Group.

World Bank. 2016a. *Managing the risks of adverse impacts on communities from temporary project induced labour influx*. Guidance Note. Washington, DC: World Bank Group.

World Bank. 2016b. *World Development Report 2016: Digital dividends*. Washington, DC: World Bank Group.

World Bank. 2019. *Belt and Road Economics: Opportunities and risks of transport corridors*. Washington, DC: World Bank Group.

World Bank. 2021a. *World Development Indicators*. DataBank. Washington, DC: World Bank Group.

World Bank. 2021b. *Worldwide Governance Indicators*. DataBank. Washington, DC: World Bank Group.

World Economic Forum (WEF). 2016. *The Global Enabling Trade Report 2016*. Geneva: World Economic Forum.

World Economic Forum (WEF). 2019. *The Global Competitiveness Report 2019*. Geneva: World Economic Forum.

World Justice Project. 2018. *Our Work*. Washington, DC, and Seattle: World Justice Project.

Wu, Z. 2018. 'Functional logic of the Belt and Road Initiative: A new interpretation based on geo-economics.' *World Economics and Politics* 9: 128–53, 160.

Xie, T. 2015. 'Is China's "Belt and Road" a strategy? When is a strategy not a strategy?' *The Diplomat*, 16 December. Available from: thediplomat. com/2015/12/is-chinas-belt-and-road-a-strategy.

Xinhuanet. 2017. 'Full text of President Xi's speech at opening of Belt and Road forum.' *Xinhuanet*, 14 May. Available from: news.xinhuanet.com/english/2017-05/14/c_136282982.htm.

Yang, J. (chair). 2019. *Belt and Road Cooperation: For A Better World—Report on the findings and recommendations from the first meeting of the Advisory Council of the Belt and Road Forum for International Cooperation.* 10 April. Geneva: Permanent Mission of the People's Republic of China to the United Nations Office at Geneva and Other International Organizations in Switzerland. Available from: www.china-un.ch/eng/zywjyjh/t1675576.htm.

Zhang, P. 2018. 'The infrastructure construction level of the Belt and Road impacts on bilateral trade from Asian countries: Analysis based on extended gravity model.' *World Economy Studies* 6: 70–82, 136.

Zhao, J. and Sun, H. 2019. 'Research on the evolution of trade relations between China and the countries along the Belt and Road.' *International Economics and Trade Research* 35(11): 36–48.

Zheng, J. and Zhou, S. 2019. 'Trade promotion effect of trade agreements between the countries along "the Belt and Road": An empirical analysis based on the propensity score matching model.' *Economic Survey* 36(6): 62–69.

3

The connectivity of the Greater Mekong Subregion: A view from the sky

Wichsinee Wibulpolprasert, Winit Theanvanichpant and Somkiat Tangkitvanich1

Countries succeed when they have a magnetic quality and an openness to the world around them: when they invest more in bridges than walls.

— Tom Fletcher (2016: 18)

Introduction

Transport infrastructure is an important element for both local and cross-border economic development. In the past 20 years, the Greater Mekong Subregion (GMS) has seen remarkable growth in the amount of transport infrastructure that connects countries in the region along numerous economic corridors, as shown in Figure 3.1.

1   We are grateful to Panu Nuangjumnong and Jirawit Wongchan-Uma from Geo-Informatics and Space Technology Development for their assistance in digitising and interpreting the satellite data. We also would like to thank Dr Watcharas Leelawath and Dr Souknilanh Keola for their helpful comments.

Figure 3.1 GMS economic corridors

Source: www.greatermekong.org.

One prominent example of this connectivity is the series of Thailand–Laos friendship bridges across the Mekong River (see Table 3.1). The first friendship bridge opened in April 1994 and connects Vientiane prefecture in Lao People's Democratic Republic (Lao PDR) to Thailand's Nong Khai Province. The second bridge opened in January 2007, connecting Suvannakhet (Lao PDR) to Mukdahan (Thailand). The third bridge connects Nakhon Phanom (Thailand) to Thakhek, Khammouan (Lao PDR), and opened in November 2011. The most recent friendship bridge was completed in December 2013, connecting Chiang Khong (Thailand) to Ban Houayxay (Lao PDR).

Table 3.1 Thailand–Laos friendship bridges

Bridge	Opening date	Thailand	Laos	Funded by
First	April 1994	Nongkhai	Vientiane	Australian Government
Second	December 2006	Mukdahan	Savannakhet	Japanese loan
Third	November 2011	Nakhon Phanom	Khammouan	Thai Government
Fourth	December 2013	Chiang Rai	Ban Houayxay	Thai, Lao and Chinese governments

Sources: Fernquest (2011); Wikipedia; Fujimura (2017).

Connective structures such as cross-border bridges allow regional trade to prosper by significantly reducing transportation times and costs. While the direct benefit of reduced transportation costs/times from enhanced connectivity is usually apparent and easily measurable, the indirect benefits that spill over to local communities are much harder to measure due to the lack of microlevel data.

Given the announcement of additional friendship bridge investments, understanding the *interactions* between the connective infrastructure investments, local economic activities and urbanisation can be informative from a cost-benefit standpoint as well as for urban planning purposes.

To our knowledge, existing studies that evaluate microlevel impacts of infrastructure in the GMS are rare due to the unavailability of fine-grained urbanisation and economic data. Most are the feasibility studies conducted by investors prior to commissioning the construction project (MOT 2008), ex-ante studies (Warr et al. 2009) or post-evaluation descriptive studies that focus on the direct trade benefits (Fujimura 2017).

For an ex-ante study, Warr et al. (2009) use a general equilibrium model to estimate the effects of the second Mekong River bridge. Their results suggest that, in the short run, transport cost reductions would produce a modest increase in interregional trade volumes in both directions and a small increase in real consumption in Thailand and Lao PDR. Over a longer period, the economic benefits to both regions would be much larger, as capital and labour become more mobile. They do not confirm the belief that the benefits of cross-border infrastructure projects occur only, or overwhelmingly, in the richer region.

The most comprehensive post-evaluation study was conducted by Fujimura (2017), which quantified the cost-benefit ratios along selected segments of the GMS economic corridors as well as the economic impacts at the country or subregional level. Despite finding a net positive economic impact from infrastructure in the GMS as a whole, the author admitted that incomplete data could compromise the robustness of the results.

The various remote sensing data that became available recently, along with the development of image classification techniques, have great potential to fill this gap and allow researchers to conduct retrospective microlevel studies of infrastructure investment that have not been possible before. For example, a study by Vernon Henderson et al. (2012) famously demonstrates that local economic activity can be estimated from satellite images of observed night light. Several other existing studies have developed classification techniques to translate raw satellite images into meaningful pixel-based identification of built-up areas and different types of land use (Goldblatt et al. 2016, 2018).

This study sets out to answer two questions that characterise the relationship between connective infrastructure, local industrialisation and local urbanisation. The first is whether connective infrastructure is a necessary condition for industrialisation, or is it industrialisation/ trade that necessitates the construction of bridges (the bridges are just enhancers)? Second, are there any indirect benefits (spillovers) from either the bridge construction or the industrialisation on the local economy?

We will focus our analysis on the impacts of the construction of the second (2007) and third (2009) Thailand–Laos friendship bridges as the time before and since their opening dates allow us long enough observation periods. Our analysis strategy follows three steps. First, we construct a measurement of urbanisation over time using publicly available data from various sources. We then characterise the interaction between connective infrastructure (the friendship bridges), industrialisation and patterns of local urbanisation. Last, we synthesise policy implications and lessons learned for the future development of connective infrastructure in the GMS.

Literature review

While this chapter will focus on the relationship between cross-border infrastructure, local industrialisation and local urbanisation, this section will review previous research more broadly to gain insights into the impacts of transport infrastructure on trade and urbanisation.

There are numerous studies of the impacts of transport infrastructure on trade, all of which seem to confirm that the presence of transport infrastructure (road networks, airports, railways and ports) has resulted in increased trade flows (for example, Ismail and Mahyideen 2015; Celbis et al. 2013). In the context of the GMS economies, Fujimura and Edmonds (2006) find that cross-border and domestic transport infrastructure together can reduce trade costs and lead directly to increased trade and investment.

However, there are far fewer studies related to the impacts of transport infrastructure on urbanisation patterns. Most empirical works are undertaken in the context of developed countries. A typical finding is that improved transport infrastructure leads to agglomeration economies of increased access to markets, innovation spillovers and a greater labour pool (for example, Duranton and Puga 2004; World Bank 2009). Most existing works also focus on intracity roads and metro lines, rather than intercity transport infrastructure. Studies of the impacts of cross-border infrastructure such as international bridges are even harder to find, especially in the context of developing countries.

Baum-Snow et al. (2012) find the configurations of urban railroads and highways have influenced urban forms in Chinese cities since 1990. In particular, each radial highway displaces about 4 per cent of the central city's population to surrounding regions and ring roads displace an additional 20 per cent or so, with stronger effects in the richer coastal and central regions. Each radial railroad reduces central-city industrial gross domestic product (GDP) by about 20 per cent, with ring roads displacing an additional 50 per cent.

More recent empirical studies are related to the impact of high-speed rail networks in China and Japan. In the case of China, Ke et al. (2017) construct hypothetical counterfactuals for per capita real GDP of cities along the high-speed rail network in the absence of their respective high-speed rail projects. They find that the gains from high-speed rail are heterogeneous with regard to location, route and region. Cities with positive effects are concentrated in the eastern coastal regions of China and in core urban agglomeration regions that allow them to become transportation hubs. In general, the gain for local economies is greater for cities that are more industrialised, with greater ability for the service sector to absorb labour and better supporting infrastructure.

Using the least-cost spanning tree to address the nonrandom route selection issue, Yu et al. (2019) find that high-speed railway connections in China have led to a reduction in GDP per capita for connected peripheral prefectures. They also find that the reduction of GDP per capita is driven by significant contractions in capital inputs, industrial outputs and skilled labour outflows.

In the case of Japan, Li and Xu (2018) show that high-speed railroads can either polarise or diffuse economic geography based on the sector and distance between cities. In other words, economic activity could agglomerate from distant to core areas or disperse from the core to the periphery at the same time. To support their findings, they cite empirical evidence from the 1982 introduction of two major high-speed railways in Japan, which halved intercity transit times. They find that noncore areas lost 3–6 per cent of their population; service sector employment declined by 7 per cent, whereas manufacturing employment increased by 21 per cent. Municipalities within approximately 150 kilometres of Tokyo expanded, while the more distant ones contracted.

Overall, previous research finds that transport infrastructure tends to increase economic activity, trade and output. However, intercity transport links often produce uneven results in economic activity and urbanisation patterns among larger cities (hubs) and smaller ones (spokes or peripheries).

Background to the friendship bridges

The second Mekong friendship bridge

The second Thailand–Laos Mekong Friendship Bridge was completed in November 2006. It connects Mukdahan and Savannakhet and was designed to be a part of the GMS's East–West Economic Corridor (EWEC), which stretches from Yangon, Myanmar, in the west to Danang, Vietnam, in the east.

The second bridge construction project, funded by a Japanese Government official development assistance (ODA) loan, aimed to promote regional economic development, logistics and trade through the corridor. Prior to the bridge's opening, a ferry service was the only transport option to cross the river. Transporting goods from Bangkok to Hanoi via ship took from one and a half to two weeks. Transport overland via the second friendship bridge reduced the time to three days (JIBTV 2014).

Apart from promoting regional connectivity, the second friendship bridge was partially built to support Japanese industries that operate in the region. The first special economic zone (SEZ) in Laos, the Savan-Seno SEZ, was completed in Savannakhet in 2003. Some Japanese factories consider the Savan-Seno SEZ a perfect location, for several reasons. First, goods can be transported overland to either Da Nang port in Vietnam (to be shipped to East Asian countries) or Laem Chabang port in Thailand. Second, labour and electricity costs are much cheaper in Laos than in Thailand (JIBTV 2014).

With these considerations in mind, the Japanese Government, via the Japan International Cooperation Agency (JICA), helped complete an improvement project for National Road No. 9 that connects Savannakhet in Laos to Vietnam. This, along with the construction of the second friendship bridge connecting Thailand to Savannakhet, naturally made the landlocked Laos a more attractive manufacturing and distribution base, which has attracted many Japanese firms to establish their factories there (JICA 2017).

The industrial and connective infrastructure development of the Savan-Seno SEZ and the second friendship bridge is considered a perfect example of the 'Thailand-plus-one business model' for Japanese firms. The model proposes that Japanese companies that operate industrial clusters in Thailand can shift some of their labour-intensive activities to SEZs in the CLM countries (Cambodia, Laos and Myanmar) near the Thai border. Such a strategy will enhance the companies' supply chain competitiveness via the lower labour costs in the CLM countries while maintaining access to the strengthened transportation infrastructure in Thailand (Oizumi 2013).

With the above context in mind, we hypothesise the relationship between connectivity, industrialisation and urbanisation for the second friendship bridge as follows: *industrialisation (the establishment of the SEZ) drives local urbanisation and the demand for connective infrastructure.*

The third Mekong friendship bridge

The third friendship bridge was commissioned in a vastly different context than the second bridge. First, it was financed by Thailand's government with the objective of strengthening regional connectivity in general. The third bridge is part of Asian Highway Route AH15, connecting Thailand's Udon Thani Province to Vinh in Vietnam. It also gives closer trade access to southern China. According to the feasibility study, the third bridge shortened ground shipping from Thailand to central Vietnam by 100 kilometres, saving approximately two hours of driving compared with crossing the second bridge (MOT 2008). Second, there was no industrial base or SEZ in the area before the bridge's construction. Instead, the Government of Laos decided to establish the Thakhek SEZ right across the Mekong River from Nakhon Phanom after the bridge was finished, with the aim of capturing the spillover benefits from the improved connectivity (Royal Thai Consulate-General 2019).

With these differences in mind, we hypothesise the relationship between connectivity, industrialisation and urbanisation for the third friendship bridge as follows: *connectivity (from the bridge) drives industrialisation and (perhaps) urbanisation*.

Data and methodology

Macrolevel data

Table 3.2 summarises the high-level indicators of the local economy and urbanisation in Thailand's provinces.

Table 3.2 High-level indicators for local urbanisation

Indicator	Description	Data period	Data source
Cross-border trade value	Export and import value of trade along the Mukdahan–Savannakhet and Nakhon Phanom–Kammouan borders	2003–16	Bank of Thailand (Bank of Thailand n.d.)
Cross-border traffic volume	Number of inbound/outbound passenger vehicles, trucks and passengers passing through the Mukdahan–Savannakhet and Nakhon Phanom–Kammouan immigration checkpoints	2008–18	Mukdahan and Nakhon Phanom immigration offices (Mukdahan Customs House 2019; Nakhon Phanom Immigration Office 2012)

Indicator	Description	Data period	Data source
Gross provincial product	Province-level measure of value added	2002–18	Office of the National Economic and Social Development Council (NESDC n.d.)
Yearly built-up area expansion	New built-up area in square kilometres that appears yearly, as identified from satellite imagery	2001–18	Landsat 5,7, 8 (details below) (USGS n.d.)

Satellite imagery data

Our satellite imagery data for the study area come from Landsat 5, 7 and 8. The Landsat satellites take pictures of the Earth's surface and record reflected energy in various wavelengths of the electromagnetic spectrum ('bands') (NASA n.d.). Each pixel represents a gridded area of approximately 30 by 30 metres (that is, a resolution of 30 metres).

Table 3.3 Examples of the various bands in Landsat 5 and 8

Band no.	Band name	Wavelength (µm)	Resolution (m)	Band applications
1	Visible Blue	0.45–0.52	30	Bathymetric mapping, distinguishing soil from vegetation and deciduous from coniferous vegetation
2	Visible Green	0.52–0.60	30	Emphasises peak vegetation, which is useful for assessing plant vigour
3	Visible Red	0.63–0.69	30	Discriminates vegetation slopes
4	NIR	0.76–0.90	30	Emphasises biomass content and shorelines
5	SWIR 1	1.55–1.75	30	Discriminates moisture content of soil and vegetation; penetrates thin clouds
6	Thermal	10.40–12.50	120	Thermal mapping and estimated soil moisture
7	SWIR 2	2.08–2.35	30	Hydrothermally altered rocks associated with mineral deposits

Source: EOSDA (n.d.).

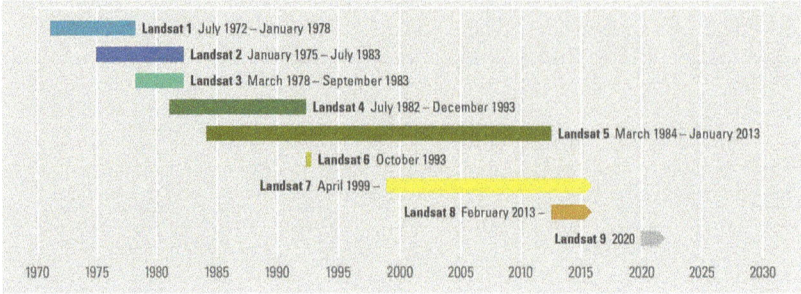

Figure 3.2 Landsat mission schedule
Source: USGS (n.d.).

Since different satellites have different mission periods (Figure 3.2), we had to combine the snapshot imagery data from three different satellites—Landsat 5, 7 and 8—to cover our entire study period, from 2000 to 2020 (De Riggi 2017).

We acquired the resulting dataset that records various bands of wavelength in the target area from the *EarthExplorer* website of the United States Geological Survey (USGS n.d.). Note that even though the images of the same location are taken every 16 days, we screened only for the best yearly snapshot with the lowest cloud cover. Table 3.4 summarises our yearly data source and the snapshot time frame.

Table 3.4 Final satellite imagery data source

Year	Data date		Satellite
	Mukdahan/Savannakhet	Nakhon Phanom/Khammouan	
2000	4 November 2000	4 November 2000	Landsat-7
2001	23 November 2001	23 November 2001	Landsat-7
2002	10 November 2002	10 November 2002	Landsat-7
2003	21 November 2003	21 November 2003	Landsat-5
2004	22 October 2004	22 October 2004	Landsat-5
2005	10 November 2005	10 November 2005	Landsat-5
2006	12 October 2006	12 October 2006	Landsat-5
2007	8 November 2007	8 November 2007	Landsat-7
2008	4 December 2008	4 December 2008	Landsat-5
2009	4 October 2009	4 October 2009	Landsat-5
2010	20 October 2010	20 October 2010	Landsat-5
2011	6 July 2011	6 July 2011	Landsat-5
2012	20 October 2012	20 October 2012	Landsat-7

Year	Data date		Satellite
	Mukdahan/Savannakhet	**Nakhon Phanom/Khammouan**	
2013	7 October 2013	7 October 2013	Landsat-7
2014	2 October 2014	2 October 2014	Landsat-8
2015	1 July 2015	1 July 2015	Landsat-8
2016	14 June 2016	14 June 2016	Landsat-8
2017	26 October 2017	26 October 2017	Landsat-8
2018	13 October 2018	13 October 2018	Landsat-8

Last, the data preparation and classification steps were performed on ENVI and ArcGIS software. Figure 3.3 summarises the data-processing steps.

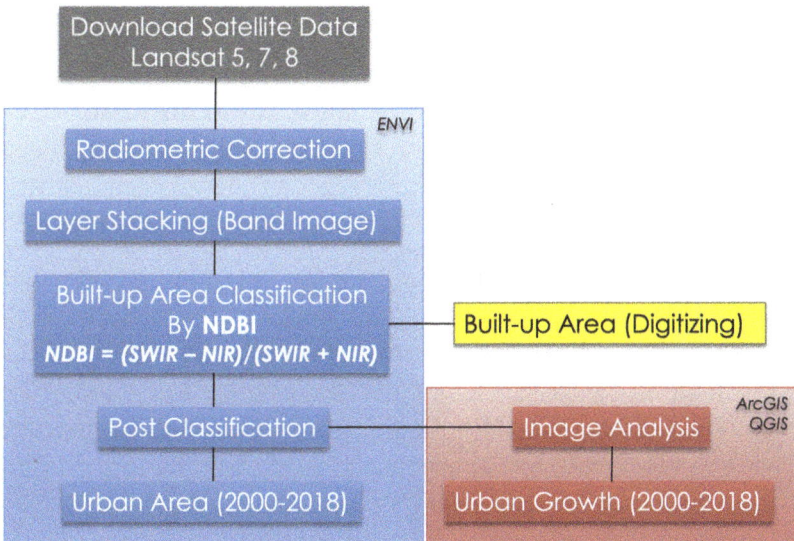

Figure 3.3 Data-processing steps

Source: Geo-Informatics and Space Technology Development team.

Built-up area classification

The next step in data processing is to translate the raw wavelength data into meaningful measures of urbanisation. We make use of the widely used Normalized Difference Built-Up Index (NDBI) to classify image pixels as built-up and non–built-up areas. The NDBI utilises the properties of built-up areas and bare soil, which reflect more shortwave infrared (SWIR) than near-infrared (NIR) waves, while green vegetation generally reflects more NIR than SWIR.

The NDBI is calculated using the formula:

$$NDBI = \frac{SWIR - NIR}{SWIR + NIR}$$

The index value ranges from −1 to 1 and can be interpreted as follows:

- NDBI > 0 and close to 1 indicates a built-up area.
- NDBI close to 0 indicates a vegetated area.
- NDBI < 0 and close to −1 indicates a water body.

This study uses an NDBI cut-off value of 0.65 to classify pixels as built-up area. Note that we finetune the cut-off values for different data years to achieve the highest classification accuracy.

After an initial classification using the NDBI, we are still left with many false-positive built-up areas. This is because the NDBI alone cannot distinguish real built-up areas from barren land with bare soil. Thus, we refine our classification results with two additional steps. First, we compare the initial classified data against verified land use data and high-resolution satellite imagery from the most recent year (2018). The logic is simple: the verified land use data and high-resolution images constitute our 'ground truth' for the real built-up area boundary, thus any built-up pixels classified initially by the NDBI that fall outside this boundary in 2018 are false positives and are excluded from our data layer in all years. Next, we perform a final visual inspection by comparing the resulting classified built-up area with the raw satellite image year by year. We then manually remove from our dataset the classified built-up areas that do not look like real built-up areas.

Strengths and limitations of using satellite imagery data

Using the satellite imagery (Landsat) data to track urbanisation progress has several strengths. First, it is publicly available online. This makes it affordable and accessible for anyone. Second, the data span a long period. This allows researchers to study land use changes before the administrative data became available. Third, the imagery data are truthful in the sense that they are recorded by the camera's sensors and are not easily manipulated.

Despite these many advantages, there are several limitations that readers should beware of when interpreting the results in this chapter. First, the Landsat data's resolution of 30 metres is considered relatively low. This property naturally lends itself to a simple classification method such as the NDBI rather than a more sophisticated/accurate classification method. Second, while the NDBI is easy to calculate and interpret, it is not highly accurate and requires additional post-classification refinements, as mentioned above. Third, even when the NDBI can classify built-up pixels correctly, it cannot distinguish between different types of built-up areas. This limitation means that, without additional information, researchers will not be able to assess the quality of urbanisation, as both highly developed and less-developed areas will be classified as built-up.

In addition to the satellite imagery data, we have explored the usability of night-time light imagery data. The main night-time light data that cover our period of interest are the OLS-DMSP night-time light series provided by the US National Centers for Environmental Information (NCEI n.d.). Unfortunately, this dataset has several limitations. First, and most importantly, the different satellites used to collect data for this series have different (unknown) baseline calibration values, which means the night-time light index is not comparable across years. This limitation is particularly noticeable when the study area is small. Second, the low resolution of the night-time light data (1 kilometre) prevent detailed geospatial analysis, which is crucial when our study areas are small.

Results and discussion

This section discusses the observed relationships between the construction of the friendship bridges, urbanisation and trade activity. Recall that our focus areas are Mukdahan (Thailand) and Savannakhet (Laos) for the second friendship bridge and Nakhon Phanom (Thailand) and Thakhek (Laos) for the third friendship bridge.

Macrolevel changes post bridge construction

We first investigate the province-level changes in different indicators of urbanisation, starting with cross-border trade volumes. Figure 3.4 shows the yearly export and import trade values (in million Thai baht, or THB) across the Mukdahan–Nakhon Phanom border. Two interesting observations stand out. First, border trade value is dominated by exports to rather than imports from Laos. Closer inspection reveals that the top export products across Mukdahan's border are computing chips and electronic circuits, while the top import products are pure copper and appliance components. On the other hand, the top export products from Nakhon Phanom are computer memory units and fruit, while the top import products into Nakhon Phanom are mainly electronic devices, memory hard disks and computers. Second, both the export and the import trade values increased exponentially shortly after the opening of the two friendship bridges. These two observations clearly indicate the direct benefit of the bridges on trade facilitation.

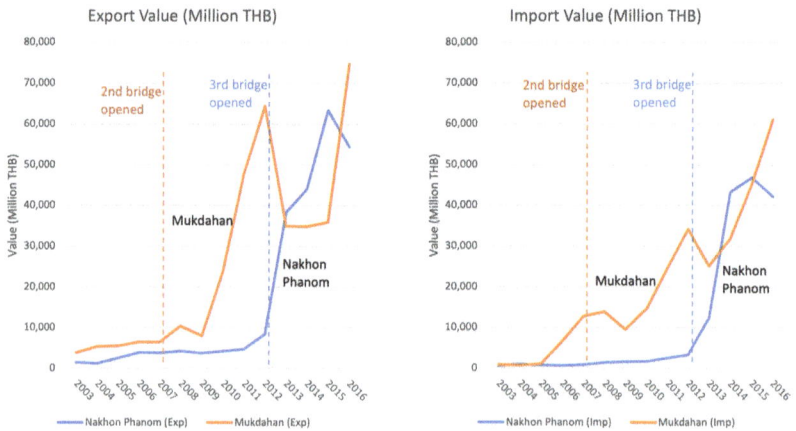

Figure 3.4 Changes in border export and import values
Source: Authors' creation.

Next, we look at the combined (inbound and outbound) cross-border traffic volume over time, in Figure 3.5. Unfortunately, no data are available before 2008, making it impossible to spot whether there was any abrupt change in traffic volume after the second bridge opened. However, if we assume that the change in traffic volume follows a pattern similar to that of the change in trade value, we expect to see the traffic volume for the second bridge spike after 2009. Unlike the change in trade value, however, the cross-border traffic volume seems to increase only gradually over time. The observed exponential growth in trade value along with a gradual increase in traffic volume (especially truck traffic) imply a significant increase in the proportion of high-value products among the goods traded or a significant improvement in truck capacity utilisation, or both.

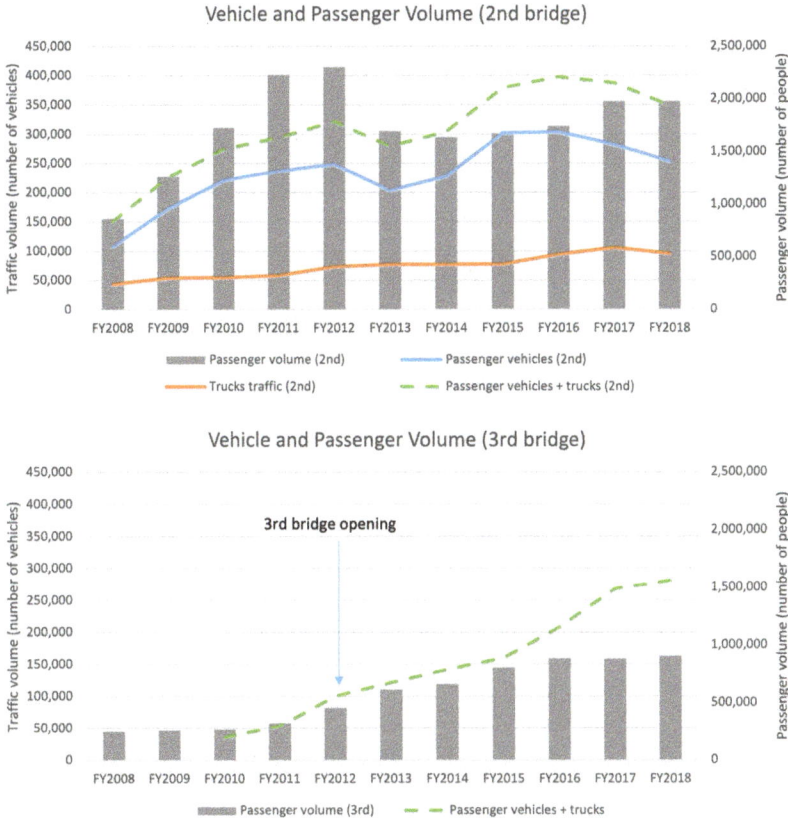

Figure 3.5 Cross-border traffic volume
Source: Authors' creation.

Last, we inspect the year-on-year change in the expansion of built-up areas and the gross provincial product (GPP) of the two Thai border provinces, in Figures 3.7 and 3.8. We notice a rapid expansion of built-up areas in the early 2000s, which gradually slows over time. This slowdown is mainly a result of the fact that there was only a very small built-up area in all the regions being studied in the base year, 2002. Therefore, a small expansion in built-up area translates to large year-on-year growth. First, similar to traffic volume, the built-up area expansion or increase in GPP does not seem to respond to the opening of the two bridges in any significant way.

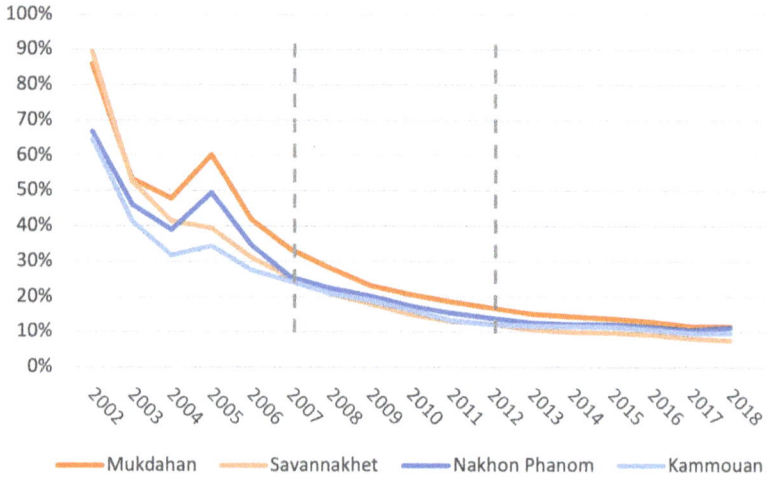

Figure 3.6 Year-on-year change in built-up area expansion
Source: Authors' creation.

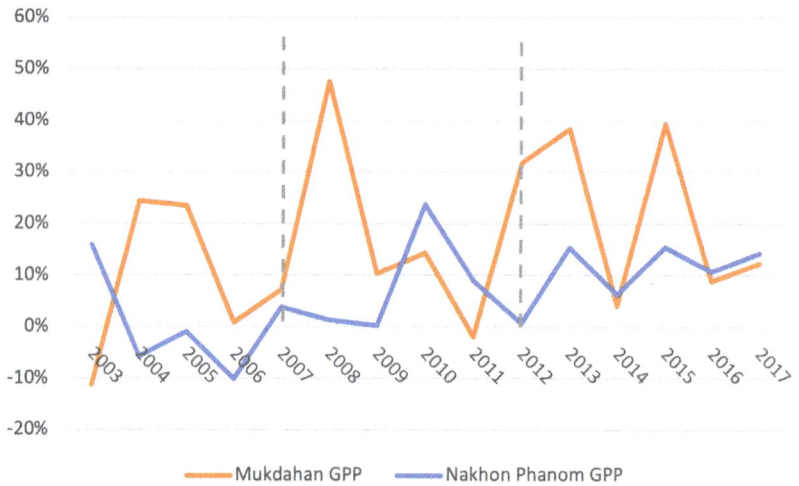

Figure 3.7 Year-on-year change in GPP
Source: Authors' creation.

Together, all the province-level data indicate that, besides providing the obvious direct trade benefits, the friendship bridges seem to have had limited impact on local urbanisation.

Built-up area growth pattern

We next turn our attention to the pattern of built-up area expansion around the two friendship bridges. Figure 3.8 shows this expansion in 2000, 2005, 2009 and 2015. Each dot represents a new built-up area created in each year. The orange or red colour indicates locations with a high density of new built-up areas ('built-up hotspots'). We can see the intense built-up hotspots in Savannakhet that occurred near the city's core in 2005, which corresponded with the opening of the Savan-Seno SEZ in 2003. New built-up hotspots in Mukdahan, on the other hand, are less intense and are scattered along the existing highways and city core. By comparing the built-up hotspot map from 2005 (before the bridge's opening) with that from 2009 (after the bridge's opening), we can see that the second friendship bridge did not seem to change the pattern of built-up area expansion in a profound way.

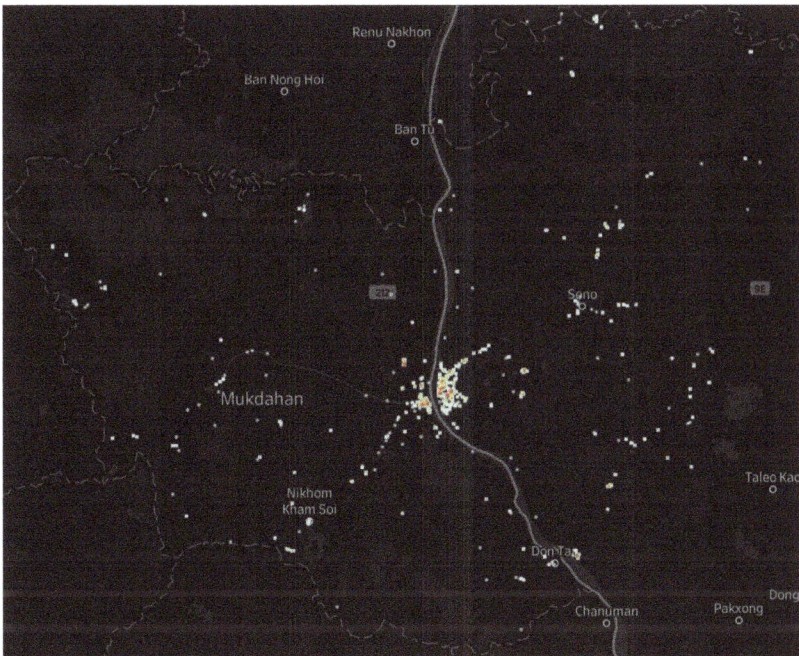

Figure 3.8a Location of newly created built-up areas in 2000 (second bridge)
Source: Authors' creation.

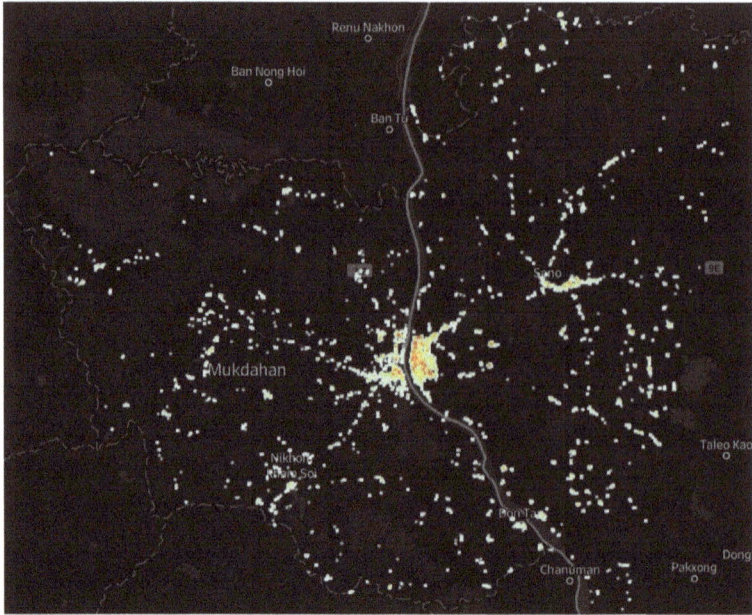

Figure 3.8b Location of newly created built-up areas in 2004 (second bridge)

Source: Authors' creation.

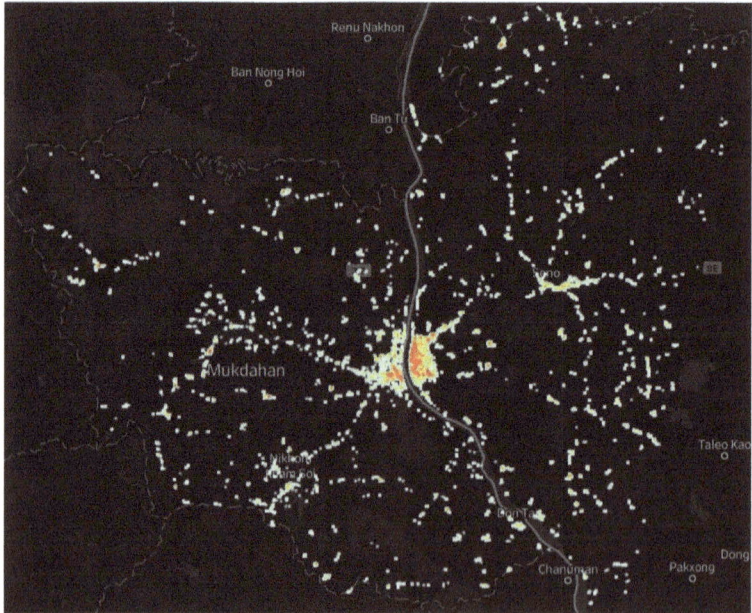

Figure 3.8c Location of newly created built-up areas in 2005 (second bridge)

Source: Authors' creation.

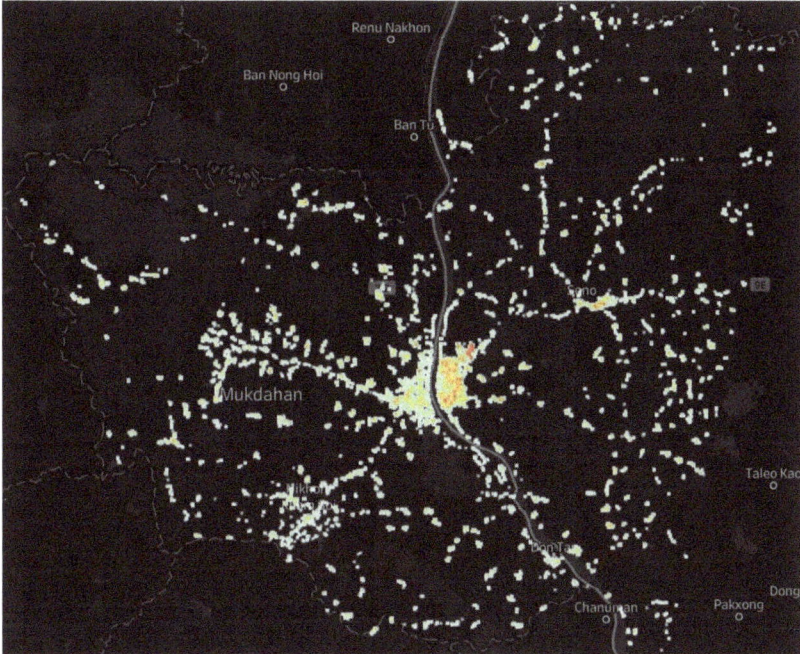

Figure 3.8d Location of newly created built-up areas in 2009 (second bridge)
Source: Authors' creation.

To quantify the observed growth pattern, we calculate the built-up area expansion within a radius of 0–10 kilometres and 11–30 kilometres north and south of the second friendship bridge. Figure 3.9 shows the radius analysis frame. Most of the existing city areas of Mukdahan and Savannakhet, as well as the Savan-Seno SEZ, lie within 10 kilometres south of the second bridge. The area in the 11–30-kilometre ring south of the bridge consists mainly of existing highways.

Figure 3.10 shows the annual increase in built-up area within various distances from the bridge between 2001 and 2018. One can see that most of the built-up area expansion occurred south of the bridge. Built-up areas in the 0–10-kilometre radius of Mukdahan and Savannakhet expanded rapidly from 2003 to 2004, which coincided with the opening of the Savan-Seno SEZ. After 2005, however, the expansion in this radius slowed while that in the 11–30-kilometre radius continued. The opening of the second friendship bridge in 2007 did not seem to alter the growth of built-up areas in any of the analysis frames.

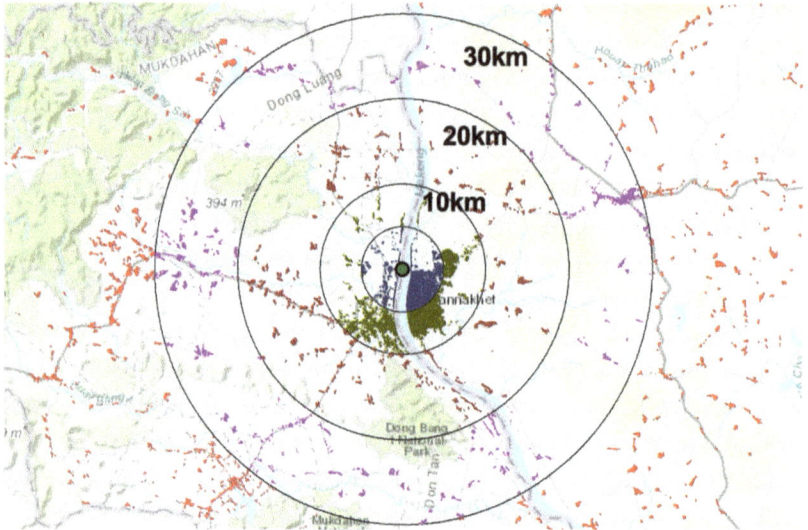

Figure 3.9 Radius analysis for Mukdahan and Savannakhet (second bridge)

Source: Built-up area map created using Landsat imagery from 2018.

Together, the analyses suggest that the creation of the Savan-Seno SEZ had a strong correlation with local urbanisation while the opening of the friendship bridges had no significant correlation with local urbanisation. Mukdahan appears to be just a throughway for the passage of goods and may benefit only from a small local spillover to communities along the highway leading up to the bridge. Therefore, we characterise the relationship for the second friendship bridge as *industrialisation (from the SEZ) that rapidly drove connectivity (the bridge) and urbanisation*.

We performed the same descriptive analysis for the third friendship bridge. Figure 3.11 plots the location of the new built-up hotspots in 2000, 2005, 2010 and 2015 in Nakhon Phanom and Khammouan. Built-up areas grew *gradually* out of the existing city cores and along major highways. The opening of the third friendship bridge in 2012 did not change the pattern of built-up area expansion in a profound way.

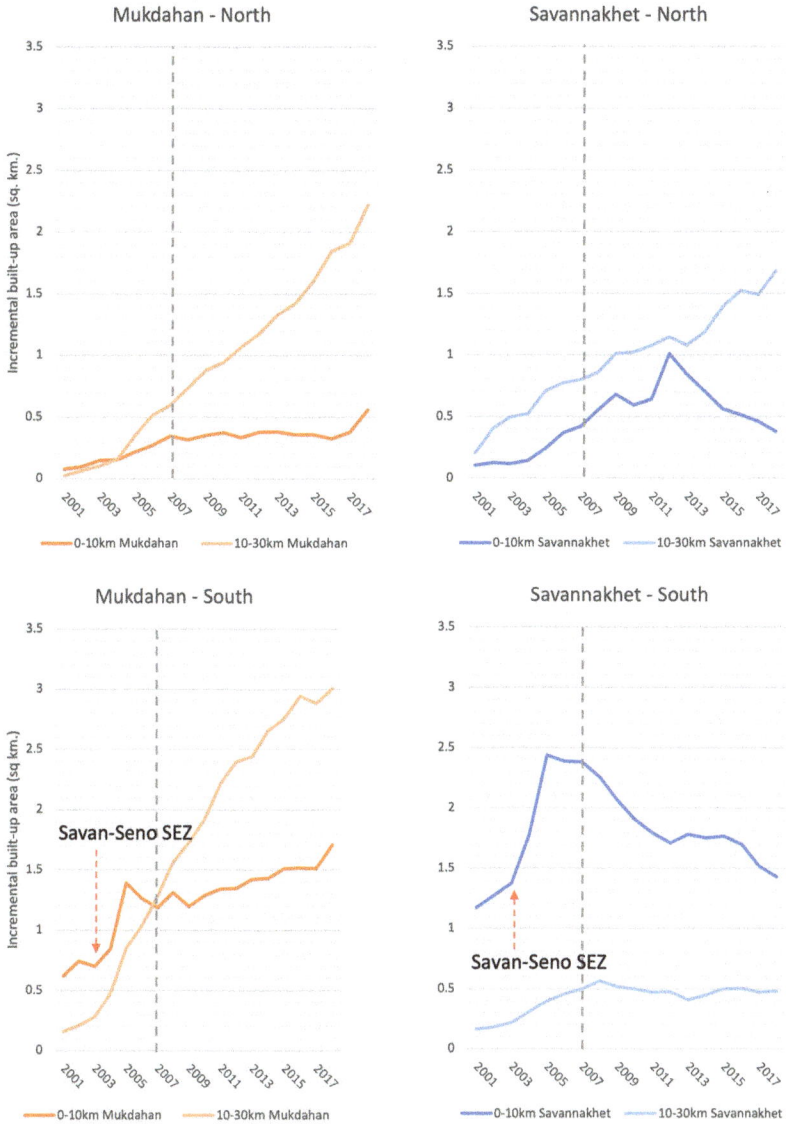

Figure 3.10 Annual increase in built-up area in Mukdahan and Savannakhet (second bridge)

Source: Authors' creation.

Figure 3.11a Location of new built-up areas in 2000 (third bridge)

Source: Authors' creation.

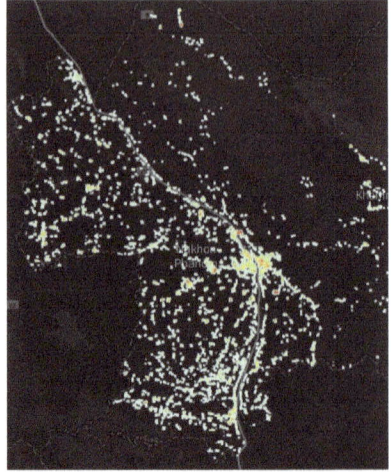

Figure 3.11c Location of new built-up areas in 2010 (third bridge)

Source: Authors' creation.

Figure 3.11b Location of new built-up areas in 2005 (third bridge)

Source: Authors' creation.

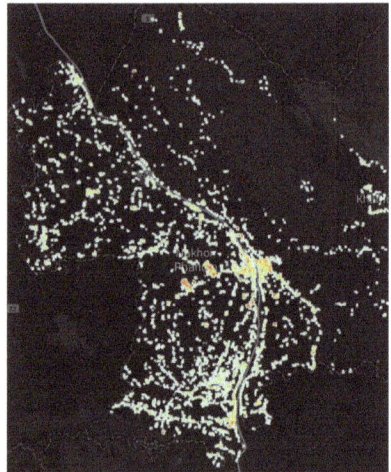

Figure 3.11d Location of new built-up areas in 2015 (third bridge)

Source: Authors' creation.

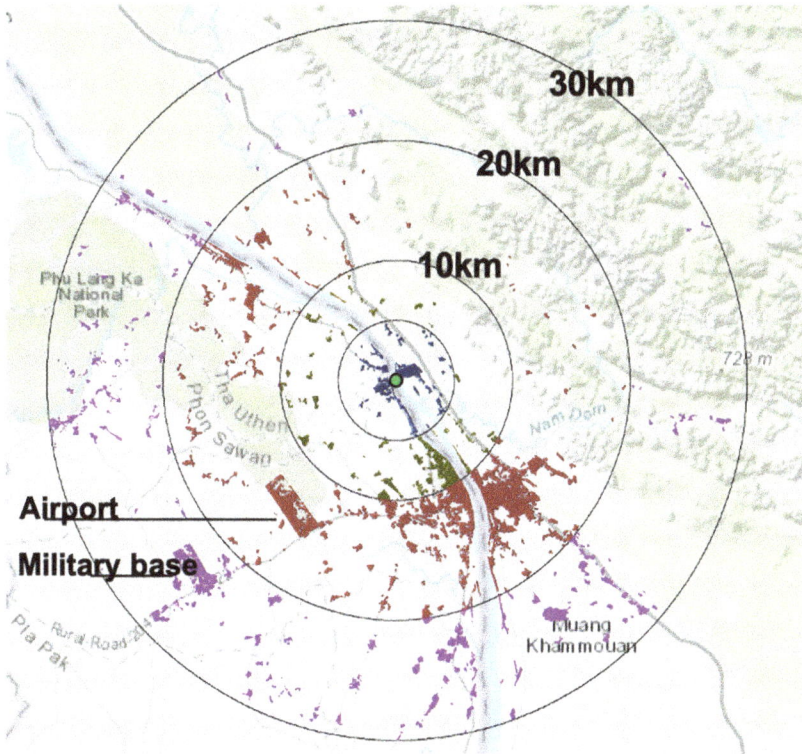

Figure 3.12 Radius analysis for Nakhon Phanom and Khammouan (third bridge)

Source: Map created using Landsat imagery for 2018.

A similar radius analysis for the third friendship bridge reveals that most of the existing city area (Nakhon Phanom and Khammouan) and major highways were located in the 10–30-kilometre ring south of the bridge (Figure 3.12). The newly created Thakhek SEZ in 2012 was in the same area.

Figure 3.13 plots the annual built-up area expansion in the 0–10-kilometre and 11–30-kilometre radii north and south of the bridge. The plots reveal that most of the new built-up hotspots in both Nakhon Phanom and Khammouan are within the 11–30-kilometre ring south of the third friendship bridge. However, the trend in built-up area expansion does not show any significant change after the opening of the third bridge and the Thakhek SEZ in 2012.

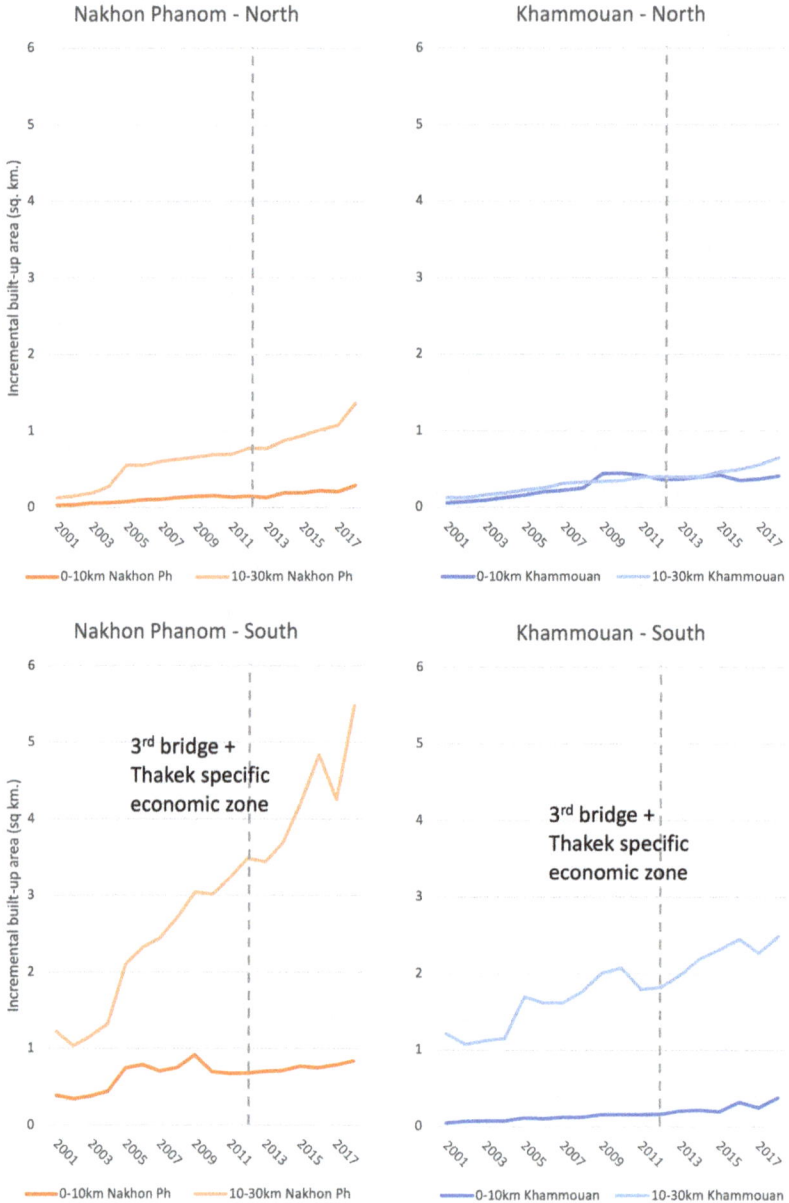

Figure 3.13 Annual increase in built-up area in Nakhon Phanom and Khammouan (third bridge)

Source: Authors' creation.

Together, the data for the third friendship bridge indicate that new built-up areas continued to expand in relation to the existing cities and highways, not in relation to the bridge or the new Thakhek SEZ. Readers should be reminded that the context and timing of the third bridge and the SEZ are very different from those of the second bridge: the third bridge was built, first, to enhance connectivity in the region in general, and then the Thakhek SEZ in Laos was established to capture the spillover benefits from the bridge. Therefore, we characterise this relationship as *connectivity (the bridge) slowly driving industrialisation and urbanisation*.

Overall, our findings show that the friendship bridges, as connective infrastructure, contributed to a clear increase in economic activity—most notably, in cross-border trade and cross-border traffic. This is broadly in line with the findings of previous work on the economic benefits of transport infrastructure. We also find that the impacts of the two bridges on patterns of urbanisation in the connected cities largely depend on the historical context of the surrounding areas. This adds a new insight to previous findings that intercity transport infrastructure often produces uneven results in urbanisation between larger cities and smaller ones.

Conclusions and policy implications

Our major descriptive findings can be summarised as follows. First, connectivity has a strong direct relationship with border trade. This can be seen from the opening of the second and third Mekong friendship bridges, which were followed by an explosion in border trade value. Second, connectivity may not have a profound impact on local urbanisation since the built-up area surrounding the bridges continued to expand in relation to the existing cities, the SEZ and highways, but not in relation to the bridges. Last, the interaction between connectivity, industrialisation and urbanisation for the second bridge is characterised as industrialisation-driven urbanisation and connectivity. On the other hand, the interaction for the third bridge is characterised as connectivity-driven (slow) urbanisation and industrialisation.

Importantly, we would like to emphasise that the relationships we characterise here represent only the *correlation* between industrialisation, bridge construction and built-up area expansion. Estimating a *causal* relationship is not possible at the local level due to the lack of other control variables. Importantly, the observed increase in the built-up areas or trade volumes after the bridges' construction cannot be entirely attributed to the bridges as several other factors also influence growth. For example, existing highways and industrial policies (for example, the Savan-Seno SEZ) could have driven the growth in these border cities even without the bridges.

The main lesson learned from these two case studies is that enhanced physical connectivity *alone* may have significant direct benefits on trade; however, the indirect benefit spillovers on the local economy may be limited. Instead, careful industrial and urban planning, along with physical connectivity enhancement, have a much greater potential to create additional local benefits and maximise the returns on the investment in such large connective infrastructure.

Last, the current study presents several limitations that can serve as areas for future study. First, due to data limitations, the relationships we characterise here only capture the *correlation (and not causation)* between industrialisation, bridge construction and built-up area expansion. A future study that aims to estimate the causal impact of the SEZ or bridge construction should gather a richer and longer dataset to control for the confounding factors of urbanisation such as local policies or institutional detail on the bridge construction decision-making process. Second, the satellite imagery data and classification method used in this study lack the resolution and depth required to assess the quality of urbanisation. A future study can make use of the commercially available higher-resolution satellite data, additional ground-truth data and a more sophisticated classification technique to differentiate building types and the quality of urbanisation. Third, the lessons learned from the two case studies might not be representative of other connective bridges in the region. Different political, cultural and social contexts can result in different interactions between connectivity, industrialisation and urbanisation. Thus, expanding the study coverage to other countries in the GMS will result in generalisable policy implications.

References

Bank of Thailand. 2019. *Value of exports and imports through Thai–Laos custom house in the north-east region.* [Statistical Database.] Bangkok: Bank of Thailand. Available from: www.bot.or.th/App/BTWS_STAT/statistics/ReportPage.aspx?reportID=549&language=th.

Baum-Snow, N., Brandt, L., Vernon Henderson, J., Turner M.A. and Zhang, Q. 2012. *Roads, railroads and decentralization of Chinese cities*. IGC Working Paper. London: International Growth Centre, London School of Economics and Political Science. Available from: www.theigc.org/wp-content/uploads/2014/09/Baum-Snow-Et-Al-2012-Working-Paper.pdf.

Celbis, M.G., Nijkamp, P. and Poot, J. 2013. *How big is the impact of infrastructure on trade? Evidence from meta-analysis*. MERIT Working Papers 2013-032. Maastricht, Netherlands: United Nations University–Maastricht Economic and Social Research Institute on Innovation and Technology. Available from: ideas.repec.org/p/unm/unumer/2013032.html.

De Riggi, J. 2017. 'Remote sensing series part 2: Landsat is the stalwart of satellite imagery platforms (and it's free!).' [Blog]. *Digital @ DAI*, 18 January. Available from: dai-global-digital.com/part-2-la-la-landsat-making-use-of-landsat-imagery.html.

Duranton, G. and Puga, D. 2004. 'Micro-foundations of urban agglomeration economies.' In J. Vernon Henderson and J.F. Thisse (eds), *Handbook of Regional and Urban Economics*. Amsterdam: Elsevier. doi.org/10.3386/w9931.

Earth Observing System Data Analytics (EOSDA). n.d. 'Landsat 5 (TM) bands.' *Earth Observing System*. Menlo Park, CA: EOSDA. Available from: eos.com/landsat-5-tm.

Fernquest, J. 2011. 'Thai–Lao friendship bridges no.3 and 4.' *Bangkok Post*, 16 February. Available from: www.bangkokpost.com/learning/advanced/221957/thai-lao-friendship-bridges-no-3-and-4.

Fletcher, T. 2016. *The Naked Diplomat: Understanding Power and Politics in the Digital Age*. London: William Collins.

Fujimura, M. 2017. *Evaluating impacts of cross-border transport infrastructure in the Greater Mekong Subregion: Three approaches*. ADB Institute Working Paper No. 771. Tokyo: Asian Development Bank Institute. Available from: www.adb.org/sites/default/files/publication/352026/adbi-wp771.pdf.

Fujimura, M. and Edmonds, C. 2006. *Impact of cross-border transport infrastructure on trade and investment in the GMS*. ADB Institute Discussion Paper No. 48. Tokyo: Asian Development Bank Institute. Available from: citeseerx.ist.psu.edu/viewdoc/download?doi=10.1.1.468.6495&rep=rep1&type=pdf.

GIS Resources. 2014. 'Why does NDVI, NDBI, NDWI ranges from −1 to 1?' [Online]. 13 April. Available from: www.gisresources.com/ndvi-ndbi-ndwi-ranges-1-1.

Goldblatt, R., Deininger, K. and Hanson, G. 2018. 'Utilizing publicly available satellite data for urban research: Mapping built-up land cover and land use in Ho Chi Minh City, Vietnam.' *Development Engineering* 3: 83–99. doi.org/10.1016/j.deveng.2018.03.001.

Goldblatt, R., You, W., Hanson, G. and Khandelwal, A. 2016. 'Detecting the boundaries of urban areas in India: A dataset for pixel-based image classification in Google Earth Engine.' *Remote Sensing* 8(8): 634. doi.org/10.3390/rs8080634.

Ishida, M. 2013. *Border Economies in the Greater Mekong Sub-Region.* London: Palgrave Macmillan. Available from: doi.org/10.1057/9781137302915.

Ismail, N.W. and Mahyideen, J.M. 2015. *The impact of infrastructure on trade and economic growth in selected economies in Asia.* ADB Institute Working Paper No. 553. Tokyo: Asian Development Bank Institute. Available from: www.adb.org/sites/default/files/publication/177093/adbi-wp553.pdf.

Japan International Broadcasting Inc. (JIBTV). 2014. 'Bridging for trade.' *JIBTV,* 17 January. Available from: www.jibtv.com/programs/mekong-bridge2014.

Japan International Cooperation Agency (JICA). 2017. '10 years after JICA assisted the construction of 2nd Thai–Lao Friendship Bridge, Japanese firms build factories, invigorating Laotian economy.' *News,* 31 July. Tokyo: JICA. Available from: www.jica.go.jp/english/news/field/2017/170731_01.html.

Ke, X., Chen, H., Hong, Y. and Hsiao, C. 2017. 'Do China's high-speed-rail projects promote local economy? New evidence from a panel data approach.' *China Economic Review* 44: 203–26. doi.org/10.1016/j.chieco.2017.02.008.

Li, Z. and Xu, H. 2018. 'High-speed railroads and economic geography: Evidence from Japan.' *Journal of Regional Science* 58(4): 705–27. doi.org/10.1111/jors.12384.

Mukdahan Customs House. 2019. 'Passenger and vehicle traffic between Thailand and Laos border.' *Annual Statistics of the Mukdahan Customs House for the fiscal year 2019.* Mukdahan, Thailand: Mukdahan Customs House. Available from: www.danmuk.org/index.php?lay=show&ac=article&Id=2147552135.

Nakhon Phanom Immigration Office. 2012. *Passenger and Vehicle Inspection Statistics.* Nakhon Phanom, Thailand: Nakhon Phanom Immigration Office. Available from: www.nakhonphanom-imm.com/2012-08-10-06-57-28.

National Aeronautics and Space Administration (NASA). n.d. 'Data.' *Landsat Science.* [Online]. Houston, TX: NASA. Available from: landsat.gsfc.nasa.gov/data.

National Centers for Environmental Information (NCEI). n.d. *Version 4 DMSP-OLS Nighttime Lights Time Series*. Boulder, CO: NCEI. Available from: ngdc.noaa.gov/eog/dmsp/downloadV4composites.html.

Office of the National Economic and Social Development Council (NESDC). n.d. 'Province-level measure of value added.' *Economic and Social Information*. Bangkok: NESDC. Available from: www.nesdc.go.th/main.php?filename=gross_regional.

Oizumi, K. 2013. 'The potential of the "Thailand-plus-one" business model: A new fragmentation in East Asia.' *Pacific Business and Industries* 8(50).

Royal Thai Consulate-General. 2019. 'Laos opens a new special economic zone at Thakhek, Khammouane Province.' Press release, 13 June. Savannakhet, Laos: Royal Thai Consulate-General.

Thailand Ministry of Transport (MOT). 2008. *Feasibility Study of the Third Mekong Bridge Construction Project (Nakhon Phanom)*. Bangkok: MOT.

United States Geological Survey (USGS). n.d. *EarthExplorer*. Reston, VA: USGS. Available from: earthexplorer.usgs.gov.

Vernon Henderson, J., Storeygard, A. and Weil, D.N. 2012. 'Measuring economic growth from outer space.' *American Economic Review* 102(2): 994–1028. doi.org/10.1257/aer.102.2.994.

Warr, P., Menon, J. and Yusuf, A. 2009. *Regional economic impacts of cross-border infrastructure: A general equilibrium application to Thailand and Lao PDR*. ADB Working Paper Series on Regional Economic Integration No. 35. Manila: Asian Development Bank. Available from: www.adb.org/sites/default/files/publication/28509/wp35-crossborder-infrastructure.pdf.

World Bank. 2009. *World Development Report 2009: Reshaping economic geography*. Washington, DC: World Bank Group.

Yu, F., Lin, F., Tang, Y. and Zhong, C. 2019. 'High-speed railway to success? The effects of high-speed rail connection on regional economic development in China.' *Journal of Regional Science* 59(4): 723–42. doi.org/10.1111/jors.12420.

4

The digital economy in Southeast Asia: Emerging policy priorities and opportunities for regional collaboration[1]

Natasha Beschorner

Introduction

Southeast Asia's digital economy[2] is expanding at an unprecedented rate. This is evidenced by the rise of technology 'unicorn' companies valued at more than US$1 billion (four of which are in Indonesia), cross-border e-commerce platforms and the growing number of entrepreneurs who are innovating and using technology to grow. The use of digital technologies has the potential to transform—indeed, disrupt—all sectors of the economy, from logistics and finance to agriculture and social services.

---

1   This chapter summarises the findings of a recent World Bank report, *The Digital Economy in Southeast Asia: Building the foundations for future growth* (Beschorner et al. 2019), focusing on key policy enablers. Also see World Bank (2019).

2   The term 'digital economy' is used to refer to private-sector utilisation of digital technologies as a driver of economic growth, innovation and other means of transforming the economy. In this sense, the digital economy is not restricted to the information and communication technology (ICT) sector, but rather encompasses the adoption of digital technology in all sectors of the economy.

These developments have also spurred increased interest from the region's governments and regional organisations, in promoting faster and more inclusive digitisation and technology adoption in various sectors. However, the full potential of technology as a driver of private-sector and wider economic growth is not yet being realised. Southeast Asia still faces significant barriers to growing its digital economy, many of which need to be addressed through enabling policies and regulations, as well as greater regional cooperation and collaboration. This chapter focuses primarily on these policy and regulatory factors.

Regional digital economy overview

The emergence and growth of the digital economy in Southeast Asia are being driven by improved internet access and usage across the region (Figure 4.1). Individuals in the region's emerging markets are spending substantial time online—more than four hours per day, for example, in Thailand, Malaysia and the Philippines.

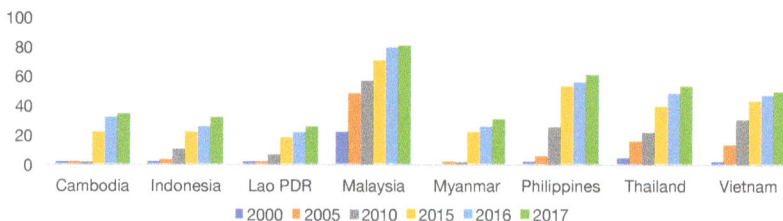

Figure 4.1 Individuals using the internet in selected Southeast Asian economies (percentage of population)

Source: World Bank staff calculations using World Bank (2021b).

According to recent surveys on internet usage, about 80 per cent of consumers regularly obtain information on products and services from social media (Kemp 2017). E-commerce spending in the region is also rising (Figure 4.2), facilitated by marketplaces/platforms where small and medium enterprises can also sell to consumers online. In big cities, the use of smartphones for messaging and social media has become ubiquitous. Ridesharing and delivery services using apps to obtain bookings are rapidly changing the face of urban transport and logistics services.

Used the internet to buy something online in the past year (% age 15+)

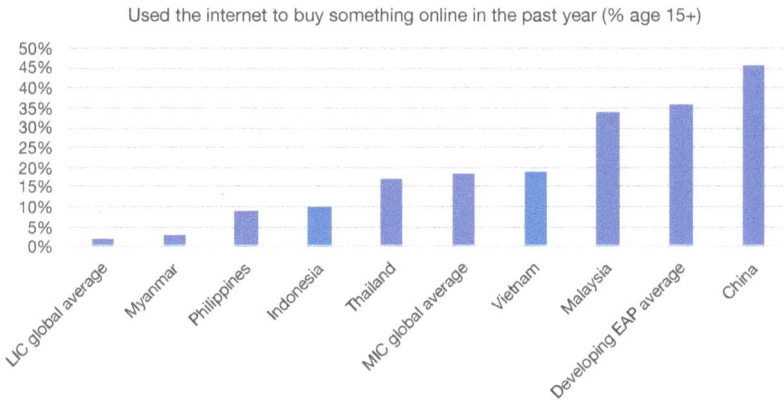

Figure 4.2 E-commerce adoption by country, 2017

LIC = low-income country

MIC = medium-income country

EAP = East Asia and the Pacific

Source: World Bank (2018a).

Digital *platforms*—a combination of technical innovation, new business models and value proposition—in the private and, in some cases, the public sectors offer a range of products and services via digital channels. Platform-based businesses have experienced remarkable growth and further expansion is projected.

The internet has dramatically lowered the cost of delivering services, as well as marketing, ordering and paying for them. Total Association of Southeast Asian Nations (ASEAN) trade in telecommunications, computer and information services (adding exports and imports) almost doubled between 2010 and 2016 (Figure 4.3) and its share of total ASEAN services trade grew by 28 per cent.

Digital technologies are facilitating payment and lending, promoting financial inclusion. In 2016, investments in the Southeast Asian fintech market increased to US$252 million—up one-third from 2015; the upward trend continued in 2017. The fintech landscape is dominated by payments and mobile wallets (43 per cent), followed by financial comparison platforms (15 per cent) and retail investment portals (11 per cent) (UOB 2017). Digital content development is another significant growth area. Ad-based video-on-demand (AVOD) or user-generated content platforms such as YouTube are very popular in Southeast Asia, with Vietnam and

Thailand ranking among the 10 markets with the highest viewership globally (Fujita 2017). The growing volume of local content highlights the increasing adoption by local media companies of digital platforms for the delivery of news and entertainment.

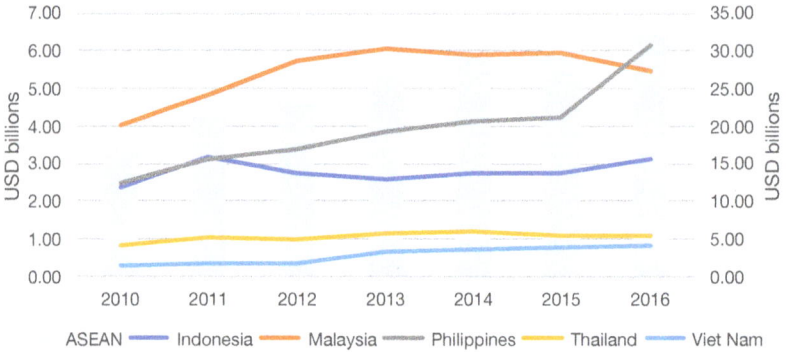

Figure 4.3 Telecommunications, computer and information services trade, ASEAN member countries

Note: Figure shows exports plus imports, for trade with all countries, to indicate the overall growth of trade rather than trade in one direction or another. The bars refer to the scale on the right axis, the lines to the scale on the left axis.

Source: Authors' calculations using information from ASEAN Secretariat.

However, the broader diffusion of digital technologies among businesses in Southeast Asia is still low, as illustrated by the World Bank's Digital Adoption Index (DAI) (Figure 4.4). The DAI measures the relative adoption of digital technologies by individuals, businesses and governments, based on a standard set of indicators across 180 countries relative to their income level. For example, Malaysia performs well in overall digital adoption in comparison with some Organisation for Economic Co-operation and Development (OECD) countries, but scores below expectations for its income level for digital adoption by businesses. These findings are also confirmed by the results of World Bank enterprise surveys. The limited use of digital technology by firms in Southeast Asia may reflect the digital divide between large and smaller firms, as globally small and medium-sized enterprises (SMEs) lag in technology adoption at all levels of economic development (OECD 2017). Other factors include the lack of necessary digital skills or limited availability of affordable broadband internet.

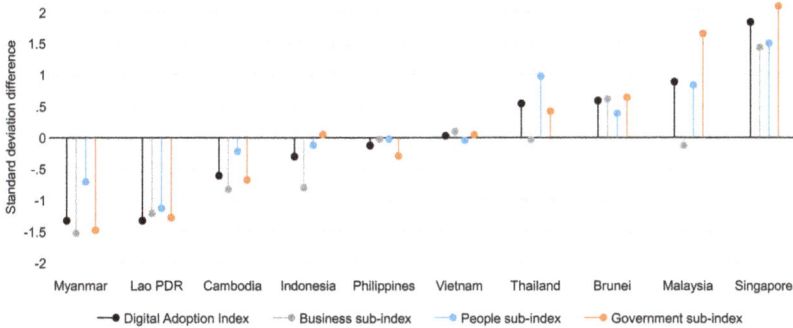

Figure 4.4 Digital adoption by individuals, governments and businesses relative to world average, ASEAN member countries[3]

Note: The diffusion of digital technologies among businesses uses proxy data such as the proportion of businesses with websites, the use of secure servers, internet bandwidth and mobile broadband.

Source: World Bank (2016b).

Looking ahead, digital technologies offer significant new opportunities for firms, including in lowering barriers to entry, particularly to global value chains (GVCs). SMEs may benefit disproportionately, as once-unaffordable computing power, storage and development platforms become cheaper (for example, via cloud computing), identifying talent becomes easier and markets become easier to reach (OECD 2017).

Emerging technologies such as fifth-generation (5G) mobile networks—particularly with their potential to expand the utilisation of device-to-device communications or the Internet of Things (IoT)—blockchain-enabled distributed data management, big data analytics and machine learning/artificial intelligence have major potential for disrupting business models across economic sectors and service delivery mechanisms.

Digital economy policy enablers … or barriers?

For the digital economy to have a significant impact on poverty reduction and inclusion in Southeast Asia, its key policy enablers or 'foundations' need to be better understood.

---

3   The overall DAI is the simple average of three subindexes, each of which comprises technologies necessary for the respective agent to promote development in the digital era: increasing productivity and accelerating broad-based growth for *business*, expanding opportunities and improving welfare for *people* and increasing the efficiency and accountability of service delivery for *government* (World Bank 2016a).

These foundations, underpinned by a stable macroeconomic environment and supportive business environment, include affordable and consistent internet *connectivity*, secure *payment* systems and mechanisms, availability of appropriate and adaptable workforce *skills*, reliable *logistics* services to facilitate the delivery of goods and a series of *crosscutting policies and regulations* supporting and securing online transactions and protecting consumers (Table 4.1). This is essentially what the *World Development Report 2016* (World Bank 2016b) refers to as the nondigital or 'analogue' complements needed to enable the digital economy and is discussed in more detail in *The Digital Economy in Southeast Asia: Building the foundations for future growth* (Beschorner et al. 2019).

Table 4.1 Digital economy foundations at a glance

Connectivity	Affordable, reliable and high-quality broadband internet access is a prerequisite for and a physical underpinning of the digital economy.
Payments	Access to safe and secure digital payment services provides the opportunity to engage in electronic transactions whether as consumers or entrepreneurs, domestically or overseas.
Digital skills	In a digitally driven economy, skills needs range from basic digital and data literacy to specialised skills to harness the productivity benefits of digital innovation.
Logistics	E-commerce is particularly dependent on well-regulated, widely available and cost-effective logistics services given the higher demand for delivery of goods, especially at low values, both within and across borders.
Digital policy and regulation	Policies that promote trust are essential for growing participation in the digital economy. These cover a range of areas, from data privacy and cybersecurity to consumer protection. Regional coordination of such policies is desirable.

There are significant differences between and within Southeast Asian countries in terms of internet access, speed and cost; in particular, differences within countries between urban and rural/remote internet access and quality can be especially large. The extent of utilisation of digital payments varies across countries. Significant gaps also exist between traditional models of education and training and the evolving demands for digital skills in the workforce. Policies and regulations for managing data, especially the flow of data across borders, are still evolving.

Table 4.2 Digital economy indicators in selected Southeast Asian countries

		Indonesia	Vietnam	Thailand	Malaysia	Cambodia	Lao PDR	Philippines
Connectivity	Mobile broadband subscribers (% of population)	100%	82%	170%	116%	67%	51%	40%
	Mobile broadband prices (500MB/month) as a percentage of GNI per capita	1.4%	1.4%	1.2%	0.9%	1.1%	n.a.	1.5%
	Fixed broadband subscribers (% of population)	3.1%	12%	11%	8%	1.5%	1%	3%
Payments	Made or received digital payment in the past year	34%	22%	62%	76%	16%	12%	23%
	Paid online for internet purchase	49%	10%	n.a.	52%	n.a.	n.a.	52%
	Percentage of online firms using digital payments	51%	51%	n.a.	57%	n.a.	n.a.	52%
Skills	Human Capital Development Index global rank (out of 120, 1 is highest)	69	68	57	52	97	105	46

		Indonesia	Vietnam	Thailand	Malaysia	Cambodia	Lao PDR	Philippines
Logistics	Logistics Performance Index score (out of 5, 1 is lowest)	2.98	2.98	3.26	3.43	2.8	2.07	2.86
	Integrated Index for Postal Development (100 = highest)	49.4	47.8	66.1	66.0	19.7	41.4	33.9
Policy and regulation	Cross-border data flow restrictions	Yes	Yes	No	Yes	No	No	No
	Data privacy regulations	Yes	Draft	Yes	Yes	No	No	Yes
	Consumer protection regulations	Yes	Yes	Yes	Yes	Yes	Draft	Yes
	Cybersecurity expenditure as percentage of GDP	0.02%	0.04%	0.05%	0.08%	n.a.	n.a.	0.04%

GNI = gross national income

n.a. not available

Note: The Integrated Index for Postal Development is a newly developed composite index that benchmarks four different aspects of postal services—reliability, reach, relevance and resilience—which was developed through an analysis of Universal Postal Union (UPU) postal big data, the UPU postal statistics database and surveys; 100 = highest performance.

Sources: ITU (2017); GSMA (2019); TeleGeography (2021); World Bank (2016a, 2018a); AT Kearney (2018); UPU (2017); WEF (2017); Record et al. (2018); UNESCO (2018).

Connectivity: Particularly high-speed (broadband) internet access

Digital connectivity in Southeast Asia is improving, driven by substantial investment primarily from the private sector. Broadband internet penetration grew 13 per cent per year in Southeast Asia between 2011 and 2016 (ITU 2017). However, as of mid-2019, about half the region's population still lacked broadband access (Figure 4.5). Mobile broadband access (notably, 4G and, prospectively, 5G) is improving as is the proliferation of smartphones, but quality and affordability remain challenging in many areas. Fixed broadband access—for example, through optical-fibre connections to the premises, which is essential for data-intensive transactions required by many businesses—is lagging.

Internet speeds—key determinants of service quality—in the largest Southeast Asian economies fall short of the global leaders, although the gap is closing. The largest middle-income developing countries in the region all fall below the OECD's average speed for mobile and fixed broadband. Thailand is the only economy ranked within the top-20 countries globally measured as the proportion of the population with broadband plans at 15 megabits per second (Mbps) or faster (Akamai 2017). Although Indonesia, the Philippines and Vietnam are currently behind, the year-on-year growth rates—520 per cent, 509 per cent and 1,222 per cent, respectively, for 2016–17—are encouraging.

Internet affordability, both in absolute terms and as a percentage of income, has seen steady improvement globally and in Southeast Asia (ITU 2016, 2018). However, while mobile broadband is becoming more affordable—less than 5 per cent of gross national income (GNI) per capita[4]—fixed broadband is typically less affordable. There are also significant variations in the availability, quality and pricing of broadband services within countries, which are attributable to geography and population distribution (particularly in Indonesia and the Philippines), technical factors (such as the type of backhaul technologies available, such as fibre, microwave or satellite), overall costs of service deployment, expected revenue for service providers, local constraints such as permits and rights-of-way requirements and lower levels of competition in particular regions.

---

4   Gross national income (GNI) is defined as the sum of value added by all producers who are residents in a nation, plus any product taxes (minus subsidies) not included in output, plus income received from abroad such as employee compensation and property income.

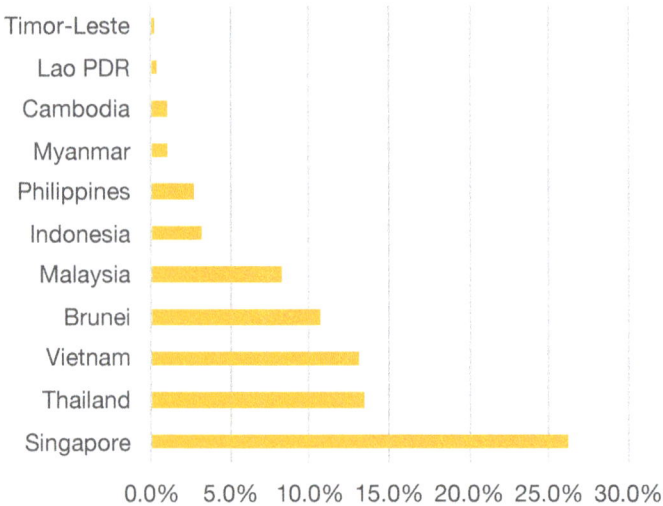

Figure 4.5 Broadband internet penetration in ASEAN member countries (percentage of population)

Notes: Mobile broadband means access to the internet using a 3G or (faster) 4G-enabled device. A GSM 2G connection means that the user has only a basic data service — that is, text messaging. Fixed broadband means access to the internet using fixed-line networks such as xDSL (digital subscriber lines) or optical fibre connected to the premises. These data show the number of mobile and fixed broadband internet subscribers as a percentage of the population for each country.

Sources: ITU (2018); GSMA (2019); TeleGeography (2021).

Governments have an important role to play in facilitating faster broadband rollout through regulatory reforms that can, for example, improve competition in the broadband value chain (wholesale and retail) and help to optimise investments in unserved and underserved locations as well as increasing the uptake of services. Sound competition policy remains highly relevant in this regard, though the nature of the competitive landscape has shifted from voice-based to platform-based service delivery. Regulatory authorities also have an important role in quality-of-service oversight.

Priority policy and regulatory reforms for improved digital connectivity include the following.

- Open access and nondiscriminatory pricing: Regulations that help to create a more level playing field for telecommunications/internet service providers to access critical infrastructure/networks at all levels of the broadband value chain. This includes the 'first mile', or international gateway, as well as the 'middle mile' or 'backbone' networks and last-mile fixed networks—for example, fibre to the home (FTTH). Open access at the wholesale level helps to promote more equitable competition among retail service provides, lowering the cost of internet services at the retail level.

- Passive infrastructure sharing: Regulations that encourage or, in some cases, mandate service providers to share tower networks (for wireless backbone infrastructure, for example, microwaves and mobile base stations) and/or fixed broadband facilities to enable more efficient utilisation of resources and reductions in the cost of network installation and maintenance. Passive infrastructure may account for up to 80 per cent of digital infrastructure investment costs, so the savings are potentially significant. There are further opportunities for sharing digital infrastructure across sectors (for example, optical-fibre cables collocated with power transmission networks, roads and pipelines).

- Radio spectrum management: Spectrum is a scare resource, particularly in densely populated urban environments, which governments allocate—for example, to telecoms and broadcasting service providers, among others, to enable them to provide communications services across designated frequencies. Evolving communications technologies may require the review and/or reallocation of spectrum among service providers to maximise efficient utilisation. For example, the 700-megahertz band—typically allocated for analogue broadcasting—is being progressively phased out globally as countries migrate to digital television. The spectrum can then be freed up for additional mobile broadband (for example, 4G) deployment.

- Foreign ownership restrictions that still apply in some countries in the telecommunications/internet sector: A review/revision of these may enable greater foreign investment in connectivity infrastructure and promote more competition in service delivery.

- National broadband plans: Several governments in the region have published such plans with indicative targets for coverage and internet speeds. Given the rapidly increasing demand, there is scope to set more ambitious targets for reducing the digital divide and to strengthen monitoring and evaluation mechanisms.

Payments

Finance is both an enabler of the digital economy and one of the main sectors where digitisation is supporting significant changes in business models and available services. For example, digital financial services can potentially offer a new pathway into the formal financial system for 'unbanked' people in the region.

The use of digital payments in Southeast Asia is still lagging, constrained by low consumer awareness and lack of trust in the security and reliability of online transactions. Vietnam, Thailand, Indonesia and the Philippines fall below the middle-income country average (27 per cent) for account holders using the internet or mobile phones to access their accounts (Figure 4.6).

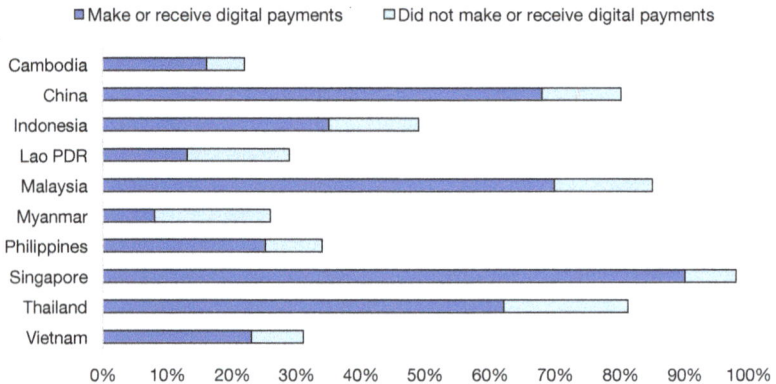

Figure 4.6 Digital payments use is still relatively limited

Source: World Bank (2018a).

The level of online payments for internet purchases in Thailand and Malaysia is roughly one-third lower than the average for middle-income countries (around 71 per cent), and around half the level in Singapore. In Vietnam, the use of online payments is 14 per cent that of the average for middle-income countries. About 85 per cent of account owners (70 per cent of adults) had made or received a digital payment in the year under review in Malaysia, but only around 35 per cent for Indonesia and 22 per cent for Vietnam (World Bank 2018a).

Policymakers face a variety of challenges in facilitating the expansion of digital payments, including the following.

- Consumer protection, given that digital financial services and products are now being delivered through new channels and business models. These models challenge traditional thinking about disclosure and recourse—for example, if the consumer suffers a loss, liability can be unclear due to the multiple parties involved in service delivery such as intermediaries and third-party providers of communications and technology services. Policymakers will need to consider how to update conventional product standards and guidelines to address these concerns.

- Increased need for cross-sectoral coordination and communication. Digital financial inclusion—which involves new providers, services and consumers—requires significant cross-sectoral coordination and communication among regulators and supervisors, both at country and global levels. This is an important agenda item for regional organisations.

- Customer identity/digital identity document (ID). Financial identity for poor people when services are delivered digitally carries the potential for both inclusion and gains for anti–money laundering and countering the financing of terrorism, but it also raises privacy and fraud risks. Meaningful and manageable laws based on privacy principles—at the national and global levels—and effective enforcement thereof offer the prospect of win-win solutions. Policymakers, development partners and other stakeholders worldwide are also recognising the need to develop comprehensive ID programs to enable access to financial and other services.

- Monitoring systems. Reporting and monitoring systems need to become more sophisticated, with a greater focus on direct linkages to financial institutions' information systems (where feasible) and development of real-time monitoring capabilities, to enable implementation of appropriate privacy and data protections for users.

- Interoperability of digital services across service providers and points of service, including agents and service providers. This issue is critical for national efforts to broaden the reach of financial services into previously underserved, often rural, areas as well as for other fund transfers—for example, government services delivery.

Skills for the digital economy

The growth of the digital economy is placing a premium on certain skills and reducing returns on others. Recent literature shows an emerging consensus around three 'tiers' of skills, outlined in Table 4.3, which are considered essential in the digital economy.[5]

Structural changes in Southeast Asian economies have already been raising the demand for workers to have more advanced skills, but the digital economy is leading to more rapid changes in business models and activities. As a result, specific occupational skills are likely to become obsolete more quickly than in the past. Thus, skills policies should aim to build adaptability among workers, not just focus on specific occupations (World Bank 2016b: 259). The skill set for the digital economy is a combination of the 'soft' skills of critical thinking and problem-solving, communication, teamwork and creativity, beyond the traditional focus on 'hard' skills such as programming and coding, science and technology. This underlines the importance of governments investing in human capital, not only to build basic literacy and numeracy, but also to develop sociobehavioural skills, which also reinforce adaptability in a rapidly changing environment (World Bank 2019).

Table 4.3 High-level digital skills categories

Types	Description	Target	Examples
Basic digital/ ICT skills	Ability to use digital technologies (for example, send emails, find work-related information on the internet, use digital apps and nonspecialised software, awareness of and ability to stay safe in cyberspace)	All citizens and workers	EU: Digital Competence Framework for Citizens, also known as DigComp
Digital/ICT complementary skills	Soft skills required to work in a technology-rich environment and to participate in ICT-enabled collaborative work (for example, communicate via social networks, market products on e-commerce platforms or analyse data gathered from the web)	Middle-skilled to high-skilled professionals	US: Partnership for 21st Century Skills US: Agenda for New Skills for Jobs

---

5   See, for example, OECD (2016); UNESCO (2018).

Types	Description	Target	Examples
Advanced and specialist skills	Skills needed to drive innovation, support digital infrastructure and the functioning of the digital ecosystem	Industry and occupation specific (for example, program software, develop applications, manage networks, data analytics)	Global: Skills Framework for the Information Age (SFIA: www.sfia-online.org/en) Singapore: Workforce Qualification scheme

ICT = information and communication technology

Key policy priorities include the following.

- Digital skills strategy development and curriculum updates. These will need to be undertaken at all levels of education systems, as well as for lifelong learning programs. Some governments in Southeast Asia are already implementing programs to build a foundation of core skills to help workers meet the demands of increasingly technology-driven economic environments. Examples include Singapore's SkillsFuture for the Digital Workplace initiative, Malaysia's #mydigitalmaker movement and Thailand's Net Pracharat skills awareness and digital literacy program. Given the rapid pace of changing skill needs, more systematic collaboration between governments and the private sector can help identify and anticipate these needs.

- Regional skills mobility. Regional efforts to promote talent mobility within ASEAN member countries, including providing for the transferability and recognition of education and skills through common certification protocols, will be important to reap the full benefits of technology and facilitate increased regional integration. Joint skills training and mutual recognition of occupational qualifications and standards between ASEAN nations also can promote talent flows from economies with specific skill surpluses to those where such skills are in short supply. This needs to be coupled with policies that support the regional movement of skilled personnel, which may require the lifting of restrictive policies in some country contexts.

Logistics

Improved connectivity, the spread of digital payments and adoption of e-commerce are all leading to higher demand for the delivery of goods within and across borders, raising the importance of logistics (trade facilitation and fulfilment) services. E-commerce consumers, whether firms or individuals, are demanding delivery services that are fast, efficient, reliable and traceable. Recent Logistics Performance Index (LPI) data[6] indicate improved overall performance from 2016 to 2018 in Thailand, Vietnam, Indonesia, the Philippines and Lao PDR. In absolute terms, performance overall for ASEAN is not especially strong; only Thailand and Vietnam placed in the top 25 per cent of performers in the LPI in 2018, and Malaysia, Indonesia and the Philippines placed in the top 50 per cent. Figure 4.7 illustrates comparative performance on two key indicators from the LPI across selected countries: customs and border management, and the competence and quality of logistics services.

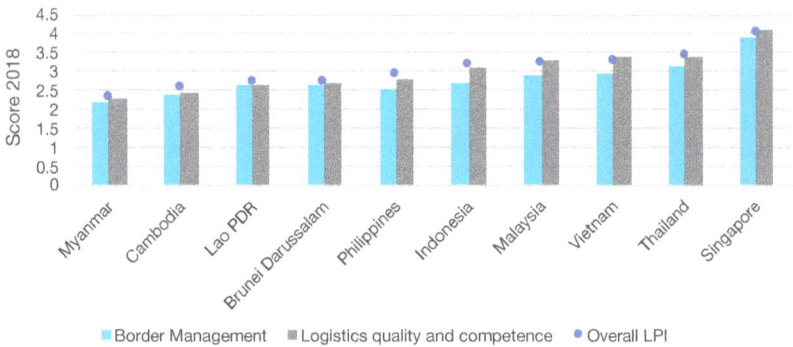

Figure 4.7 Logistics performance indicators: Selected key indicators, 2018

Source: World Bank (2018b).

Key policy and regulatory issues for governments related to logistics include the following.

- Harmonisation of 'de minimis' thresholds across countries. A particular feature of the growth of e-commerce is that it is leading to an increase in shipments of low-value, small consignments, both within and across borders. At present, most governments have *de minimis* thresholds in place, setting a value for individual shipments below which customs duties and other taxes are not charged. As the volume of goods falling below these thresholds grows, many governments perceive this as

---

6   The LPI collects the perceptions of logistics service providers about several aspects of logistics performance: 1) the efficiency of customs and border management clearances, 2) the quality of trade-related and transport-related infrastructure, 3) the ease of arranging competitively priced international shipments, 4) the competence and quality of logistics services, 5) the ability to track and trace consignments and 6) the frequency with which shipments reach consignees within the scheduled or expected delivery time.

generating risk—for community protection and safety, revenue collection and intellectual property enforcement, among other areas. This has led to widely varying standards across countries. A common approach in Southeast Asia (for example, by ASEAN) is needed, and governments could facilitate cross-border e-commerce.

- Maintaining risk-based approaches to managing border clearances, including simplified procedures for low-value, low-risk goods and 'trusted trader' schemes for frequent traders with strong compliance records. Efficiency and control can be facilitated by ensuring that logistics operators or e-commerce firms provide data to customs agencies in advance of a parcel's arrival. The majority of small parcels crossing borders through e-commerce are likely to be legitimate shipments and inspecting all or most parcels will not only impede trade but also entail high administrative costs for customs and other agencies.

- Reducing internal regulatory barriers. These include phasing out fragmented licensing arrangements for logistics services and reducing market entry barriers—for example, foreign equity limits and minimum capital requirements that increase logistics costs in some countries, such as Indonesia.

- Facilitating provision of space, especially in urban areas, for warehouse and distribution facilities would enable more timely delivery of small parcels (e-commerce companies require up to three times the inventory space of 'offline' retailers) (Prologis 2016).

- Facilitating last-mile delivery in those Southeast Asian economies that still have large gaps in postal addressing, such as Indonesia and Myanmar, is critical, given the heavy reliance on postal networks for e-commerce deliveries. In Indonesia, for example, the lack of standardisation in addressing systems and parcel sizes requires the use of manual rather than automatic sorting, which is likely to push costs up as e-commerce demand grows. Alternative solutions (for example, pick-ups at supermarkets or parcel lockers) will be needed and in some cases have already been developed by private-sector firms and consumers.

Crosscutting digital economy policy and regulation

Policies to promote trust in the internet and digital activities are essential for growing participation in the digital economy and for managing risks associated with technologies such as cloud computing, big data analytics, the IoT and, prospectively, artificial intelligence (AI) and machine learning. This includes policies and regulations on electronic transactions more broadly, but also specific measures addressing data protection and privacy—particularly the issue of cross-border data flows—cybersecurity and consumer protection. Other relevant crosscutting policies relate to digital entrepreneurship, digital government and digital identity programs.

Southeast Asian governments have generally adopted policies and regulations pertaining to e-commerce. This focus is also evident in ASEAN's regional digital agenda, which has a strong focus on e-commerce rather than the digitisation of industries. ASEAN member countries have adopted two UN Commission on International Trade Law (UNCITRAL) instruments, the Model Law on Electronic Commerce (MLEC) and, more recently, the Convention on Electronic Contracting. Both instruments prohibit discrimination against contracts originating in electronic form and disparity of treatment between electronic communications and paper documents.[7] These prohibitions are regarded as 'enabling' e-commerce by removing doubts about the enforceability of online contracts. While multiple ASEAN jurisdictions have enacted domestic legislation based on either the MLEC or the convention, the adoption of the MLEC has not been uniform.

Most Southeast Asian countries—except Cambodia, Lao PDR and Myanmar—have general legal frameworks for secure electronic transactions, data protection and privacy and consumer protection for online purchases (see Table 4.4). Challenges include implementation and enforcement and development of subsidiary legislation and regulations to address the detailed issues outlined above.

---

7   See UNCITRAL (1999: Article 8, Explanatory Note, para. 129).

Table 4.4 Legal frameworks in ASEAN countries for electronic transactions, data protection, privacy and online purchases

Country	Does the country have a legal framework for electronic transactions/ e-signatures?	Does the country have a legal framework for data protection/ privacy online?	Does the country have a legal framework for consumer protection when purchasing online?	Does the country have a legal framework for cybercrime prevention?
Brunei Darussalam	Yes	No	Yes	Yes
Cambodia	Draft	No	Draft	Draft
Indonesia	Yes	Yes	Yes	Yes
Lao PDR	Yes	Yes	Draft	Yes
Malaysia	Yes	Yes	Yes	Yes
Myanmar	Yes	No	Yes	Yes
Philippines	Yes	Yes	Yes	Yes
Singapore	Yes	Yes	Yes	Yes
Thailand	Yes	Yes	Yes	Yes
Vietnam	Yes	Yes	Yes	Yes

Source: UNCTAD (n.d.).

Data protection and privacy

The use of data is central to the digital economy. Accordingly, a robust legal and regulatory regime that addresses issues of data ownership, protects personal data and builds trust, while allowing the legitimate use of data, is a critical requirement. The extent to which countries in the region have legal and regulatory frameworks on the ownership, governance and privacy of data varies. Malaysia, Singapore and the Philippines adopted comprehensive data protection laws earlier last decade. Thailand's personal data protection law was to come into force in May 2020. In Indonesia, sectoral regulations applicable to electronic service providers are already in place and a draft law on data protection is pending presidential approval. Vietnam has a variety of specific regulations in place but no crosscutting data protection law. Cambodia, Brunei, Lao PDR and Myanmar lack publicly announced plans to introduce comprehensive data protection frameworks.

The ease of transmitting data across borders is central to the growth of cross-border business models. At the transactional level, data underpin the flow of goods and services within countries around the region and between Southeast Asia and its major trading partners. Effective use of data is also a necessary condition for the adoption of cloud technologies that can reduce upfront capital costs and boost productivity (Meltzer and Lovelock 2018). Cross-border data flows generate more economic value than traditional flows of traded goods, according to some estimates. These flows accounted for US$2.8 trillion of global GDP in 2014 and have the potential to reach US$11 trillion by 2025 (Manyika and Chui 2015).[8] Indeed, the ability to move data rapidly and globally is the new growth engine for many businesses.

The region has seen a push by some governments to restrict cross-border data flows, especially of sensitive personal data. The regulatory regimes in Indonesia and Vietnam include data localisation requirements under which businesses are obliged to ensure that various forms of data are processed and stored on servers/facilities physically located within national borders or that at least a copy of the data are available locally and accessible for law enforcement purposes ('data mirroring'). The arguments for such regulations include enhancing national security, protecting personal privacy, aiding law enforcement and preventing foreign surveillance, in addition to appeals to the principle of sovereignty. But governments have also imposed restrictions to support domestic technology sectors or to promote the construction of in-country data centres and the creation of highly skilled technical jobs (FTI Consulting 2017). Such restrictions have economic and trade costs and, according to the European Centre for International Political Economy, may reduce GDP by 0.5 per cent in Indonesia, 0.4 per cent in South Korea and 1.7 per cent in Vietnam (Bauer et al. 2014).

Blanket data localisation restrictions can have widespread impacts beyond the digital economy because of the increasingly central importance of data to economic activity—for example, the use of data to monitor the efficiency of production processes or the performance of engineering parts to identify needs for maintenance or replacement. Moreover, many services critical for increasing productivity (including for SMEs)—for example, research and development services provided from a subsidiary

---

8   There is no consensus on estimates of the value and impact of data flows and gathering such data is highly challenging.

to a domestic manufacturing firm, design services for an engineering company or marketing for an agricultural producer—are accessed through cross-border data transfers.

Data localisation regulations should be designed to reduce risk—whether to privacy, from cyberattack or from delays due to law enforcement—to an acceptable level relative to the economic and social benefits, including innovation, expected from the use of the data.[9] In most cases, legitimate regulatory goals can be achieved at lower costs to growth and trade than those involved in blanket requirements on data localisation. For example, in most countries, only certain types of data are required to be held on local servers (for example, data of national security importance), rather than mandating a blanket requirement. Such approaches should avoid excessive regulatory complexity—for example, by introducing multiple categories of data that are not clearly defined—or relying on imprecise provisions.

The negative impacts of regulations that impede data flows often go unobserved, as many governments do not have the capacity to adequately measure the contributions of data to the digital economy. Governments could improve their measurement of the effects of cross-border data flows and thus the impact of data localisation requirements by increasing the sample sizes used when measuring trade in services and collecting data more often and at a more granular level. They could also collect more detailed and specific data on cross-border data flows and develop better measures to capture how the digital economy contributes to GDP, job growth and productivity. ASEAN could support measurement and data collection by developing a standard nomenclature for terms, standard metrics and indicators related to the digital economy.

A key challenge is finding ways for data to flow freely between countries in the region with different regulatory approaches to privacy. There are ongoing efforts to facilitate data flows through self-regulatory instruments—notably, through the Asia-Pacific Economic Cooperation (APEC) Cross-Border Privacy Rules (CBPR) system, which enables personal data to flow freely even in the absence of two governments having recognised the other's privacy laws as equivalent. Instead, APEC relies on businesses to ensure that data sent to third parties, either domestically or abroad, continue to be protected consistent with APEC privacy principles.

---

9   This principle has been adopted by the OECD (OECD Secretariat 2015: Principle 5).

The APEC CBPR regime also requires accountability agents accredited by their local government to monitor and hold businesses accountable for privacy breaches.[10] To date, in Asia, only Japan has effectively joined the scheme, but it will soon be operational in Singapore and South Korea once their governments appoint accountability agents. The Philippines and Vietnam have expressed an interest in joining the scheme.

Another, complementary approach is to work towards the convergence of data privacy laws across countries. Some Southeast Asian jurisdictions have effectively implemented the high-level principles and concepts embedded in various international legal instruments, frameworks or guidelines into their national legal systems, including the OECD Privacy Principles, EU Directive 95/46/EC (now the General Data Protection Regulation, or GDPR), the APEC Privacy Framework and the ASEAN Data Protection Framework. However, divergence has increased as jurisdictions have prescribed more and more detailed requirements to ensure enforcement and compliance (Hogan Lovells 2018: 4). Local or regional actions seeking to promote the convergence of existing data protection laws should be encouraged.

Cybersecurity

Cybersecurity threats have wideranging implications for commercial activities and personal privacy and have triggered a range of regulatory responses. Cybersecurity is a function of multiple elements—technical, financial, physical and human resources.

Countries in the region have to date underinvested in the 'hard' and 'soft' infrastructure of cybersecurity. In 2017, expenditure on cybersecurity ranged from 0.22 per cent of GDP in Singapore (the third highest globally) to 0.02 per cent in Indonesia. Overall, ASEAN member countries spent about 0.07 per cent of GDP on cybersecurity—below the global spending average of 0.13 per cent (AT Kearney 2018). According to an assessment by AT Kearney, ASEAN member countries need to increase spending on cybersecurity to between 0.35 per cent and 0.61 per cent of collective GDP—or about US$171 billion—between 2017 and 2025.

---

10   Trustarc and JIPDEC have been recognised as accountability agents in the United States and Japan, respectively.

Singapore, Malaysia, Thailand, the Philippines and, more recently, Indonesia have established national cybersecurity strategies and agencies to coordinate cybersecurity agendas, but specific governance mechanisms and policies are still underdeveloped. One major contributing factor is the global and regional shortage of skills in these areas.

To address current and emerging threats, Southeast Asian governments will need to accelerate the development of national cybersecurity strategies with a well-defined vision, scope, objectives and a practical roadmap for implementation. An approach based on the identification, analysis and evaluation of risk will be crucial.

A regional governance framework to address cybersecurity is also yet to be established. The focus to date has been on including cybercrime in existing frameworks, particularly ASEAN mechanisms. ASEAN is working on a more coordinated approach to develop a comprehensive cybersecurity framework that establishes regional cybersecurity standards and encourages intelligence sharing.

Consumer protection

Complementing e-commerce and e-transaction laws, consumer protection laws and regulations are essential for building an ecosystem of trust and confidence in electronic transactions. Concerns about potentially greater consumer vulnerabilities through the rise of the digital economy have driven a growing focus on consumer protection related to e-commerce and other aspects of the digital economy. For example, online consumer protection has featured in several ASEAN initiatives and is also a theme in Indonesia's E-Commerce Roadmap (2017).

Consumer concerns about trust and reliability in e-commerce appear to be a barrier to further growth. The overall lack of trust in online transactions is demonstrated by the fact that, despite an increase in the use of some digital payments—for example, in Thailand and Malaysia—cash on delivery remains the preferred payment mode in emerging Southeast Asian markets, as noted in the section above.

The main effort at the regional level to address these issues is the ASEAN Strategic Action Plan for Consumer Protection 2025, the implementation of which has focused on information-sharing between regulators, although there are also more ambitious goals, such as creating a cross-border redress system and a rapid alert system on product safety. However, ASEAN's initiatives can only advance as far and as quickly as the members themselves can enforce laws and regulations that protect transactions both online and offline, and not all countries have consumer protection laws in place.

Digital entrepreneurship

Many governments in Southeast Asia are considering options to improve the 'digital entrepreneurship ecosystem' through strengthening the wider business environment and facilitating access to staff with skills appropriate for the digital economy. In addition, governments are increasingly interested in issues specific to digital startups, including access to finance for entrepreneurs, awareness-raising of the potential of the digital economy or targeted financial or other support to help firms grow.

Support to strengthen the foundations of the digital economy, along with the wider business environment, must be balanced with providing targeted support for digital startups. For example, a recent World Bank report on Malaysia's digital economy (Record et al. 2018) recommends the government shift its role from providing a wide range of support programs for entrepreneurship to addressing structural reforms, especially to supply-side factors like access to skills and finance, while avoiding crowding out private investment, channelling government funds into ineffective programs or putting burdensome regulations in place.

Digital government[11] and digital identification

The provision of online services to citizens and businesses, typically via a digital government 'platform' or portal (such as www.gov.sg in Singapore or www.malaysia.gov.my in Malaysia), can boost the growth of the digital economy. Developing online business registration platforms and shifting from paper-based to online systems for government approval of cross-border trade shipments can encourage firms to adopt digital technologies. The provision of digital services can help raise digital awareness and literacy. And the digitisation of government payments can increase financial inclusion. For example, 14 per cent of bank account holders in Thailand opened their account to enable receipt of a government transfer. There is considerable potential for increasing financial inclusion through

---

11 There are numerous definitions of this concept. The term 'e-government' is used to refer to the use of information and communication technologies, specifically the internet, to deliver services to individuals and businesses. The term 'digital government' is used more holistically to refer to 'the use of digital technologies, as an integrated part of governments' modernisation strategies, to create public value' (OECD 2014).

digitising government payments. For example, in the Philippines, six million unbanked people receive government payments in cash, even though 58 per cent of them own a mobile phone (Demirguc-Kunt et al. 2018). The adoption of government-issued digital IDs can boost financial inclusion by helping to meet 'know your customer' and other regulatory requirements.

Digital ID systems are widely recognised as key enablers for the development of digital government, e-commerce and the digital economy (World Bank 2016b: 194–97). Digital ID systems facilitate reliable authentication of a person's identity on demand and bind users of online transactions with their 'real world' or legal identities. E-commerce and the IoT have also created a need for verifiable digital identities for legal entities and devices. Interoperability of digital IDs across borders can accelerate economic integration and create opportunities for new markets.

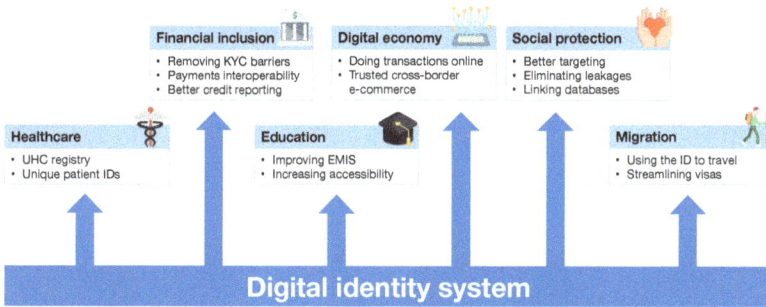

Figure 4.8 Digital IDs in the digital economy ecosystem

KYC = know your customer

EMIS = educational management information system

UHC = universal health coverage

Source: Prepared by the Identification for Development (ID4D) team at the World Bank presentation in 2019.

Digital ID is also associated with advancing a range of other development outcomes, including comprehensive social safety nets, streamlined public administration, financial inclusion and the empowerment of women. Five ASEAN member states—Brunei, Indonesia, Malaysia, Singapore and Thailand—have fully digitised their foundational ID system and have established an associated public key infrastructure. The foundational

ID is widely used in public and private-sector face-to-face transactions, including ubiquitous use of the unique identification number. All these systems, except for Singapore's, use smartcards with data such as private keys and biometrics stored on the chip. Cambodia, Lao PDR and Vietnam are currently piloting digitised foundational ID systems. Myanmar has listed the development of a digital ID system as one of 12 priorities in its national economic policy.[12]

Towards a regional digital economy?

Almost all governments in Southeast Asia have developed national strategies or high-level plans, endorsed at the head of government or a similar level, for growing the digital economy, but implementation remains a challenge. A robust assessment of where the market is adjusting well to digital transformation would help determine where government intervention would be most useful and where it is not required. Such a targeted approach to intervention would be less challenging to implement and would help establish a logical sequence for the implementation of various initiatives. Furthermore, more effective consultation and feedback mechanisms are required for policymakers to gain the perspectives of private-sector firms at every stage of national digital economy strategies—from conception to implementation and monitoring. Government strategies on the digital economy will need to include implementation plans with concrete targets, timelines and institutional coordination to ensure delivery and accountability.

Given a range of potentially important cross-country dimensions of the digital economy, regional cooperation—for example, through ASEAN—could be leveraged to strengthen the enabling environment for the growth of the digital economy in individual Southeast Asian countries as well as to facilitate deeper integration between national economies. Digital platforms—for example, for e-commerce, transport and financial services—are increasingly transnational. Greater regional cooperation

---

12 'Foundational ID system' is an ID system used for general purposes (for example, national IDs and birth certificates) as the root of someone's identity. By comparison, a functional ID system is intended for a specific purpose—for example, a passport is for travel, a driver's licence is for permission to drive. Public key infrastructure is widely known in digital ID and ICT circles. Essentially, it is a technology for authenticating people or things by using cryptography to match a private key (a digital certificate held by a user) and a public key (held by an authority). A unique ID number (for example, a national ID number) is one type of credential issued by a foundational ID system. Other examples include a card or a username (World Bank 2021a).

could help address many of the issues identified in this chapter, including data privacy (to improve the coherence of legal frameworks), cybersecurity (to prevent and respond to threats) and consumer protection (to improve cross-border appeal and redress mechanisms), among others. Identifying concrete measures that can be taken in these areas is an important area for future analysis and policy cooperation in Southeast Asia.

ASEAN could encourage its members to develop the necessary infrastructure for information and communication technology (ICT) development, reduce barriers to participation in digital markets and harmonise regulations. Supporting development of the digital economy will also strengthen ASEAN's overall objective of promoting regional economic integration. ASEAN has adopted initiatives to support the growth of the digital economy, including the first and second ASEAN ICT masterplans (AIM2015 and AIM2020) and the Master Plan on ASEAN Connectivity 2025, while high-level ASEAN agreements—notably, the 2015 and 2025 economic blueprints—demonstrate a broadening of the vision for the digital economy in the region.

However, there is scope to go further in cooperation on the digital economy at the ASEAN level, especially in terms of detailed actions, timelines and targets. There are no monitoring or ranking mechanisms to evaluate progress at the national or regional level in developing critical enablers, such as the impact of privacy laws, data protection or incentives to support universal broadband access, mobile financial services, e-commerce and other key areas of the digital economy. Though the current approach recognises the importance of regulatory harmonisation, it offers no concrete principles for how regulations need to be extended and harmonised to create a single digital market, including by taking interim steps such as developing a common standard that applies to digital services, like the European Union's privacy directive or the streamlined sales tax system in the United States for interstate e-commerce transactions. Clearer links could be drawn between digital economy efforts and longstanding ASEAN priorities in areas such as trade facilitation. The ASEAN E-commerce Consultative Committee offers a forum to pursue this. ASEAN is currently developing a digital data governance framework for consideration by member states.

APEC has made more rapid progress than ASEAN in developing specific, in-depth guidelines, principles and capacity-building programs to facilitate the adoption of digital economy principles—namely, in key areas such as data privacy, cybersecurity, electronic trade, digital infrastructure and micro, small and medium-sized enterprise development. ASEAN could learn from this experience in developing a common, unified approach to issues like data privacy.

Conclusion

The digital economy is widely seen as presenting significant opportunities to propel future growth in Southeast Asia. The region already has rapidly rising internet usage, although business, and indeed government, use of digital technology remains below its potential.

A concerted effort by the region's governments, both individually and collectively, to strengthen the foundations of the digital economy could address five key areas: connectivity, digital payments, digital skills, logistics, and crosscutting digital policies and regulations. Some regulatory gaps need to be filled (such as on consumer protection and data privacy) and some regulations could be adjusted to more effectively achieve policy goals (such as on cross-border data localisation). In some areas, governments should step back and allow the private sector to innovate and invest in digitisation. The development and implementation of national and regional digital economy plans could be improved by shifting from high-level planning to strengthened implementation and coordination across governments, by fostering greater private-sector participation in planning, implementation and monitoring of plans, and pursuing concrete initiatives to address policy and regulatory blockages. Beyond setting the overall policy and regulatory framework for the digital economy, governments have a direct role to play, including through supporting digital entrepreneurship and other digital initiatives.

Governments, businesses and citizens alike are increasingly concerned about various risks associated with digitisation, some of which—like inadequate protection of personal data and cybersecurity threats—are directly linked to the technologies associated with the digital economy. Others relate to the new types of business models developing in the digital economy—for example, the challenges to the protection of consumer rights when buyers and sellers are physically separated and, increasingly, in different countries. Similarly, the slow pace of consumer adoption of digital payments is in part due to perceived risks and lack of trust in new payment systems. While thinking about potential responses to these challenges has begun, further analysis at the country level is required on these risks and the appropriate responses.

Other risks are longer term, with the nature of the risk and the appropriate responses less well defined. For example, automation is widely perceived as presenting risks to workers, although concrete evidence of this in Southeast Asia is limited. Further analysis is required to understand how skills demands and jobs change as the digital economy grows and what the implications are for national education systems, training and skills upgrading initiatives and national social protection schemes.[13] Growing concerns about the risks presented by using the internet to spread misinformation could lead to responses that restrict the medium's potential as a means of open exchange of ideas and information. The discussion on data flows and cybersecurity highlighted that heavy restrictions on the use of the internet—for example, through data localisation requirements—are not necessary to protect citizens' interests and would impair the growth of the digital economy.

Finally, digitisation offers various ways to boost inclusiveness. The rapidly decreasing cost of broadband (especially mobile broadband) is helping more people access information and connect to economic opportunities. For example, e-commerce platforms are bringing new entrepreneurs into international trade. At the same time, there are still significant disparities in the cost and quality of internet access—most visible between central and more remote regions of large, geographically dispersed countries like Indonesia, but also between urban and rural areas of countries like Thailand, Vietnam and Malaysia. Similarly, the wide discrepancies in quality and affordability of internet access between countries also needs to be addressed to boost the inclusiveness of the digital economy in the region. While the digital economy can help create new opportunities to overcome barriers in the offline economy, those who lack adequate connectivity or the skills to participate risk being left behind.

---

13   Another area for future analysis is the issue of digital economy taxation. Governments in Southeast Asia are becoming concerned that e-commerce could be eroding the tax base and creating disadvantages for locally based firms. As policy responses in the region are evolving, this chapter does not address this topic in detail.

Table 4.5 Policy priorities summary for developing Southeast Asian countries

	Cambodia, Lao PDR, Myanmar	Indonesia, Malaysia, Thailand, Vietnam, Philippines	Regional cooperation
Connectivity	Address barriers and strengthen enabling conditions for accelerated private investment in broadband	Allow greater competition along the broadband value chain	Cross-border connectivity including regulatory harmonisation
		Management of radio spectrum (frequencies for mobile communications)	
		Passive infrastructure sharing and rights-of-way	
Payments	Facilitate innovation in digital payments	Promote use (for example, payments for government services) and address regulatory gaps	Promote interoperability
Skills	Continue upgrading basic education, including a focus on building digital skills at the primary school level	Integrate digital skills development across the curriculum including technical as well as 'soft' skills. Implement approaches for lifelong learning through the education system	Enable greater regional mobility of skilled workers, including through mutual recognition of qualifications
	Targeted digital skills training, especially for small and medium-sized enterprises	Deepen industry–business collaboration to identify future skills needs and meet short-term gaps	
Logistics	Issue clear regulations for small-parcel trade	Risk-based approach to facilitating small-parcel trade	Harmonised regional de minimis thresholds and simplified procedures
	Address regulatory barriers to entry in logistics	Enable innovation in digitised logistics services	

	Cambodia, Lao PDR, Myanmar	Indonesia, Malaysia, Thailand, Vietnam, Philippines	Regional cooperation
Data policies	Ensure legal regime exists for data privacy and protection	Build regulatory capacity and raise consumer and business awareness	Pathway to regulatory coherence
	Caution on introducing data localisation	Roll back blanket data localisation policies and introduce data classification–based approaches	Open regional regime on data
Cybersecurity	Ensure laws cover cybercrime and build enforcement capacity	Boost public and private spending on cybersecurity and address skills gaps	Regional regulatory and enforcement collaboration, including overarching governance framework
Consumer protection	Establish legal regime for consumer protection	Strengthen regulatory capacity for consumer protection, awareness and outreach	Regional complaint and enforcement mechanisms
Supporting digital entrepreneurs	Provide targeted support for skills upgrading and technology adoption as overall digital foundations are strengthened	Ensure coordination of SME support programs while still focusing on structural reforms	Support internationalisation of SMEs through regional integration
Digital ID	Consolidate implementation of digital IDs	Digital ID as a basis for transactions	Regional compatibility of digital IDs
Plans and strategies	Develop actionable digital economy strategies with the participation of government and private-sector stakeholders	Identify concrete actions and institutional responsibilities to implement and monitor digital economy strategies or master plans	Regional vision for open, integrated digital economy

References

Ahsan, A., Mattoo, A., Gootiiz, B., Saez, J.S., Molineuvo, M. and Walkenhorst, P. 2015. *ASEAN services integration report: A joint report by the ASEAN Secretariat and the World Bank.* Working Paper No. 100637. Washington, DC: World Bank Group. Available from: documents.worldbank.org/curated/en/759841468178459585/ASEAN-services-integration-report-a-joint-report-by-the-ASEAN-Secretariat-and-the-World-Bank.

Akamai. 2017. *Akamai's [State of the Internet]: Q1 2017 report.* Vol. 10, no. 1. Cambridge, MA: Akamai.

AT Kearney. 2018. *Cybersecurity in ASEAN: An urgent call to action.* Singapore: Kearney Southeast Asia. Available from: www.kearney.com/web/southeast-asia/article?/a/cybersecurity-in-asean-an-urgent-call-to-action.

Bauer, M., Hosuk, L.-M., van der Marel, E. and Verschelde, B. 2014. *The costs of data localisation: Friendly fire on economic recovery.* ECIPE Occasional Paper No. 3/2014. Brussels: European Centre for International Political Economy. Available from: ecipe.org/wp-content/uploads/2014/12/OCC32014__1.pdf.

Beschorner, N., Bartley Johns, M., Guermazi, B., Treadwell, J.L., Prakosa, P.W.B., Abdul Karim, N.A.B., Van Tuijll, D.A., Bennis, L., Nicoli, M., Van Rees, J. and Girot, C.A.H.M. 2019. *The digital economy in Southeast Asia: Strengthening the foundations for future growth (English).* Working Paper No. 137143. Washington, DC: World Bank Group. Available from: documents.worldbank.org/curated/en/328941558708267736.

Demirguc-Kunt, A., Klapper, L., Singer, D., Ansar, S. and Hess, J.R. 2018. *The Global Findex Database 2017: Measuring financial inclusion and the fintech revolution (English).* Washington, DC: World Bank Group. Available from: documents.worldbank.org/curated/en/332881525873182837/The-Global-Findex-Database-2017-Measuring-Financial-Inclusion-and-the-Fintech-Revolution.

FTI Consulting. 2017. *Localization to Fragment Data Flows in Asia.* Washington, DC: FTI Consulting. Accessed from: www.fticonsulting-asia.com/~/media/Files/apac-files/insights/articles/localization-to-fragment-data-flows-asia.pdf [page discontinued].

Fujita, A. 2017. 'YouTube bets its future on Asia.' *CNBC,* 26 April. Available from: www.cnbc.com/2017/04/26/youtube-bets-its-future-on-asia.html.

Girot, C. (ed.). 2018. *Regulation of Cross-Border Transfers of Personal Data in Asia*. Singapore: Asian Business Law Institute. Available from: abli.asia/ PUBLICATIONS/Regulation_of_Cross-border_Transfers_of_Personal_Data _in_Asia.

Google, Temasek and Bain & Company. 2019. *e-Conomy SEA 2019*. Available from: www.blog.google/documents/47/SEA_Internet_Economy_Report_2019.pdf.

GSM Association (GSMA). 2019. *State of the Industry Report on Mobile Money 2018*. London: GSMA. Available from: www.gsma.com/mobilefordevelopment/ wp-content/uploads/2019/02/2018-State-of-the-Industry-Report-on-Mobile-Money.pdf.

Hogan Lovells. 2018. *Asia Pacific Data Protection and Cyber Security Guide 2018: Shifting landscapes across the Asia-Pacific region*. London: Hogan Lovells.

International Telecommunication Union (ITU). 2016. *Measuring the Information Society Report 2016*. Geneva: ITU. Available from: www.itu.int/en/ITU-D/ Statistics/Pages/publications/mis2016.aspx.

International Telecommunication Union (ITU). 2017. *Measuring the Information Society Report 2017. Volume 1*. Geneva: ITU. Available from: www.itu.int/en/ ITU-D/Statistics/Pages/publications/mis2017.aspx.

International Telecommunications Union (ITU). 2018. *Measuring the Information Society Report 2018. Volume 1*. Geneva: ITU. Available from: www.itu.int/en/ ITU-D/Statistics/Pages/publications/misr2018.aspx.

Kemp, S. 2017. *Digital in Southeast Asia in 2017*. Special Report. New York: We Are Social Inc. Available from: wearesocial.com/special-reports/digital-southeast-asia-2017.

Manyika, J. and Chui, M. 2015. 'By 2025, Internet of things applications could have US$11 trillion impact.' *Fortune*, 23 July. Available from: www.mckinsey. com/mgi/overview/in-the-news/by-2025-internet-of-things-applications-could-have-11-trillion-impact.

Manyika, J., Lund, S., Bughin, J., Woetzel, J., Stamenov, K. and Dhingra, D. 2016. *Digital globalization: The new era of global flows*. Report, 24 February. New York: McKinsey Global Institute. Available from: www.mckinsey.com/ business-functions/digital-mckinsey/our-insights/digital-globalization-the-new-era-of-global-flows.

Meltzer, J.P. and Lovelock, P. 2018. *Regulating for a digital economy: Understanding the importance of cross-border data flows in Asia*. Global Economy and Development Working Paper 113. Washington, DC: Brookings Institution. Available from: www.brookings.edu/wp-content/uploads/2018/03/digital-economy_meltzer_lovelock_web.pdf.

Organisation for Economic Co-operation and Development (OECD). 2014. *Recommendation of the Council on Digital Government Strategies*. Paris: OECD Publishing. Available from: www.oecd.org/gov/digital-government/Recommendation-digital-government-strategies.pdf.

Organisation for Economic Co-operation and Development (OECD). 2016. *New skills for the digital economy: Measuring the demand and supply of ICT skills at work*. Digital Economy Papers No. 258. Paris: OECD Publishing. doi.org/10.1787/5jlwnkm2fc9x-en.

Organisation for Economic Co-operation and Development (OECD). 2017. *OECD Southeast Asia Regional Forum: Opportunities and policy challenges of digitalisation in Southeast Asia, 24 August 2017, Anantara Siam Bangkok Hotel, Bangkok, Thailand*. Background Note. Paris: OECD. Available from: www.oecd.org/southeast-asia/events/regional-forum/Forum_Note_Digital_Transformation_STI.pdf.

Organisation for Economic Co-operation and Development (OECD) Secretariat. 2015. *New skills for the digital economy: Measuring the demand for ICT skills at work*. Paper, 8 July. Paris: Directorate for Science, Technology and Innovation Committee on Digital Economy Policy, OECD. Available from: one.oecd.org/document/DSTI/ICCP/IIS(2015)4/en/pdf.

Prologis. 2016. *Global E-Commerce Impact on Logistics Real Estate*. September. San Francisco: Prologis. Available from: www.prologis.com/about/logistics-industry-research/global-e-commerce-impact-logistics-real-estate.

Record, R.J.L., Larson, B.R., Teh Sharifuddin, S.B. and Chong, Y.K. 2018. *Malaysia's digital economy: A new driver of development (English)*. Working Paper No. 129777. Washington, DC: World Bank Group. Available from: documents.worldbank.org/curated/en/435571536244480293/Malaysias-Digital-Economy-A-New-Driver-of-Development.

Schwab, K. (ed.). 2016. *The Global Competitiveness Report 2015–2016: Insight report*. Geneva: World Economic Forum. Available from: www3.weforum.org/docs/gcr/2015-2016/Global_Competitiveness_Report_2015-2016.pdf.

TeleGeography. 2021. Website. Carlsbad, CA: PriMetrica, Inc. Available from: www2.telegeography.com.

United Nations Commission on International Trade Law (UNCITRAL). 1999. *Model Law on Electronic Commerce, with Guide to Enactment, 1996: With additional articles as adopted in 1998.* New York: United Nations.

United Nations Conference on Trade and Development (UNCTAD). n.d. 'Summary of adoption of e-commerce legislation worldwide.' *UNCTAD Global Cyberlaw Tracker.* Geneva: UNCTAD. Available from: unctad.org/en/Pages/ DTL/STI_and_ICTs/ICT4D-Legislation/eCom-Global-Legislation.aspx.

United Nations Educational, Scientific and Cultural Organization (UNESCO). 2018. *A global framework of reference on digital literacy skills for Indicator 4.4.2.* Information Paper No. 51, June. Montreal: UNESCO Institute for Statistics. Available from: uis.unesco.org/sites/default/files/documents/ip51-global-framework-reference-digital-literacy-skills-2018-en.pdf.

United Overseas Bank (UOB). 2017. *State of fintech in ASEAN.* FinTech White Paper R2a. Singapore: UOB. Available from: www.uobgroup.com/ techecosystem/pdf/UOB-State-of-FinTech-in-ASEAN.pdf.

Universal Postal Union (UPU). 2017. *Integrated Index for Postal Development (2IPD): 2016 results.* Bern: UPU. Available from: www.upu.int/en/Publications/2IPD/ Integrated-Index-for-Postal-Development-(2IPD)---2016-results.

We Are Social and Hootsuite. 2019. *Digital 2019.* Global Digital Report. New York: We Are Social Inc. Available from: wearesocial.com/global-digital-report-2019.

World Bank. 2016a. *Digital Adoption Index.* Washington, DC: World Bank Group. Available from: wbgfiles.worldbank.org/documents/dec/digital-adoption-index.html.

World Bank. 2016b. *World Development Report 2016: Digital dividends.* Washington, DC: World Bank Group. Available from: documents.worldbank.org/curated/ en/896971468194972881/pdf/102725-PUB-Replacement-PUBLIC.pdf.

World Bank. 2018a. *The Global Findex Database 2017.* Washington, DC: World Bank Group. Available from: globalfindex.worldbank.org.

World Bank. 2018b. *Logistics Performance Index (LPI) 2018.* Washington, DC: World Bank Group. Available from: lpi.worldbank.org/international/global.

World Bank. 2019. *World Bank East Asia and Pacific Economic Update, October 2019: Weathering growing risks (English).* Washington, DC: World Bank Group. Available from: documents.worldbank.org/curated/en/598201570731087175/ World-Bank-East-Asia-and-Pacific-Economic-Update-October-2019-Weathering-Growing-Risks.

World Bank. 2021a. *Identification for Development (ID4D)*. Washington, DC: World Bank Group. Available from: id4d.worldbank.org/.

World Bank. 2021b. *World Development Indicators*. DataBank. Washington, DC: World Bank Group. Available from: databank.worldbank.org/source/world-development-indicators.

World Economic Forum (WEF). 2017. *The Global Competitiveness Report 2016–17*. Geneva: WEF.

5

Connecting locals to locals: Market discovery through e-commerce

Voraprapa Nakavachara and Santitarn Sathirathai

Introduction

The digital economy, once a fringe market, has experienced remarkable growth globally. Technological advancements and the increasing ubiquity of affordable internet and internet-enabled devices have led to a spate of industries being disrupted and digitised. Though its introduction in Southeast Asia occurred far later than in the West, the digital economy throughout the region has seen a massive leap in growth. A report by Google and Temasek (2018) estimates that the internet economy within ASEAN+6 (defined as Indonesia, Malaysia, the Philippines, Singapore, Thailand and Vietnam) more than doubled, from US$32 billion in 2015 to US$72 billion in 2018. One of the digital economy's most successful constituents, accounting for roughly 31 per cent of ASEAN+6's digital economy in 2018, is e-commerce, which refers to the activity of transacting goods and services over the internet.

Despite the unprecedented proliferation of e-commerce, there has been little detailed academic research on it within the region. While there is some literature on e-commerce's effects on buyers, there has been little attention given to the sellers on these platforms in ASEAN. This chapter therefore aims to contribute to the literature by examining the e-commerce industry in Thailand through the perspective of its impact on online sellers. More specifically, the objective of the chapter is to assess the effects of e-commerce on the broader economy through changes in firm-level efficiency and market connectivity. In particular, we explore the impact of e-commerce adoption on the sellers' geographical reach, business revenue, profit growth and, ultimately, household income.

We chose to focus on Thailand for a number of reasons. First, Thailand has a burgeoning e-commerce industry that is rapidly growing. This is partly due to a large number of aspiring entrepreneurs and social sellers.[1] Second, Thailand has an ideal composition of traditional, brick-and-mortar small and medium-sized enterprises (SMEs) and 'pure' online sellers (defined as sellers with no offline stores). Third, the government is pushing for the development of the digital economy, especially for SMEs, under the 'Thailand 4.0' plan.

One problem that is common to much of the previous literature on e-commerce sellers is sourcing data. A combination of limited access to sellers and low response rates results in relatively small sample sizes. These sample sizes were often not large enough for researchers to extensively analyse and address their research questions. To overcome this problem, we have worked closely with Sea Group and its e-commerce platform, Shopee, to construct a dataset from a novel and large-scale survey of sellers on Shopee. The benefit of collaborating with Shopee is that not only is it one of the largest e-commerce platforms in Southeast Asia, but also it has one of the most diverse seller communities. Sellers on Shopee range from pure online microentrepreneurs to traditional SMEs and larger companies, and cover various product categories. With the help of the Shopee team, we were able to get close to 7,000 merchant responses—enough to construct a sizeable microdataset for in-depth and unique analyses. The richness of the data also allows for connectivity analysis using mapping visualisations as well as regression analyses on various subsamples.

---

1   Social sellers are online sellers who participate in social commerce. Social commerce can refer to transactions on social media platforms (for example, Facebook, Instagram), sellers promoting products and sales through social media but transacting on an e-commerce platform or using social networking services (for example, live chat, live stream) native to the e-commerce platform before completing the transaction on the said platform. For disambiguation, we will henceforth refer to the first case as social commerce and the latter two as socially enabled e-commerce.

Utilising the constructed dataset, this chapter finds that e-commerce adoption is associated with improvement in sellers' household incomes. The benefits come from two channels. First, e-commerce empowers existing SMEs by significantly boosting their revenue, efficiency and profit growth. The improvement in profitability goes beyond a one-off gain as moving online seems to also result in stronger profit growth rates. Second, our trade connectivity analysis illustrates how e-commerce allows merchants, especially those in poorer regions, to discover new market opportunities outside their own region.

Due to data limitations, we were only able to analyse the sellers who eventually engaged in e-commerce. We were not able to examine the traditional sellers that had not yet gone online and compare the results. We note this as a limitation of our current study and encourage future research to revisit this issue once the required data are available.

The chapter is structured as follows. Section two provides an overview of the e-commerce landscape within the region and in Thailand. Section three provides a brief literature review, while section four outlines the survey methodology and data. Section five begins the main empirical investigation and explores the economic impact of e-commerce using regression analysis, by looking at the impact on sellers' revenue, profit growth and efficiency (proxied by revenue per employment). Section six delves into the impact of e-commerce on seller connectivity, by way of market discovery, through the use of connectivity diagrams. Section seven discusses this chapter's overall findings and is followed by conclusions, policy implications and recommendations.

E-commerce landscape

E-commerce is defined as 'the activity of transacting goods and services over the internet'. The most common forms of e-commerce are business-to-consumer (B2C), consumer-to-consumer (C2C), consumer-to-business (C2B) and business-to-business (B2B) (UNESCAP and ADB 2018).

This chapter will focus on B2C and C2C due to data availability. B2C is where businesses sell to consumers and more naturally lends itself to electronic retailing (e-tailing) and marketplace e-commerce. On the other hand, C2C is where users (consumers) of an e-commerce platform can be the buyer, seller or both, and is most commonly done through marketplace e-commerce or social commerce.

E-commerce in Southeast Asia

E-commerce has seen unprecedented growth within the region, with total gross merchandise value (GMV) of B2C and C2C estimated to have more than doubled in a single year, from US$11 billion in 2017 to US$23 billion in 2018, and it is projected to grow to US$102 billion by 2025 (Google and Temasek 2018). However, despite its current scale, e-commerce in Southeast Asia still lags far behind more mature e-commerce markets. According to Sathirathai and Wan (2018), in 2017, e-commerce penetration within the region averaged approximately 2 per cent of the population, which is far below both China and the United States, at roughly 23 per cent and 8 per cent, respectively. In context, e-commerce penetration of 2 per cent would put ASEAN+6 where China was in 2010—roughly seven years behind. This number only serves to highlight the nascence of the industry and, despite an already impressive compound annual growth rate of 39 per cent from 2015 to 2018, the industry is expected to grow even further.

It is important to note, however, that ASEAN+6 has characteristics unique to the region that have led to the evolution of business models different from those in other regions. The recent development of low-cost entry-level smartphones has led to a population that accesses the internet with a mobile phone first and, in most cases, a mobile only. Data from Google's *Consumer Barometer* (Think with Google 2017) reveal that smartphone ownership is at 74 per cent in the region, while only 40 per cent of people use a computer. In addition, 63 per cent of respondents claim they access the internet more often via smartphone than via computer or tablet. This trend is also reflected in mobile e-commerce penetration, for which around 68 per cent of internet users in ASEAN+6 have made a purchase online via mobile in the past month, while China and the United States · have penetration rates of 74 per cent and 44 per cent, respectively (Kemp 2019b).

Lack of offline retail in ASEAN+6 and low urbanisation rates have supported the growth of C2C marketplaces. This form of e-commerce is made up almost entirely of independent sellers, the majority of which are SMEs. In Indonesia, McKinsey & Company (2018) estimates that, of the 4.5 million active sellers in 2017, 99 per cent were microenterprises. Furthermore, they estimate that 15 per cent of all sellers are selling their own products. The region is also highly social media–centric, resulting in the popularity of both social commerce and socially enabled e-commerce.

For example, McKinsey & Company (2018) estimates that more than 37 per cent of Indonesia's e-commerce value is generated through social commerce, with roughly one-third of all online shoppers being purely social commerce users.

E-commerce in Thailand

Thailand had an estimated e-commerce GMV of US$3 billion in 2018, which was roughly 13 per cent of the region's total. Many of the drivers of the prosperity of e-commerce in the region can be found in Thailand. On top of already favourable demographics, a report by Sea and the World Economic Forum (WEF) (2018) finds that Thailand has the greatest propensity for entrepreneurship within Southeast Asia, with 36 per cent of youths aspiring to be entrepreneurs in the future, compared with a regional average of 25 per cent. Additionally, Thailand boasts a social media–centric population that is largely mobile-first. It is estimated that approximately 51 per cent of consumers buy goods through social media and the value of social commerce is roughly half of the total e-commerce market.

In terms of connectivity drivers, Thailand completed its Village Broadband Internet Project (Net Pracharat) in 2017. The government installed and provided free broadband internet to 24,700 rural villages throughout the country. In 2018, Thailand's internet penetration rate was 82 per cent (Kemp 2019a), which grew significantly from 27 per cent in 2011 (Kemp 2011). The country's average fixed internet connection speed is 57.6 megabits per second (Mbps)—higher than the world average of 54.3 Mbps. Thailand's mobile broadband connectivity (broadband mobile connections per capita) is 133 per cent, which is higher than the global average of 74 per cent.

Thailand also has unique online consumer behaviour. Banking penetration is relatively high in Thailand at 81 per cent of the population aged above 15 years, compared with a regional average of 55 per cent (World Bank 2017). While bank transfers are the most popular form of online payment, constituting 28 per cent of all online payments, cash on delivery remains highly preferred, at 20 per cent (Worldpay 2018). A survey conducted by ecommerceIQ (2018) finds the top two things Thai online shoppers value most are cheap product prices and great product selection. This may reflect the fact that more than half of online shoppers are outside Bangkok and may be more sensitive to price and product diversity.

Despite its already impressive growth, the outlook for Thailand's e-commerce industry is still very positive. While Thailand's e-commerce market is estimated to account for less than 1 per cent of retail sales, it is expected to rise to 5 per cent over the next five years (Jones and Pimdee 2017). This is expected to be further supported by the government's recent launch of the Thailand 4.0 initiative, announced in October 2018 (Royal Thai Embassy n.d.). The third of the five agendas outlined in the announcement of the initiative focuses on incubating entrepreneurs and developing 'networks of innovation-driven enterprise'. One objective of the agenda is to increase the current contribution of SMEs from 37 per cent of total GDP to 50 per cent within 10 years through access to financing, skills development and supporting the enhancement of digital transformation. The government has also announced plans to develop 100 smart cities within two decades as part of another agenda within the Thailand 4.0 initiative, thus further connecting more individuals and creating a more supportive environment for digital ventures (Christopher 2018).

Literature review

The digital revolution has changed society in many ways. From a communication standpoint, online connectivity has led to the 'death of distance' in that the physical distance between people is becoming less relevant and no longer constrains our ability to communicate and interact with one another.

Focusing on international trade, the literature has documented that the value and amount of trade are inversely related to the distance between the locations of the parties involved in the trade transaction (Lendle et al. 2016). This is because the further the distance between the parties, the higher are the costs of communication and trade arrangements. With e-commerce taking off in the past decade, the costs of trade have dramatically reduced. In addition, e-commerce benefited the economy as a whole in terms of lowering trade barriers, increasing employment and enhancing economic development (McKinsey & Company 2018).

The literature also documents the benefits of e-commerce from both the sellers' and the buyers' perspectives. From the sellers' point of view, e-commerce eliminates the cost of setting up actual physical stores, provides alternative means of earning and makes it easier to become an entrepreneur (Fan et al. 2018; Dai and Zhang 2016). From the buyers' point of view, e-commerce reduces search costs, allows access to a broader variety of products and makes it easier to buy things from far away (Dolfen et al. 2019).

Most of the recent literature on e-commerce has focused on China, as the country's e-commerce sector recently experienced accelerated growth. Fan et al. (2018), using data from Alibaba Inc., document that e-commerce increases domestic trade within China. In addition, the adoption of e-commerce increases welfare from the sellers' perspective. Couture et al. (2018) evaluated the Chinese Government's nationwide e-commerce expansion program and conclude that it reduced logistical barriers and resulted in sizeable welfare gains. However, the young and the rich appeared to benefit more from the program than any other group of people. Dai and Zhang (2016), using firm registry data, show that e-commerce helps people with limited financial and social capital to become entrepreneurs. Huang et al. (2018) find that people residing in areas with higher levels of e-commerce adoption are more likely to be entrepreneurs.

Despite explosive growth in e-commerce in Southeast Asia in recent years, only a limited number of studies have investigated the impact of e-commerce in the region. Wong (2003) argues that Singapore's infrastructure and its people's readiness should allow the country to be a very fast adopter of e-commerce. Rowe et al. (2012) studied the factors driving e-commerce adoption in Vietnam and found that, among others, the knowledge and resources available to enterprises and the positive attitude of management towards technology were the most important factors. McKinsey & Company (2018) explore the Indonesian e-commerce market and conclude that e-commerce helps increase sales and employment. For Thailand, Cheewatrakoolpong and Mallikamas (2019) study factors determining whether e-commerce sellers would export their products. Among others, the factors determining whether they would export are the number of years in operation and the types of products they sell.

To the best of our knowledge, this chapter is the first to utilise a relatively large survey (close to 7,000 observations) of e-commerce sellers in Thailand to analyse the impact of e-commerce on sellers' household income, revenue, profitability, efficiency and connectivity. Many of the previous studies that tried to investigate impacts from the sellers' side were unable to collect a decent-sized survey due to low response rates. We overcome this problem by working closely with Sea Group and Shopee, its e-commerce platform, to launch and collect the survey data.

The survey and data

The data used in this chapter are from a survey we conducted with the assistance of Sea Group and its Shopee team. The survey was prepared and conducted during 2018–19. The questions were sent (via the Shopee platform) to Shopee sellers who sold a minimum number of items over a six-month period. The sellers were provided with small incentives to participate in the survey.[2]

We would like to point out that, although we were able to launch an extensive survey, we were not able to build an actual panel dataset. Since this was a voluntary survey, we needed to find a balance between the information we wanted to get and the information the respondents would be willing to comfortably provide. Therefore, there was a limitation on the data we could obtain. To measure the changes associated with engaging in e-commerce, we asked sellers about their current situation (now they were online) and their previous situation (when they were not online or when they were just starting out). This information would allow us to visualise the impact—although not as accurately as if we were able to construct a panel dataset. Also, respondents could find some questions, such as those relating to profit, sensitive. Therefore, instead of asking about actual profits, we asked how their profits had changed after they engaged in e-commerce.

Survey questions

The survey questionnaire included three sets of broad questions as follows (see Appendix 5.1 for the full questionnaire).

Questions on basic demographics

We asked sellers for their basic demographic information such as age, gender, education, employment status, whether they were a primary earner for their household, their province of residence, and so on.

---

2   Although we launched the survey in a systematic way, we were not able to control who decided to answer the survey. Therefore, we cannot claim that the results represent the population of Shopee sellers or all Thai SMEs. However, in the section titled 'Thailand's SMEs versus our data', we compare the basic statistics in our data with those for all Thai SMEs to illustrate how they fit.

Questions on economic impacts of e-commerce

To measure the economic impact of e-commerce, we have to segregate the sellers into two groups: existing SMEs and new entrepreneurs.

Existing SMEs are sellers with a prior offline business before going online. For these sellers, we asked questions about their prior offline business such as revenue, profit growth, the number of people employed including the owner, the location of the customers to whom they used to sell and so on. We asked when they started their online business. We then asked about their business since they moved online—information that included current revenue, profit growth, employment, the location of customers and so on. In addition, we asked them about the size of their online business relative to their entire business. In this chapter, we will call these questions 'Set A questions' and we will call these SMEs 'Group A sellers'.

New entrepreneurs are sellers with no prior offline business who are just starting their business purely online (a few may have subsequently set up an offline business). For these sellers, we asked questions about their current online business, including the year they started, current revenue, profit growth, employment, the location of their customers and so on. In this chapter, we will call these questions 'Set B questions' and these entrepreneurs 'Group B sellers'.

For both groups, we also asked whether entering into e-commerce (that is, selling online) had changed their household income. The response choices were: 'Decreased significantly', 'Decreased somewhat', 'Not much impact', 'Increased somewhat' and 'Increased significantly'.

Other miscellaneous questions

We are also interested in why the sellers decided to enter into e-commerce, so we asked them about the factors that motivated them to do so. Among the responses are 'External pressure (others are doing it)', 'Flexibility and better work–life balance' and 'Financial security'. We also asked questions about how they intended to spend the profits earned.

Thailand's SMEs versus our data

To discuss how our data fit with those for all of Thailand's SMEs, we first discuss the overall summary statistics of Thailand's SMEs as provided by the Office of Small and Medium Enterprise Promotion (OSMEP). The aggregate data for Thailand's small enterprises (SEs), medium enterprises and SMEs in 2018 are shown in Table 5.1 (left panel).[3] We separate the statistics for all enterprises and for enterprises in the wholesale and retail sector.[4] According to the enterprise promotion office, there are 3,077,822 SMEs in the Thai economy (1,279,557 of which are in the wholesale and retail sector). Only 23.03 per cent of the SMEs are registered as juristic entities. Thailand's SMEs accounted for THB7,013,971 in GDP and employed 13,950,241 people. The imputed average monthly sales are THB189,906 and the imputed average employment is 4.53 people.

Most of the SMEs (99.5 per cent) are actually small enterprises. Their imputed average monthly sales are THB136,302 and their imputed average employment is 4.14 people. Of the 3,063,651 small enterprises, 1,275,470 are in the wholesale and retail sector. Their imputed average monthly sales are THB122,749 and their imputed average employment is 3.33 people.

According to a ministerial regulation issued by Thailand's Ministry of Industry in 2002, SMEs in the retail sector are defined as enterprises with up to 30 employees or with assets (excluding land) of up to THB60 million. In our survey data, we have the information on employment but not on assets. Therefore, we applied this employment threshold to eliminate sellers who are not SMEs. We were able to gather 6,860 observations from the survey. Among them, 2,049 observations (29.9 per cent) belong to Group A and 4,811 observations (70.1 per cent) belong to Group B.[5]

---

3   Note that we were only able to gather the annual GDP and total employment. Therefore, we had to impute the estimated monthly sales (GDP/12/Number of enterprises) and the average employment (Total employment/Number of enterprises).

4   We were not able to segregate the retail sector from the wholesale sector.

5   We were able to collect the initial sample of 7,226 observations; however, we dropped those observations missing important information like gender and age. We also dropped observations that were extreme outliers (possibly due to input errors)—for example, negative age, negative revenue, negative employment and extremely high revenue growth (more than 10,000 per cent). Finally, we kept only the observations that were between the ages of 10 and 70. We also excluded observations that were not SMEs by definition. After the cleaning process, we had 6,860 observations.

Table 5.1 All Thai SMEs versus our sample

Variables	Unit	Thailand's Office of Small and Medium Enterprise Promotion data¹						Our data		
		Small enterprises (2018)		Medium enterprises (2018)		Small–medium enterprises (2018)				
		All	Wholesale & retail sector	All	Wholesale & retail sector	All	Wholesale & retail Sector	All	Group A	Group B
No. of enterprises		3,063,651	1,275,470	14,171	4,087	3,077,822	1,279,557	6,860	2,049	4,811
Registered as juristic entity	%	22.78	18.79	78.58	54.51	23.03	18.90	n.a.	n.a.	n.a.
Sole proprietor/others	%	74.51	81.01	21.42	45.49	74.27	80.90	n.a.	n.a.	n.a.
Community enterprises	%	2.72	0.20	0	0	2.70	0.20	n.a.	n.a.	n.a.
Total										
GDP	Million THB per year	5,010,991	1,878,750	2,002,980	324,118	7,013,971	2,202,900	n.a.	n.a.	n.a.
Employment	Persons	12,670,351	4,246,714	1,279,890	191,844	13,950,241	4,438,558	n.a.	n.a.	n.a.
Average										
Sales²	THB per month	136,302	122,749	11,778,632	6,608,719	189,906	143,468	58,073	123,147	30,298
Employment²	Persons	4.14	3.33	90.32	46.94	4.53	3.47	2.04	2.86	1.69

¹ All Thai SME statistics are from the Office of Small and Medium Enterprise Promotion (OSMEP) White Paper on SME 2019.

² Average monthly sales and average employment for all Thai SMEs are not provided in the OSMEP White Paper but are imputed by the authors.

n.a. = not available

The basic summary statistics of our data are shown in Table 5.1 (right panel). Overall, average monthly sales are THB58,073 and average employment is 2.04 people. These statistics are lower than those for the total of Thai SMEs. However, looking at Group A and Group B separately, we find that Group A's statistics are comparable with those of Thailand's small enterprises in the wholesale and retail sector. Group A's average sales are THB123,147 and average employment is 2.86 people, whereas imputed average sales of Thailand's small enterprises in the wholesale and retail sector are THB122,749 and imputed average employment is 3.33. On the other hand, Group B's average sales of THB30,298 and average employment of 1.69 are far below those of Thailand's total SMEs. They are also lower than the average of Thailand's small enterprises.

Summary statistics of the sellers

Table 5.2 provides the detailed summary statistics of the sellers in our data. For the overall sample, the average age is 32.46 years. About 27.9 per cent of the survey respondents are male and about 45.3 per cent are the primary earner for their household. The majority (68.3 per cent) have a bachelor's degree as their highest education level. Also, the majority (43.4 per cent) are employed by organisations.

Table 5.2 Summary statistics

Variables		All	Group A	Group B
No. of observations		6,860	2,049	4,811
Age	Average (years)	32.46	34.16	31.74
Male	(%)	27.9	35.7	24.5
Primary earner	(%)	45.3	52.0	42.5
Education	Below high school (%)	2.5	2.5	2.5
	High school (%)	7.0	6.0	7.5
	Vocational (%)	4.9	5.1	4.8
	Bachelor (%)	68.3	68.1	68.3
	Advanced degree (%)	17.3	18.3	16.8
Employment	Employed full-time (%)	41.6	25.1	48.7
	Employed part-time (%)	1.8	1.9	1.8
	Not employed: Homemaker (%)	7.0	4.3	8.2
	Not employed: Retired (%)	0.5	0.2	0.6
	Not employed: Student (%)	7.9	3.4	9.8
	Other (%)	3.9	3.8	3.9
	Self-employed (%)	31.7	58.5	20.2
	Unemployed (%)	5.7	2.8	6.9

As mentioned above, we segregated our respondents into existing SMEs (Group A) and new entrepreneurs (Group B); therefore, we also computed the summary statistics for each of the groups separately. The average age of Group A is 34.16 and the average age of Group B is 31.74 years; 35.7 per cent of Group A and 24.5 per cent of Group B are male. Approximately 52 per cent of Group A and 42.5 per cent of Group B are the primary earner in their household. We conducted T-tests (of the difference in means) and can conclude that Group A is older than Group B, Group A has more men than Group B and Group A has more primary earners than Group B.[6] The majority of both groups (68.1 per cent of Group A and 68.3 per cent of Group B) have a bachelor's degree as their highest level of education; Group A appears to be mostly self-employed (58.5 per cent) whereas Group B appears to be mostly employed by an organisation (50.5 per cent).

Economic impact analysis

In this section, we explore the potential economic impact of going online for individual sellers. We start by examining the impact on household income of e-commerce adoption. One of the survey questions we asked was how entering into e-commerce business (that is, starting to sell online) had changed each seller's household income; Table 5.3 summarises the responses.[7] Overall, entering into e-commerce appears to have had a positive impact on household income for most sellers—in particular, 72 per cent reported that their household income increased due to e-commerce, with 16.3 per cent of respondents reporting a 'significant' increase. Looking at Group A (existing SMEs) and Group B (new entrepreneurs) separately, the former saw a higher proportion of households reporting income gains due to e-commerce. Among Group A, 82.4 per cent of households indicated income gains, with 22.8 per cent seeing a significant increase, while for Group B the numbers were 67.5 per cent and 13.5 per cent, respectively.

---

6   Specifically, the T-statistics are 11.906, 9.107 and 7.244 for the difference in the means of age, male (dummy) and primary earner (dummy), respectively.
7   See Appendix 5.1, Question 18 (for Set A) and Question 16 (for Set B).

Table 5.3 Change in household income after entering e-commerce

Answer	All		Group A		Group B	
	Freq.	%	Freq.	%	Freq.	%
Decreased significantly	18	0.3	18	0.9	0	0.0
Decreased somewhat	137	2.0	33	1.6	104	2.2
Not much impact	1,755	25.8	308	15.1	1,447	30.3
Increased somewhat	3,793	55.7	1,212	59.6	2,581	54.0
Increased significantly	1,110	16.3	464	22.8	646	13.5
Total	6,813	100.1	2,035	100.0	4,778	100.0

Next, we explore the mechanisms through which e-commerce adoption could contribute to higher household income for merchants. For existing SMEs, the key mechanism is likely to be improvement in profitability coming from rising sales and higher efficiency—that is, generating more revenue without ballooning costs. For new entrepreneurs, online channels may help provide additional income. We employ different empirical investigation methods to examine each group below.

Economic analysis for existing SMEs (Group A)

Recalling that Group A sellers had an offline business before moving online, we were able to collect data related to their business performance before and after they went online. The dependent variable of interest for Group A sellers is the change in their performance measures. Specifically, we will first explore the economic impact on sellers via increased revenue and profit growth. Then we explore how entering into e-commerce helped improve their business efficiency (as proxied by revenue per employment).

The empirical model used for the analysis is Equation 5.1.

Equation 5.1

$$\Delta y_i = \alpha + \beta \cdot x_i + \theta_p + \gamma_c + \varepsilon_i$$

In Equation 5.1, Δy_i represents changes in the dependent variables of seller I, which are: 1) percentage change in revenue before versus after the seller went online, 2) change in profit growth before versus after the seller went online and 3) change in efficiency (change in revenue per employee before versus after the seller went online). Note that, for profits, we can only compare change in the *growth rates*—that is, acceleration—and not the level of profit due to the nature of the survey questions. This means the measure will not capture any potential level shift in profits after merchants go online.

In Equation 5.1, x_i is a vector of observable characteristics of seller i. The key variable of interest is the *degree of digital integration* measured by the size of the online business relative to the entire business (constructed as group dummies with the base group being the sellers who have at most 20 per cent of their business online; other groups are 20–40 per cent, 40–60 per cent, 60–80 per cent and 80–100 per cent).[8] We anticipate that the higher the degree of digital integration, the higher will be the positive impact of e-commerce on the SME in terms of revenue, profit and efficiency.

The other variables (which are the components of the vector x_i) include the number of people employed (including the seller) prior to going online and years in operation of the business. The first variable is a control for the size of the business prior to going online. The second variable is a control for how long the SME has been in operation. It is possible that older SMEs are more likely to be traditional and may not be able to adjust quickly to e-commerce. We also include the information on the age and gender of the seller, their highest education level (constructed as group dummies with the base group being sellers with lower than high school education; other groups are high school, vocational, bachelor and an advanced degree) and a dummy indicating whether they entered e-commerce because of external pressure. In Equation 5.1, θ_p is the province dummy; γ_c is the main product category dummy; and ε_i is the error term. We use the robust standard errors clustered by province. For each of the dependent variables, we run three regressions; the first regression (the base analysis) has neither the province nor the product category dummies, the second regression has the province dummies but no product category dummies and the last regression has both the province dummies and the product category dummies.

The results are shown in Table 5.4. Columns (1) to (3) display the results for the percentage increase in revenue. The SMEs with a moderate to high online presence (40 per cent or higher) are more likely to experience

---

8   Specifically, the base group are sellers with at most 20 per cent of their business online. The subsequent groups are sellers with more than 20 per cent but not more than 40 per cent online, sellers with more than 40 per cent but not more than 60 per cent online, sellers with more than 60 per cent but not more than 80 per cent online and sellers with more than 80 per cent up to 100 per cent online.

a higher revenue increase after going online. Specifically, the SMEs that have 40–60 per cent of their business online experienced a 42.2 to 45.3 percentage point higher change in revenue compared with the base group (sellers with at most 20 per cent of their business online). SMEs that have 60–80 per cent of their business online and those with 80–100 per cent experienced a 99.72 to 103.5 percentage point and 280 to 284.6 percentage point higher percentage change, respectively, in revenue compared with the base group. This confirms our hypothesis that the higher the degree of digital integration, the higher is the positive impact of e-commerce on the SMEs in terms of revenue increase.

Table 5.4 Impact on sellers (Group A)

Variable	(1) Percent_Inc_ Rev	(2) Percent_Inc_ Rev	(3) Percent_Inc_ Rev
PercentOnline_A_20_40	5.635	4.665	9.980
	(33.10)	(35.96)	(35.59)
PercentOnline_A_40_60	42.18*	38.82	45.32**
	(22.78)	(25.29)	(22.71)
PercentOnline_A_60_80	99.72***	103.5***	100.9***
	(20.88)	(22.09)	(22.10)
PercentOnline_A_80_100	280.0***	281.5***	284.6***
	(68.62)	(71.59)	(70.53)
PriorEmp_A	−2.209	−2.360	−2.574
	(1.719)	(1.866)	(1.922)
YearsInOperation_A	−0.684	−0.840	−0.976
	(0.874)	(0.962)	(1.273)
Age	−2.350	−2.431	−2.325
	(1.751)	(1.829)	(1.914)
Male	−14.26	−21.68	−27.89
	(13.84)	(15.43)	(17.78)
RC_Education = 2, High School	−10.46	4.888	12.84
	(27.99)	(31.71)	(32.99)
RC_Education = 3, Vocational	4.575	16.05	27.27
	(39.07)	(41.11)	(43.60)
RC_Education = 4, Bachelor	18.70	32.84	32.74
	(27.87)	(26.99)	(30.37)

Variable	(1) Percent_Inc_ Rev	(2) Percent_Inc_ Rev	(3) Percent_Inc_ Rev
RC_Education = 5, Advanced degree	13.91	24.64	23.83
	(28.59)	(27.05)	(28.60)
ExtPressure_W	−0.322	1.470	4.021
	(17.23)	(18.47)	(19.89)
Constant	171.8***	470.8***	689.9***
	(56.61)	(65.25)	(86.51)
Observations	1,964	1,964	1,919
R-squared	0.030	0.048	0.057
Province dummies	No	Yes	Yes
Product dummies	No	No	Yes
Sample	Group A	Group A	Group A

Variables	(4) Inc_ ProfitGrowth	(5) Inc_ ProfitGrowth	(6) Inc_ ProfitGrowth
PercentOnline_A_20_40	2.613***	2.688***	2.650***
	(0.475)	(0.473)	(0.457)
PercentOnline_A_40_60	3.705***	3.760***	3.779***
	(0.346)	(0.346)	(0.371)
PercentOnline_A_60_80	6.662***	6.692***	6.695***
	(0.524)	(0.526)	(0.526)
PercentOnline_A_80_100	4.574***	4.652***	4.558***
	(0.763)	(0.789)	(0.801)
PriorEmp_A	−0.0938**	−0.0916*	−0.0878*
	(0.0463)	(0.0463)	(0.0495)
YearsInOperation_A	−0.0281*	−0.0315*	−0.0331
	(0.0167)	(0.0175)	(0.0271)
Age	−0.0318**	−0.0339***	−0.0294**
	(0.0128)	(0.0123)	(0.0129)
Male	0.514	0.667	0.688
	(0.566)	(0.561)	(0.490)
RC_Education = 2, High school	1.409	1.622	1.390
	(1.413)	(1.520)	(1.554)

Variables	(4) Inc_ProfitGrowth	(5) Inc_ProfitGrowth	(6) Inc_ProfitGrowth
RC_Education = 3, Vocational	1.370	1.754	1.770
	(1.434)	(1.494)	(1.606)
RC_Education = 4, Bachelor	0.875	0.976	0.827
	(1.257)	(1.380)	(1.457)
RC_Education = 5, Advanced degree	0.783	0.948	0.826
	(1.212)	(1.335)	(1.409)
ExtPressure_W	0.694	0.812*	0.914*
	(0.470)	(0.477)	(0.461)
Constant	1.106	−0.401	0.759
	(1.402)	(1.737)	(2.950)
Observations	2,047	2,047	1,996
R-squared	0.107	0.134	0.147
Province dummies	No	Yes	Yes
Product dummies	No	No	Yes
Sample	Group A	Group A	Group A

Variables	(7) Inc_RevPerEmp	(8) Inc_RevPerEmp	(9) Inc_RevPerEmp
PercentOnline_A_20_40	6,329*	6,007	6,545*
	(3,217)	(3,634)	(3,748)
PercentOnline_A_40_60	7,966	9,038	9,375
	(5,310)	(5,887)	(6,065)
PercentOnline_A_60_80	10,169**	10,541**	9,180**
	(4,054)	(4,122)	(3,905)
PercentOnline_A_80_100	20,295***	20,836***	21,309***
	(3,249)	(3,473)	(3,745)
PriorEmp_A	143.9	119.9	97.08
	(241.2)	(232.4)	(271.5)
YearsInOperation_A	55.86	17.35	194.2
	(154.6)	(171.0)	(234.8)
Age	68.36	35.70	−5.682
	(209.7)	(206.6)	(221.7)

Variables	(7) Inc_ RevPerEmp	(8) Inc_ RevPerEmp	(9) Inc_ RevPerEmp
Male	1,218	901.3	1,684
	(2,523)	(2,767)	(2,893)
RC_Education = 2, High school	2,988	7,432	10,498
	(6,483)	(6,888)	(6,600)
RC_Education = 3, Vocational	3,290	3,263	5,822
	(4,078)	(5,307)	(6,100)
RC_Education = 4, Bachelor	5,310	9,169	10,761
	(5,943)	(6,722)	(6,461)
RC_Education = 5, Advanced degree	1,778	4,972	4,719
	(4,234)	(4,847)	(4,500)
ExtPressure_W	−1,545	−1,198	610.5
	(1,999)	(2,065)	(2,169)
Constant	−4,664	3,701	14,090**
	(4,260)	(6,153)	(6,177)
Observations	2,043	2,043	1,992
R-squared	0.010	0.048	0.068
Province dummies	No	Yes	Yes
Product dummies	No	No	Yes
Sample	Group A	Group A	Group A

*** $p < 0.01$

** $p < 0.05$

* $p < 0.1$

Notes: PercentOnline_A_20_40 is a binary variable that takes the value of 1 for Group A sellers who generate 20–40 per cent of total sales from online channels; YearsInOperation_A represents the age of the firm in years; ExtPressure_W is a binary variable that takes the value of 1 if the seller cited external pressure as a motivation to join e-commerce and 0 otherwise. Robust standard errors are in parentheses.

Columns (4) to (6) display the results for change in profit growth. The results reveal that SMEs with more than 20 per cent of their business online experienced a larger increase in profit growth. Specifically, the SMEs that had 20–40 per cent of their business online experienced a 2.6–2.7 percentage point higher increase in profit growth compared with the base group (sellers with at most 20 per cent of their business online). SMEs with 40–60 per cent online, 60–80 per cent online and 80–100 per cent online experienced a 3.7–3.8, 6.7–6.9 and 4.6–4.7

percentage point higher increase in profit growth, respectively, than the base group. Interestingly, for most groups, the higher the degree of digital integration, the higher was the increase in profit growth, except for the last group (80–100 per cent online), in which the increased profit growth became slightly lower. The longer the SMEs have been in operation, the lower is the increase in profit growth. Specifically, an additional year of operation is associated with a 0.03 percentage point lower increase in profit growth. Older sellers appeared to be doing worse than their younger peers (about 0.03 to 0.04 percentage points lower for an additional year of age). For some specifications, those who went online due to external pressure appeared to have a higher increase in profit growth (about 0.8 to 0.9 percentage point higher), but the results are only slightly significant.

Columns (7) to (9) display the results for increased efficiency (change in revenue per employment before versus after the seller went online). For all specifications, the SMEs with a high online presence (60 per cent or higher) are associated with a larger increase in efficiency. Specifically, SMEs with 60–80 per cent and 80–100 per cent of their business online experienced a THB9,180–10,541 and THB20,295–21,309 per person higher value in terms of increased efficiency, respectively, compared with the base group. (Note that for the 20–40 per cent group, the significance is only minor and not robust across all specifications.)

In terms of increased efficiency, one may be concerned that efficiency comes at the cost of a reduction in employment. Table 5.5 addressed this concern, revealing changes in employment of Group A sellers after they went online. Only 8.8 per cent reported a decrease in employment. The majority (72.3 per cent) did not have any change in employment, whereas 18.9 per cent reported an increase in employment.

Table 5.5 Change in employment after adopting e-commerce (Group A)

Change in employment	Group A	
	Freq.	%
Decrease in employment	180	8.8
No change	1,482	72.3
Increase in employment	387	18.9
Total	**2,049**	**100.0**

Recall from our discussion regarding Table 5.1 that Group A sellers' characteristics are similar to those of Thailand's small enterprises operating in the wholesale and retail sector as a whole. Although we cannot claim that our data sample represents the population of Thai SMEs, we may consider the results as what could have happened to the small enterprises operating in the wholesale and retail sector. However, as already mentioned, due to data limitations, we were not able to examine and compare the results for the traditional sellers who did not go online. We cannot exclude the possibility that the SMEs that went online are the more able ones and thus our results could be overestimated. We note this as a limitation of our study and encourage future research to revisit this issue once the required data are available.

Economic analysis for new entrepreneurs (Group B)

For Group B, the sellers started online and did not have an offline business,[9] therefore, we were only able to gather the data for their current business. For the empirical analysis, we are not able to compare their business before they went online with after they went online in the same way as we analysed Group A.

Recall from our discussion regarding Table 5.1 that Group B sellers are much smaller than the average for Thailand's SMEs. Our interest here is to examine whether these smaller or individual sellers in Group B have augmented their household income by selling online. For this group, we will use logistical regressions to assess whether certain attributes of their online business are associated with any increase in their household income.

The empirical model used for the analysis is Equation 5.2.

Equation 5.2

$$y_i = \alpha + \beta \cdot x_i + \theta_p + \gamma_c + \varepsilon_i$$

In Equation 5.2, y_i represents the dependent variable of seller i that takes the value of 1 if the seller reported an increase in household income and 0 otherwise; x_i is a vector of observable characteristics of seller i's business. The key variables of interest are current revenue, current employment, years online (in this case, the same as years in operation) and whether

---

9   Very few of them may have set up an offline business later on.

the seller is the primary earner in their household. In the equation, θ_p is the province dummy; γ_c is the main product category dummy; and ε_i is the error term. We use the robust standard errors clustered by province. We run three regressions—the first (the base analysis) has neither the province nor the product category dummies, the second has the province dummies but no product category dummies and the last has both the province dummies and the product category dummies.

The results are shown in Table 5.6. Columns (1) to (3) report the results of the base analysis and the augmented analyses, respectively. The results reveal that having high revenue and high employment (proxied for the size of the business) are associated with an increase in household income. The increase is also more likely if the sellers are the primary earners in their household.

Table 5.6 Impact on sellers (Group B)

Variables	(1) IncreaseHHInc	(2) IncreaseHHInc	(3) IncreaseHHInc
Ln_CurrentRev_B	0.391***	0.401***	0.395***
	(0.0197)	(0.0225)	(0.0208)
CurrentEmp	0.0992***	0.104***	0.114***
	(0.0268)	(0.0272)	(0.0268)
YearsOnline	–0.00404	–0.00853	–0.00919
	(0.0103)	(0.0105)	(0.0110)
PrimaryEarner	0.540***	0.558***	0.542***
	(0.0688)	(0.0646)	(0.0701)
Constant	–2.694***	–3.136***	–2.372**
	(0.115)	(0.181)	(0.966)
Observations	4,763	4,747	4,651
R-squared	0.133	0.148	0.149
Province dummies	No	Yes	Yes
Product dummies	No	No	Yes
Sample	Group B	Group B	Group B

*** $p < 0.01$

** $p < 0.05$

* $p < 0.1$

Note: Robust standard errors are in parentheses.

Connectivity analysis: E-commerce's role in increasing market discovery

In this section, we examine how e-commerce can help existing SMEs (Group A) discover new market opportunities through two main potential mechanisms:

- **Reducing geographical barriers:** Through e-commerce, buyers are able to discover new products from distant provinces and regions more easily, in part due to reduced search costs. Sellers are also able to find new markets that they could not access in the past—for instance, through lower marketing costs and greater economies of scale in logistics.

- **Reducing information asymmetry:** Services on e-commerce platforms such as functions for chatting, payments (for example, escrow) and data analytics can help reduce information asymmetry and improve trust among buyers and sellers, resulting in more efficient transactions.

Trade connections defined

As already mentioned, in our survey, we asked our Group A sellers about the location of the customers to whom they sell (prior to going online versus the current period). Specifically, we asked respondents to select the regions to which they sell products, with eight options representing the various regions in Thailand.[10] Due to the potential sensitivity of this question, we did not ask sellers about the value of sales to each region. As such, we only know whether the seller sells to a particular region or to their own province, but not the value of sales.

A 'trade connection' exists if the seller indicates they sell to a particular region in our survey. For instance, if a seller based in Bangkok selects the province of their residence, North Thailand and Northeast Thailand, we define this seller as having three trade connections.[11] We asked the sellers

---

10 These options are: 1) province of own residence, 2) Bangkok, 3) other provinces in north Thailand, 4) other provinces in northeast Thailand, 5) other provinces in east Thailand, 6) other provinces in south Thailand, 7) other provinces in west Thailand and 8) provinces in central Thailand.

11 For sellers from Bangkok who selected both 'Bangkok' and 'province of own residence', we kept just one option.

for data for two periods: before the seller went online and the current period. Changes in responses for these periods are used to determine the impact of e-commerce on trade connectivity.

The survey shows total trade connections increased materially after sellers adopted e-commerce. This increase was driven almost exclusively by trade outside the seller's region. The number of trade connections roughly doubled after sellers went online, rising from 4,400 to 8,600. In addition, the average number of trade connections per seller increased from 2.1 to 4.2—that is, entrepreneurs in Thailand sold to two more regions, on average, after utilising e-commerce. The maps in Figure 5.1 show how trade intensity has risen across Thailand, before and after going online, while Figure 5.2 shows how trade has changed before and after e-commerce separately for Thailand's regions. Figures 5.3 and 5.4 show how the increase in trade connections was driven by an increase in activity outside the seller's own region.

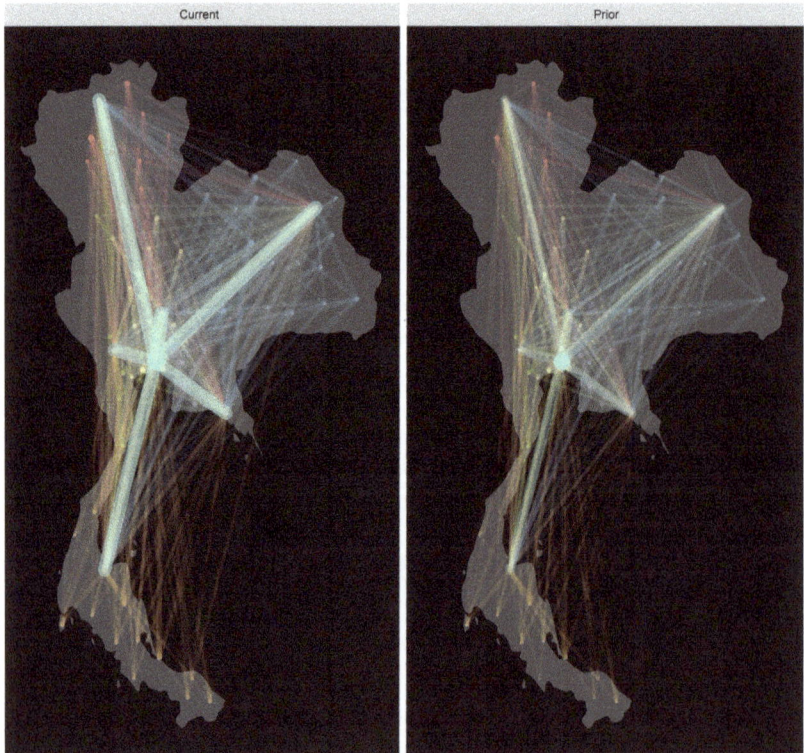

Figure 5.1 Increase in trade connections: Whole of Thailand
Source: Prepared by the authors based on the survey data.

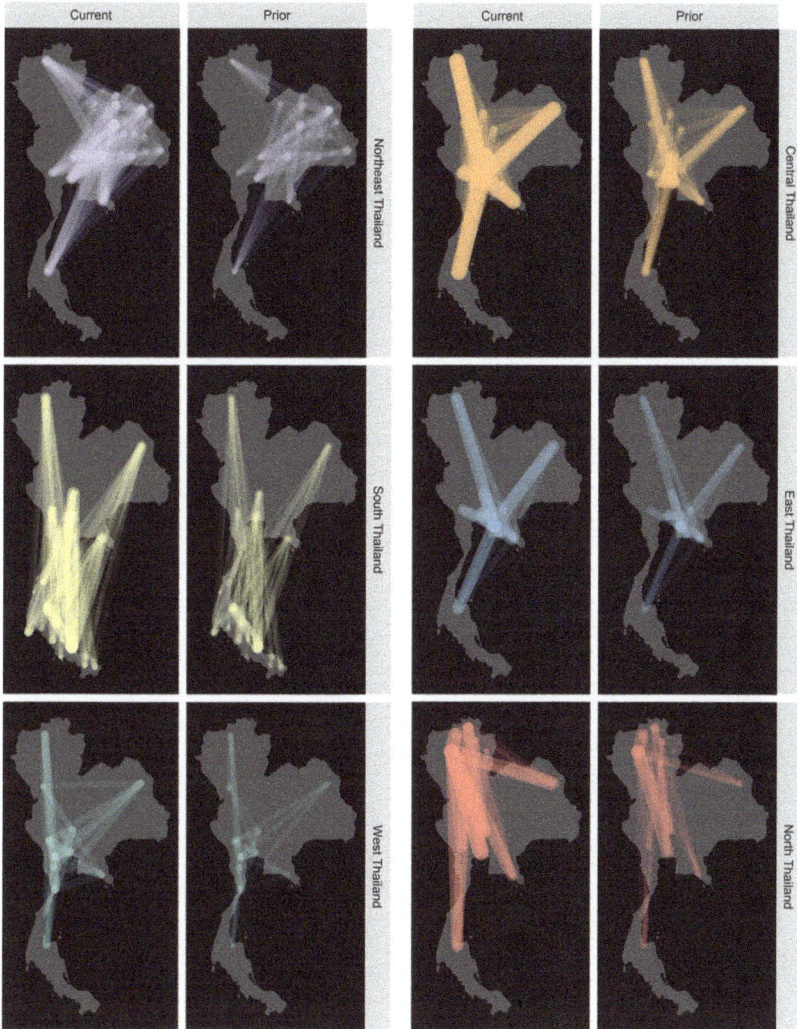

Figure 5.2 Increase in trade connections by region in Thailand
Source: Prepared by the authors based on the survey data.

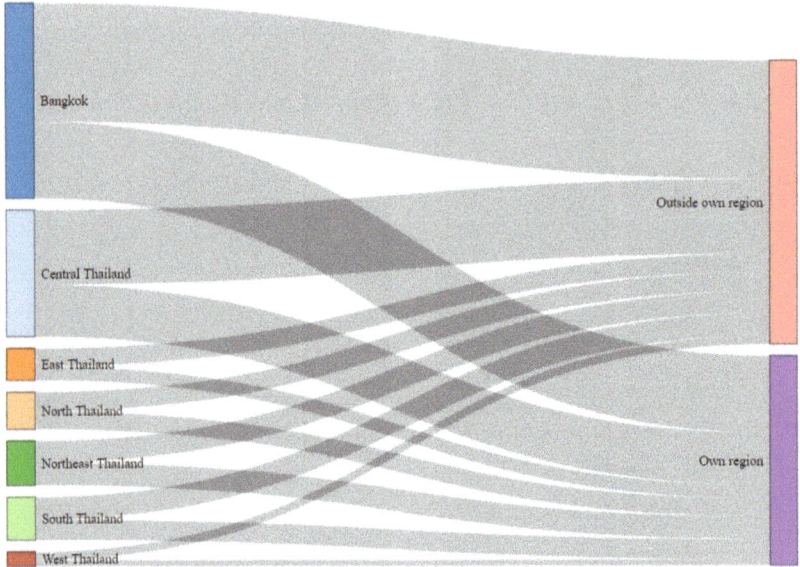

Figure 5.3 Sankey diagram: Own region versus outside own region—before e-commerce

Source: Prepared by the authors based on the survey data.

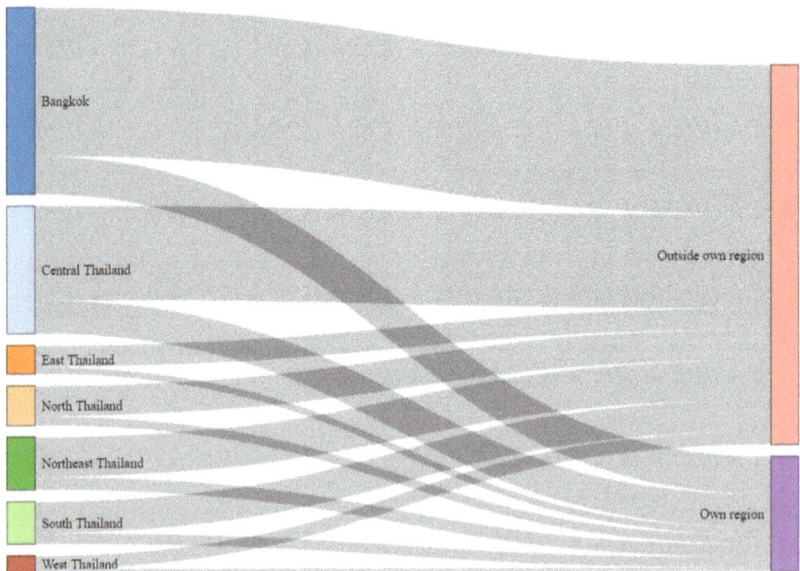

Figure 5.4 Sankey diagram: Own region versus outside own region—after e-commerce

Source: Prepared by the authors based on the survey data.

Extensive versus intensive margins

To examine the trade connections in detail, we first defined extraregional sellers (ERS) as sellers who sell goods outside their own geographic region. We then tried to capture the increased trade connections from two aspects:

1. **Extensive margin—the new ERS:** The extensive margin can be measured by the increase in trade connections by sellers who were not originally ERS and then became ERS after going online.

2. **Intensive margin—preexisting ERS:** The intensive margin can be measured by the increase in trade connections by sellers who were ERS and then sold to more regions after going online.

The increase in trade connections was driven much more by the 'new ERS' (extensive margin) than by the 'preexisting ERS' (intensive margin). The extensive margin accounted for around 76 per cent of the increase in trade connections for Thai sellers after moving online. The rest of the increase in trade connections was due to the intensive margin (24 per cent) (see Figure 5.5 for a waterfall chart decomposing the change in trade connections to the extensive and intensive margins). Figure 5.6 shows the share of trade connection increase based on extensive versus intensive margins.

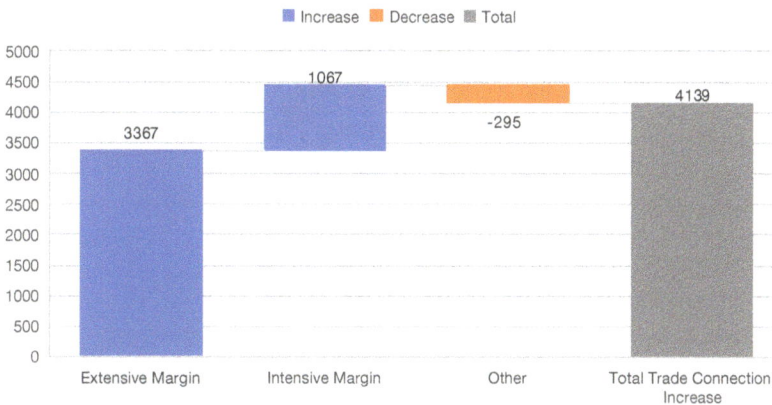

Figure 5.5 Waterfall chart: Decomposing into extensive versus intensive margins
Source: Prepared by the authors based on the survey data.

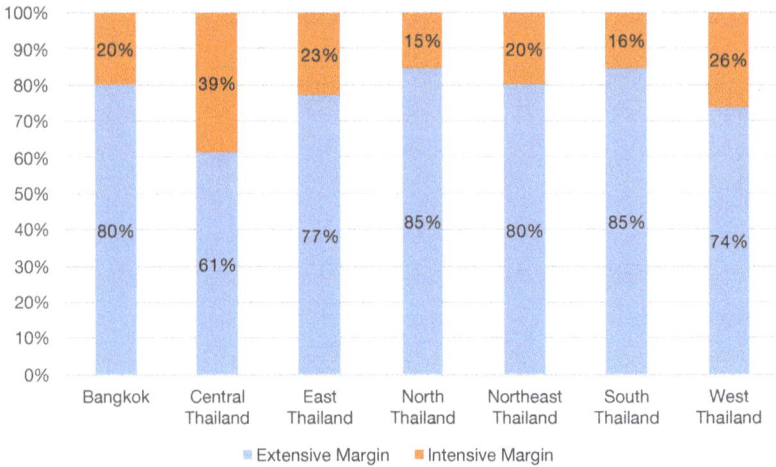

Figure 5.6 Share of trade connection increase based on extensive versus intensive margins

Source: Prepared by the authors based on the survey data.

Another way to look at the extensive margin is from the seller's perspective. Before moving online, around 44 per cent of sellers in Thailand sold outside their own region. After moving online, close to 81 per cent of sellers in Thailand are now selling outside their own region (see Table 5.7 for more details).

Table 5.7 Share of sellers selling outside own region (per cent)

Location of seller	Share of sellers selling outside own region		
	Before moving online	Current period	Change in share (pp)
Bangkok	37.92	71.86	33.94
Central Thailand	57.17	86.87	29.70
East Thailand	49.23	86.15	36.92
North Thailand	44.10	91.93	47.83
Northeast Thailand	41.18	85.78	44.61
South Thailand	38.41	84.76	46.34
West Thailand	47.76	86.57	38.81
Whole of Thailand	44.46	80.87	36.41

Market discovery

The largest increase in trade connectivity and market discovery after moving to e-commerce was for sellers in upcountry areas such as north and northeast Thailand, which are the two poorest regions.[12]

For instance, the shares of sellers in the north and northeast selling outside their own region increased by 48 percentage points and 45 percentage points, respectively—higher than the nationwide increase of 36 percentage points (see Table 5.7). Sellers in the north and northeast were also among the top three regions seeing the largest increase in average trade connections per seller, at 2.3 and 2.6, respectively (see Table 5.8). For the northern sellers, 85 per cent of the expansion in trade connections came from extensive margins (high counts of ERS) versus only 61 per cent for merchants in central Thailand.

Table 5.8 Average number of trade connections

Location of seller	Average number of trade connections		
	Before moving online	Current period	Increase
Bangkok	2.16	3.98	1.82
Central Thailand	2.21	4.47	2.26
East Thailand	2.12	3.78	1.66
North Thailand	1.98	4.28	2.30
Northeast Thailand	1.88	4.48	2.60
South Thailand	2.26	4.48	2.22
West Thailand	1.88	4.39	2.51
Whole of Thailand	2.12	4.21	2.09

This is important as it points to the possibility that e-commerce could help increase the reach of merchants who need the connections most—those from the more remote and poorer regions. While we cannot establish causality from our analyses, it is interesting to note that the north and northeast saw the largest proportions of sellers reporting an increase in household income after adopting e-commerce: 86.1 per cent of merchants in the north and 83.8 per cent in the northeast reported an increase in household income after going online, both of which are higher than the nationwide average of 82.4 per cent (see Figure 5.7 and Table 5.9 for the data by region).

---

12   Based on the latest GDP per capita data (2016).

■ Share of respondents saying they experienced household income increase

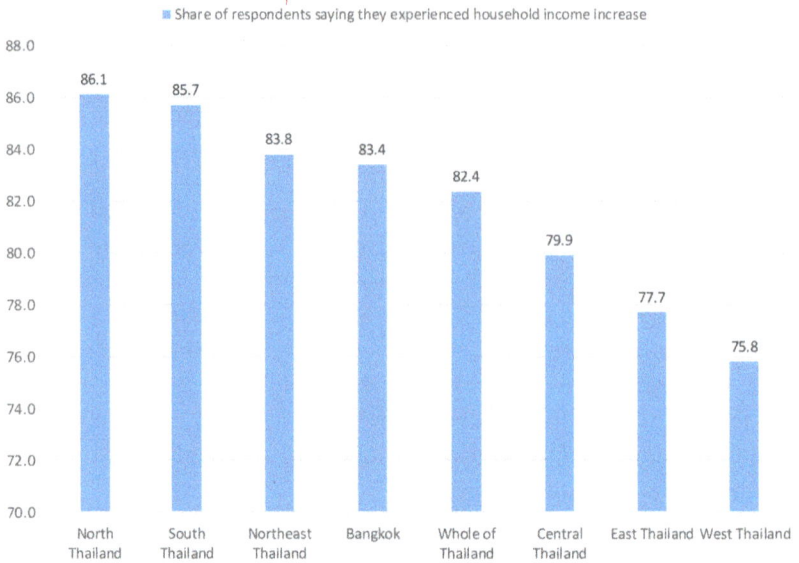

Figure 5.7 Impact on household income from e-commerce by region

Source: Prepared by the authors based on the survey data.

Table 5.9 Share of households reporting an increase in income, by region (per cent)

Location of seller	Percentage of households that report an increase in income		
	Group A	Group B	Whole sample
Bangkok	83.4	64.6	69.6
Central Thailand	79.9	69.8	72.8
East Thailand	77.7	67.6	70.5
North Thailand	86.1	72.0	76.6
Northeast Thailand	83.8	70.7	75.5
South Thailand	85.7	70.8	76.9
West Thailand	75.8	72.9	73.9
Whole of Thailand	82.4	67.5	72.0

Discussions

Our analyses show that e-commerce can help improve merchants' household income: 72 per cent of sellers reported an increase in income due to e-commerce, while 16.3 per cent reported significant improvement in household earnings. The improvement in income potentially works through different mechanisms for existing SMEs and new entrepreneurs.

Existing SMEs (Group A)

For existing SMEs, e-commerce empowers the business, raising profitability by lifting sales and improving efficiency. Generally, our models suggest the higher the degree of digital integration—measured by the share of e-commerce in the total business—the stronger are the benefits of e-commerce. Due to data limitations, we were unable to estimate the potential shift in the *level* of profits after merchants go online. But the significant jump in revenue and efficiency gains could indicate improvement in the level of profit. On average, merchants experienced a 163.4 per cent boost to revenue by going online, and could attain as much as a 284.6 per cent rise in sales if their degree of digital integration reached 80–100 per cent. The surge in revenue came with improvement in efficiency—here measured as revenue per employee. In addition, we showed that, for most sellers, such increased efficiency did not come at a cost of reduction in employment.

Moreover, our analyses point to the potential improvement in profitability that goes beyond a one-off level shift. We found that merchants experience acceleration in profit growth as the share of e-commerce in total sales rises, with the benefit peaking at 6.9 per cent when the ratio hits 60–80 per cent. This implies that digital integration may provide more than just a *static* boost to business performance, but also a more *dynamic* improvement. Perhaps the rise in the share of online sales indicates that firms are going through broader and/or deeper digital transformation (for example, digitisation of business processes) that brings about longer-lasting efficiency gains.

Our connectivity analysis provides important clues to why such a boost to revenue is possible. E-commerce helps reduce the 'distance' between sellers and buyers resulting in market discovery beyond their immediate location. On average, businesses saw their number of trade connections double after moving online. This is predominantly through extensive margins—the share of sellers who sell to customers outside their own region rose from 44 per cent to 81 per cent after going online. But those who were already selling outside their own region also expanded the number of destinations.

Interestingly, we found that the poorest regions in Thailand, the north and northeast, experienced the greatest increase in trade connections after sellers adopted e-commerce. Note that these two regions also contain among the highest shares of households reporting an improvement in income due to e-commerce. This points to the possibility that e-commerce can be utilised to develop more remote and lower-income regions, contributing to more inclusive economic growth.

The basic characteristics of Group A sellers resemble those of all Thailand's small enterprises operating in the wholesale and retail sector; however, we cannot claim they are truly representative of the population. Due to data limitations, we were not able to examine traditional sellers who had not moved online. We note this as a limitation of our study and would like to leave this for future research to explore once the necessary data are available.

New entrepreneurs (Group B)

For the new entrepreneurs, we found that e-commerce could provide a source of additional income. In addition, the larger the sales and the number of employees, the better was the probability that the sellers experienced higher household income. The evidence is strengthened in the case where the sellers are the primary earner in their household.

The basic characteristics of Group B sellers are not similar to the average characteristics of all Thailand's SMEs. In fact, Group B sellers are much smaller in terms of sales and number of employees. The authors conjecture that these sellers may be operating as sole proprietors or individuals trying to supplement their income by selling items online. Our empirical results revealed that the more they can sell online the better chance they have of increasing their household income.

E-commerce: Different strokes for different folks

There is also evidence suggesting that these new entrepreneurs (Group B sellers) are using e-commerce as a means of supplementing their income rather than it being the main business for the household.

According to our data, the majority of Group B sellers are people with other full-time responsibilities. The shares of people with full-time employment or who are homemakers in Group B are twice those in Group A. The share of students is three times higher in Group B than Group A. Second, these new entrepreneurs (Group B sellers) use profits from their business in a different way to those in the existing SMEs (Group A sellers) (see Table 5.10 for details). When asked what their profits are used for, 60.6 per cent of respondents from Group B indicated they were used for 'personal reasons', including saving, caring for family and education. Existing SMEs, on the other hand, have a higher tendency to use the profits for business purposes such as reinvestment and hiring staff. Third, the two groups have different motives for adopting e-commerce (see Table 5.11 for details). When asked about their motivations to participate in e-commerce, 59.9 per cent of respondents from Group B nominated 'personal reasons'—quality of life, convenience, flexibility and so on—while only 40.1 per cent mentioned business motivations including cutting costs or business expansion. For Group A, the numbers are 53.2 per cent for personal reasons and 46.8 per cent for business-related purposes. In addition, the majority of Group B sellers are people with other full-time jobs.

Table 5.10 Use of profits

	Personal reasons	Business reasons	Mixed reasons	Total responses
Group A	2,372	1,412	473	**4,357**
	(55.7%)	(33.2%)	(11.1%)	
Group B	5,295	2,700	741	**8,736**
	(60.6%)	(30.9%)	(8.5%)	

Notes: Personal uses of profits include saving, paying for education and helping care for family. Business uses include reinvestment in the business, hiring more employees and increasing employees' salaries. Mixed reasons refer to using profits to repay outstanding loans, where it is not possible to determine whether the loan is personal or business-related. Respondents to this question were allowed to select multiple answers, with no minimum or maximum limit to the number of choices selected. Therefore, the total responses could be larger or smaller than the total number of respondents.

Table 5.11 Motivation for entering into e-commerce

	Personal reasons	Business reasons	Total responses
Group A	4,334	3,812	**8,146**
	(53.2%)	(46.8%)	
Group B	9,711	6,491	**16,202**
	(59.9%)	(40.1%)	

Notes: Personal motivations include ease of online shop setup, flexibility of working hours, greater time for household work, shorter commute and better quality of life. Business motivations include the ability to expand the business, lowering business costs, external pressure (for example, other companies going online), financial security and to reduce business risk. Respondents to this question were allowed to select multiple answers, with no minimum or maximum limit to the number of choices selected. Therefore, the total responses could be larger or smaller than the total number of respondents.

Conclusions and policy implications

Using unique and large-scale survey data on merchants in Thailand, this chapter found that e-commerce adoption can result in improvement in household incomes for sellers. In particular, by reducing distance, time and cost constraints, e-commerce can result in two types of benefit. First, e-commerce empowers existing SMEs by significantly boosting their revenue, efficiency and profit growth. The improvement in profitability seems to go beyond a one-off gain as going online also results in stronger profit growth rates. Second, our trade connectivity analysis illustrates how e-commerce allows merchants, especially those in poorer regions, to discover new market opportunities outside their own region. In addition, e-commerce allows people of various employment status—including full-time employees, homemakers and students—to earn additional income, while maintaining other responsibilities.

While existing SMEs have a greater tendency to reinvest additional profits in their business, part-time entrepreneurs are more likely to use their extra earnings to care for family and pay for education. Our research also points to the possibility that e-commerce could help spread development to remote areas such as upcountry in the north and northeast of Thailand. Connectivity analyses showed that these two poorest regions saw the largest boost to trade connectivity and were among the top regions to report improvement in household income after e-commerce adoption.

Our study is, however, subject to certain limitations. Since our survey was voluntary, we need to find a balance between the information we would like to get and the information the respondents were willing to provide. First, we were not able to build a panel dataset. We were only able to ask the sellers about their current situation (now they were online) and their previous situation (when they were not online or when they were just starting off). This information allowed us to visualise the impact, although not as accurately as if we were able to construct a panel dataset. Second, sellers may consider some information sensitive, so we avoided asking about it; however, we tried to ask the 'second-best' questions. For example, we avoided asking sellers about actual profit and instead asked about profit growth. Third, we were only able to analyse the sellers who had engaged in e-commerce and not those who are yet to go online to compare the results. We note all these as limitations of our current work and encourage future research to revisit this issue once the appropriate data are available.

However, it is still undeniable that e-commerce can potentially serve as a tool to contribute to economic growth, by empowering SMEs, new entrepreneurs and those in more remote areas. This is particularly important for emerging markets such as ASEAN member states, where 99 per cent of enterprises are SMEs (Bain & Company 2018) and urbanisation is relatively low at only 51 per cent compared, for example, with 85 per cent in Latin America (UN 2019). E-commerce adoption by entrepreneurs is by no means automatic. To fully unlock the potential of e-commerce, governments and the private sector need to work together to address two types of constraints entrepreneurs face to selling online: those that prevent the adoption of e-commerce, such as limited internet access and lack of digital skills, and those that hold back the effectiveness of e-commerce, including underdeveloped logistics, payment systems and regulatory environments (World Bank 2019).

Promoting e-commerce adoption

We observed from our results that existing businesses gained by going online in terms of increases in revenue, profit growth and efficiency. In addition, individuals can also earn extra income by selling online that could increase their total household income. Therefore, promoting e-commerce adoption should be a key recommendation for policymakers. This can be achieved in two ways: increased digital access and increased digital literacy.

In terms of increasing digital access, the Thai Government implemented the Village Broadband Internet Project (Net Pracharat) in 2017, through which it provided free broadband internet to 24,700 rural villages throughout the country. In 2018, Thailand's internet penetration rate was 82 per cent (Kemp 2019a). In addition, Thailand's mobile broadband connectivity (mobile broadband connections per population) is 133 per cent, which is higher than the global average of 74 per cent.

Improving internet access through better digital infrastructure is essential but not sufficient. According to Bain & Company (2018), although 75 per cent of ASEAN SMEs see digital tools as an opportunity, only 16 per cent truly utilise them to their full potential. The same report found that 45 per cent of ASEAN SMEs lack an understanding of technology, while 40 per cent see a gap in digital skills (Bain & Company 2018). The authors see this lack of digital literacy as the last-mile barrier to e-commerce adoption. Improving digital skills is crucial to ensure that the rapid growth in the digital economy is inclusive, benefiting everyone and not just those with the knowhow to unlock its potential.

Governments and the private sector can collaborate to provide relevant training for would-be online entrepreneurs. For instance, policymakers can work with e-commerce platforms in the region to scale up offline training programs to teach SMEs how to sell online. Partnerships between academia and industry are also crucial. Given how rapidly skillsets change, higher education institutions should partner with private institutions to adjust their curriculums to ensure what is taught in the lecture theatre is relevant to industry.

Enhancing the effectiveness of e-commerce

Although the sellers in our sample who went online were able to discover new market opportunities, the benefits they could achieve are still limited by the effectiveness of e-commerce. Therefore, our policy recommendations would be to increase logistics efficiency, improve the regulatory environment and increase the adoption of digital payment systems.

The Thai Government has a crucial role to play in improving logistics infrastructure to reduce the costs of shipping items across the country. This goes beyond building hard infrastructure and includes improving the general regulatory environment for businesses such as by cutting red tape, streamlining approval processes and dismantling tariff and nontariff barriers. For example, Thailand's ongoing effort to use the Regulatory Guillotine and remove outdated laws is a step in the right direction.

Another key constraint on e-commerce growth is the lack of digital payment systems and a high reliance on cash on delivery in ASEAN countries. The good news is that governments across the region, including in Thailand, are already taking steps to improve the digital payments ecosystem through initiatives such as QR-code standardisation and enabling e-KYC (know-your-customer). The next steps for policymakers include promoting digital IDs and improving the interoperability of payment systems to promote efficiency.

References

Bain & Company. 2018. *Advancing towards ASEAN digital integration.* Report. Boston: Bain & Company.

Cheewatrakoolpong, K. and Mallikamas, S. 2019. บทบาทของ ต่อการค้าระหว่าง ประเทศ [*The Role of E-Commerce in International Trade*], [in Thai]. TRF Project. Bangkok: Thailand Research Fund.

Christopher, M. 2018. 'Thailand 4.0: The smart grid project.' *OpenGov Asia*, 20 July. Available from: www.opengovasia.com/thailand-4-0-the-smart-grid-project.

Couture, V., Faber, B., Gu, Y. and Liu, L. 2018. *E-commerce integration and economic development: Evidence from China.* NBER Working Paper No. w24384. Cambridge, MA: National Bureau of Economic Research.

Dai, R. and Zhang, X. 2016. E-commerce expands the bandwidth of entrepreneurship. Paper presented to American Economic Association Conference, San Francisco, CA, 3–5 January.

Dolfen, P., Einav, L., Klenow, P., Klopack, B., Levin, J., Levin, L. and Best, W. 2019. *Assessing the gains from e-commerce.* NBER Working Paper No. 25610. Cambridge, MA: National Bureau of Economic Research. doi.org/10.3386/w25610.

ecommerceIQ. 2018. *eIQ Consumer Pulse: Uncovering the value of Thailand's top online platforms.* Bangkok: ecommerceIQ.

Fan, J., Tang, L., Zhu, W. and Zou, B. 2018. 'The Alibaba effect: Spatial consumption inequality and the welfare gains from e-commerce.' *Journal of International Economics* 114: 203–20. doi.org/10.1016/j.jinteco.2018.07.002.

Google and Temasek 2018. *e-Conomy SEA 2018: Southeast Asia's internet economy hits an inflection point.* 3rd edn. Singapore: Google Asia-Pacific.

Huang, B., Shaban, M., Song, Q. and Wu, Y. 2018. *E-commerce development and entrepreneurship in the People's Republic of China.* ADBI Working Paper Series No. 827. Tokyo: Asian Development Bank Institute.

Jones, C. and Pimdee, P. 2017. 'Innovative ideas: Thailand 4.0 and the fourth industrial revolution.' *Asian International Journal of Social Science* 17(1): 4–35.

Kemp, S. 2011. *Digital 2011: Thailand.* 28 December. New York: We Are Social Inc. Available from: datareportal.com/reports/digital-2011-thailand.

Kemp, S. 2019a. *Digital 2019: Essential insights into how people around the world use the internet, mobile devices, social media, and e-commerce.* New York: We Are Social Inc.

Kemp, S. 2019b. *Digital 2019: Global internet use accelerates.* Blog, 30 January. New York: We Are Social Inc. Available from: wearesocial.com/blog/2019/01/digital-2019-global-internet-use-accelerates.

Lendle, A., Olarreaga, M., Schropp, S. and Vézina, P.L. 2016. 'There goes gravity: eBay and the death of distance.' *The Economic Journal* 126(591): 406–41. doi.org/10.1111/ecoj.12286.

McKinsey & Company. 2018. *The Digital Archipelago: How online commerce is driving Indonesia's economic development.* New York: McKinsey & Company.

Office of Small and Medium Enterprises Promotion (OSMEP). 2019. *White Paper on SME.* www.sme.go.th/upload/mod_download/download-20190919 092631.pdf.

Rowe, F., Truex, D. and Huynh, M.Q. 2012. 'An empirical study of determinants of e-commerce adoption in SMEs in Vietnam: An economy in transition.' *Journal of Global Information Management* 20(3): 23–54. doi.org/10.4018/jgim.2012070102.

Royal Thai Embassy. n.d. *Thailand 4.0: What is Thailand 4.0?* Washington, DC: Royal Thai Embassy. Available from: thaiembdc.org/thailand-4-0-2.

Sathirathai, S. and Wan, M. 2018. 'ASEAN e-commerce: Hidden tigers meet tech dragons.' *The Nation Thailand*, 5 February. Available from: www.nation thailand.com/business/30338037.

Sea and World Economic Forum (WEF). 2018. *ASEAN Youth and the Future of Work*. Singapore & Bern: Sea Limited & WEF.

Think with Google. 2017. *Consumer Barometer*. Mountainview, CA: Google. Available from: www.consumerbarometer.com/en/graph-builder/?question= N1&filter=country:vietnam,indonesia,philippines,taiwan,thailand,singapore ,malaysia.

United Nations (UN). 2019. *Population Dynamics: World population prospects 2019*. New York: Department of Economic and Social Affairs. Available from: population.un.org/wpp.

United Nations Economic and Social Commission for Asia and the Pacific (UNESCAP) and Asian Development Bank (ADB). 2018. *Embracing the E-Commerce Revolution in Asia and the Pacific*. Bangkok: UNESCAP.

Wong, P.K. 2003. 'Global and national factors affecting e-commerce diffusion in Singapore.' *The Information Society* 19(1): 19–32. doi.org/ 10.1080/01972240309471.

World Bank. 2017. *The Global Findex Database 2017*. Washington, DC: World Bank Group. Available from: globalfindex.worldbank.org/node.

World Bank. 2019. *The Digital Economy in Southeast Asia: Strengthening the foundations for future growth*. Washington, DC: World Bank Group.

Worldpay. 2018. *Global Payments Report*. Jacksonville, FL: Worldpay from FIS.

Appendices

Appendix 5.1 Survey questionnaire

Demographics		
Questions and options		**Type of variable**
1. What is your gender?	F/M	
2. When were you born?	DD/MM/YYYY	Date option in SurveyGizmo
3. What is the highest level of education you have attained?	No schooling/Elementary/Junior high/Senior high/ Vocational/Bachelor/Higher than Bachelor/Other	
4. Are you the primary income earner of your household?	Yes/No	

Demographics		
Questions and options		**Type of variable**
5. How many people are there in your household?	Fill in: _____ (number)	From 1 to maximum 20
6. What is your current employment status?	Employed full-time (35 hours/week or more)/Employed part-time (less than 35 hours/week)/Self-employed or Work for my own business/Unemployed—Looking for work/Not employed—Student/Not employed—Doing household work or taking care of dependents/Not employed—Retired/Other (please specify)	
7. Is e-commerce your primary source of income?	Yes/No	
8. What is your estimated monthly household income?	[See Appendix 5.2]	Dropdown option
9. In which province are you currently located?	[See Appendix 5.2]	Dropdown option
10. When did you start selling online?	DD/MM/YYYY	Date option in SurveyGizmo
11. Do you have an offline business?	Yes/No	
If you answered 'Yes' to Question 11, go to Question 12		
If you answered 'No' to Question 11, go to Question Group B		
12. Did you start selling offline before selling online?	Yes/No	
If you answered 'Yes' to Question 12, go to Question Group A		
If you answered 'No' to Question 12, go to Question Group B		

Economic and social impacts of e-commerce		
Question group A (Traditional business goes online)		
Questions and options		**Type of variable**
13. When did you start selling offline?	DD/MM/YYYY	Date option in SurveyGizmo
14. Question about monthly sales of your business (online + offline):		
Currently, your business has average sales per month of:	[Local currency] _____	Number
Just before your business went online, your business had average sales per month of:	[Local currency] _____	Number

Economic and social impacts of e-commerce	
Question group A (Traditional business goes online)	
Questions and options	**Type of variable**
15. Online sales as a percentage of total monthly sales of your business are currently:	
Percentage: _____ (0% to 100%)	Percentage: 0% to maximum 100%
16. Question about the number of employees of your business:	
Currently, the number of employees hired by your business is:	Number _____	No negative number
Just before your business went online, the number of employees hired by your business was:	Number _____	No negative number
17. Question about increasing profits of your business:	
Currently, average profit increases per year by:	No increase/Increase by 1–3%/ Increase by 4–6%/Increase by 7–9%/ Increase by 10–12%/Increase by 13–15%/Increase by 16–18%/Increase by 19–21%/Increase by 22–24%/ Increase by 25–27%/Increase by 28–30%/Increase by more than 30%	Dropdown option
Just before your business went online, average profits increased per year by:	No increase/Increase by 1–3%/ Increase by 4–6%/Increase by 7–9%/ Increase by 10–12%/Increase by 13–15%/Increase by 16–18%/Increase by 19–21%/Increase by 22–24%/ Increase by 25–27%/Increase by 28–30%/Increase by more than 30%	Dropdown option
18. How has selling online changed your household income?	
a) Increased significantly; b) Increased somewhat; c) Not much impact; d) Decreased somewhat; e) Decreased significantly	
19. From which regions do your customers come?	
Currently	[See Appendix 5.2]
Just before your business went online	[See Appendix 5.2]

Economic and social impacts of e-commerce	
Question group B (Businesses that launched online only)	
Questions and options	**Type of variable**
13. Question about monthly sales of your business:	
Currently, your business has sales revenue per month of:	[Local currency] _____	Number

197

Economic and social impacts of e-commerce		
Question group B (Businesses that launched online only)		
Questions and options		**Type of variable**
When you started your online business, your business had average sales per month of:	[Local currency] _____	Number
14. Question about the number of employees of your business:		
Currently, the number of employees hired by your business is:	Number _____	No negative number
When you started your online business, the number of employees hired by your business was:	Number _____	No negative number
15. Question about increasing profits of your business:		
Currently, average profit increases per year by:	No increase/Increase by 1–3%/Increase by 4–6%/Increase by 7–9%/Increase by 10–12%/Increase by 13–15%/Increase by 16–18%/Increase by 19–21%/Increase by 22–24%/Increase by 25–27%/Increase by 28–30%/Increase by more than 30%	Dropdown option
When you started your online business, average profits increased per year by:	No increase/Increase by 1–3%/Increase by 4–6%/Increase by 7–9%/Increase by 10–12%/Increase by 13–15%/Increase by 16–18%/Increase by 19–21%/Increase by 22–24%/Increase by 25–27%/Increase by 28–30%/Increase by more than 30%	Dropdown option
16. How has selling online changed your household income?		
a) Increased significantly; b) Increased somewhat; c) Not much impact; d) Decreased somewhat; e) Decreased significantly		
17. From which regions do your customers come?		
Currently	[See Appendix 5.4]	
When you started your online business	[See Appendix 5.4]	

Motivations for entering e-commerce and criteria for choosing e-commerce platform	
Continue from Question group A + B	
Questions and options	**Type of variable**
19. What are your main motivations for choosing to sell via e-commerce? (Click all that apply)	
a) Ease of setting up an online business	
b) Flexibility and better work–life balance	

Motivations for entering e-commerce and criteria for choosing e-commerce platform	
Continue from Question group A + B	
Questions and options	**Type of variable**
c) More time to handle household work and take care of children	
d) Opportunity to expand the business	
e) Lower cost of doing business	
f) External pressure (others are doing it)	
g) Shorter commute to work	
h) Quality of life	
i) Financial security	
j) Reduced risks	
20. How do you use profits gained through e-commerce? (Click all that apply)	
a) Reinvest into e-commerce business	
b) Hire more employees	
c) Increase employee salaries and/or benefits	
d) Save the additional profits	
e) Pay down loans (e.g., mortgage and car loans)	
f) Pay for education	
g) Care for family members (e.g., supporting dependants)	
h) Other, please specify _____	
21. How many platforms do you use to sell your goods? Include both e-commerce and social media platforms. (Fill in the blanks)	
No. of platforms: _____	No negative number
22. Please rank the top-three platforms in terms of how good you think they are (Rank 1 to 3, 1 being the best)	
___ Shopee ___ Lazada ___ JD Central ___ Instagram ___ Twitter ___ Facebook	Rank in SurveyGizmo
23. Please rank the five most important criteria when considering an e-commerce platform on which to sell. (Rank 1 to 5, 1 being the best)	

Motivations for entering e-commerce and criteria for choosing e-commerce platform	
Continue from Question group A + B	
Questions and options	Type of variable
___ Customer traffic ___ Ease of use ___ Used or recommended by peers ___ Logistics support ___ Free shipping ___ Workshops and training ___ Chat and related social functions ___ Ability to link with Instagram/Facebook ___ Support and promotion campaigns ___ Advertising services ___ Ease of payments ___ Financing and loan products	Rank in SurveyGizmo
24. Please rank the three most crucial aspects that require business support. (Rank 1 to 3, 1 being the best)	
___ Funding ___ Business knowledge ___ Operation management ___ Sales & marketing ___ Distribution channel ___ Logistics ___ Customer & business insights ___ Connection & business community	Rank in SurveyGizmo

Appendix 5.2 Household income brackets

Monthly household income (baht)	
Less than 2,500	70,001–90,000
2,500–5,000	90,001–110,000
5,001–7,500	110,001–130,000
7,501–10,000	130,001–150,000
10,001–30,000	More than 150,000
30,001–50,000	Prefer not to say
50,001–70,000	

Appendix 5.3 Thai provinces

Thai provinces		
Amnat Charoen	Nakhon Pathom	Rayong
Ang Thong	Nakhon Phanom	Roi Et

Thai provinces		
Bangkok	Nakhon Ratchasima	Sa Kaeo
Bueng Kan	Nakhon Sawan	Sakon Nakhon
Buri Ram	Nakhon Si Thammarat	Samut Prakan
Chachoengsao	Nan	Samut Sakhon
Chai Nat	Narathiwat	Samut Songkhram
Chaiyaphum	Nong Bua Lam Phu	Saraburi
Chanthaburi	Nong Khai	Satun
Chiang Mai	Nonthaburi	Si Sa Ket
Chiang Rai	Pathum Thani	Sing Buri
Chon Buri	Pattani	Songkhla
Chumphon	Phangnga	Sukhothai
Kalasin	Phatthalung	Suphan Buri
Kamphaeng Phet	Phayao	Surat Thani
Kanchanaburi	Phetchabun	Surin
Khon Kaen	Phetchaburi	Tak
Krabi	Phichit	Trang
Lampang	Phitsanulok	Trat
Lamphun	Phra Nakhon Si Ayutthaya	Ubon Ratchathani
Loei	Phrae	Udon Thani
Lop Buri	Phuket	Uthai Thani
Mae Hong Son	Prachin Buri	Uttaradit
Maha Sarakham	Prachuap Khiri Khan	Yala
Mukdahan	Ranong	Yasothon
Nakhon Nayok	Ratchaburi	

Appendix 5.4 Thai regions

Thai regions	
Province of residence	Other provinces in the eastern region
Bangkok	Other provinces in the western region
Other provinces in the north region	Other provinces in the central region
Other provinces in the northeast region	Other provinces in the southern region

Note: Regions are macroregions and include options for 'Province of residence' and 'Capital city'.

6

Digital connectivity in China and Asia: The case of mobile payments

Yiping Huang and Xun Wang

Introduction

China seems unlikely to develop a new payment system, especially given its state-owned bank–dominated financial system. Many individuals hold at least two bank accounts (with 5.46 cards per person in 2018), as different banks provide differentiated services with different fees. Additionally, Union Pay, a bank card–based network that connects the accounts of different banks in China, has been functioning since 2002.

While China has the largest card system in the world, with nearly 9 billion cards, according to the People's Bank of China (PBC 2020), 91 per cent of these are debit cards—indicating an underdeveloped social credit system. To access this card-based payment system, merchants are supposed to be equipped with card-reader terminals connected via the internet to communicate and pay the processing fee for each transaction. These are two main reasons many merchants show little interest in this payment system.

Most small businesses do not have access to the card-based payment system and cash remains a dominant medium of exchange. Cash has disadvantages, however, including losses due to theft and the fact it is cumbersome for merchants to handle large amounts. In these circumstances, an alternative payment system that lowers the processing cost and simplifies transactions might become more popular in China.

Smartphones and QR-codes are vital components in the revolution of mobile payment systems. Smartphones provide a network of communication thanks to the rapid development of the internet and QR-codes allow small businesses that are not connected to the internet to access the payment system. More importantly, the adoption of QR-codes significantly reduces the processing fees for merchants.

In this chapter, we introduce the innovation and development of China's mobile payment system, especially from the perspective of the development path of Alipay. We argue that the mobile payment system has complemented the traditional bank-based financial sector by improving individual and household risk-sharing and promoting entrepreneurship in China. We explore the prospects for cooperation in mobile payments between Asian and other emerging and developing economies and also analyse issues and challenges to be addressed to further digital connectivity in this region.

The rise of China's mobile payment system

Alipay and WeChat Pay are now the two dominant platforms for payments in the Chinese market. As shown in Figure 6.1, the number of active users of both platforms has grown substantially since 2013. After the advent of the payment code in 2017, the number of Alipay's active users experienced sharp growth, rising from 520 million to 900 million in 2018. And it has been estimated that WeChat Pay, as part of the largest social network platform, has about 1 billion regular active users.

Estimates suggest more than 90 per cent of residents in large cities in China use Alipay or WeChat Pay as their primary payment method, with cash second and debit/credit card third (Klein 2019). The transaction volume of mobile payments in China reached RMB277 trillion (more than US$41 trillion) in 2018 (Figure 6.2), 92.6 per cent of which were made via Alipay (53.8 per cent) and WeChat Pay (38.9 per cent).

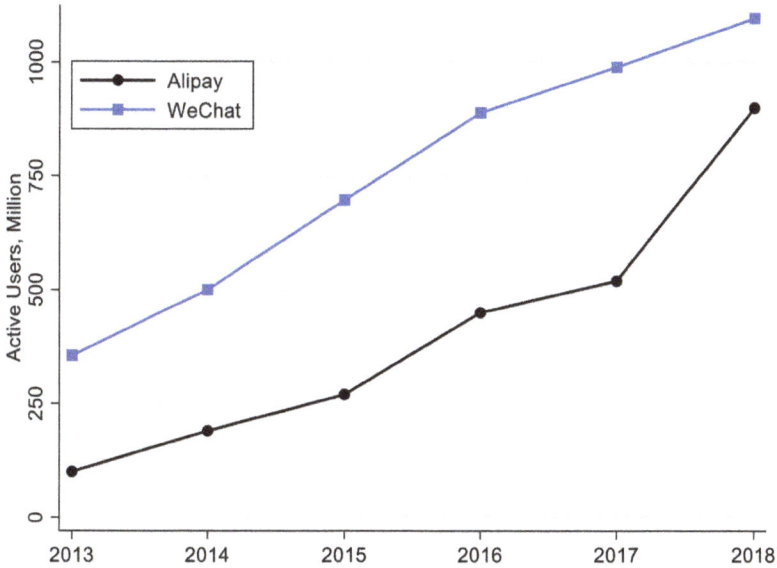

Figure 6.1 Active users of Alipay and WeChat, 2013–18 (million persons)

Sources: Statista (www.statista.com); China.org.cn; Xinhua News Agency (www.xinhuanet. com); Techinasia (www.techinasia.com).

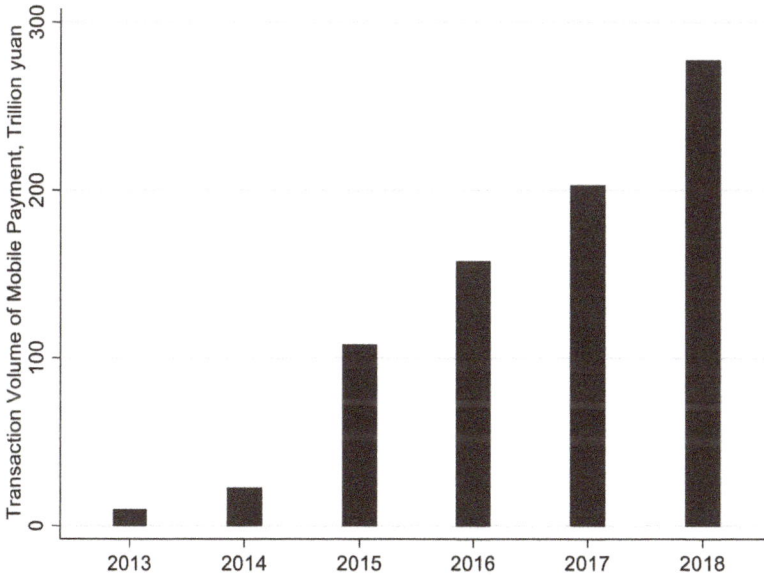

Figure 6.2 Transaction volume of mobile payments in China (RMB trillion)

Sources: CEIC; PBC (www.pbc.gov.cn/en/3688006/index.html).

Making a cross-country comparison, China has ranked number one in mobile payment markets (for transaction volume and penetration rate) in the world. The proportion of adults using mobile payments in China was as high as 76.9 per cent, and the proportion in rural areas was 66.51 per cent in 2017. The penetration rate of mobile payments in China was 77 per cent in 2016, while the rate was 48 per cent in the United States, 47 per cent in the United Kingdom, 48 per cent in Germany and 38 per cent in France. The penetration rate in Japan was only 27 per cent—far lower than in China.

Mobile payments in China have played an increasingly important role in the settlement system. According to a report on the overall operation of the payment system, the number of mobile payment transactions grew at an annual rate of 61 per cent, reaching 60.5 billion, in 2018. Mobile payment platforms have evolved into their own ecosystems, covering businesses such as financing, financial management, credit references and big data, which will continuously reshape China's financial structure.

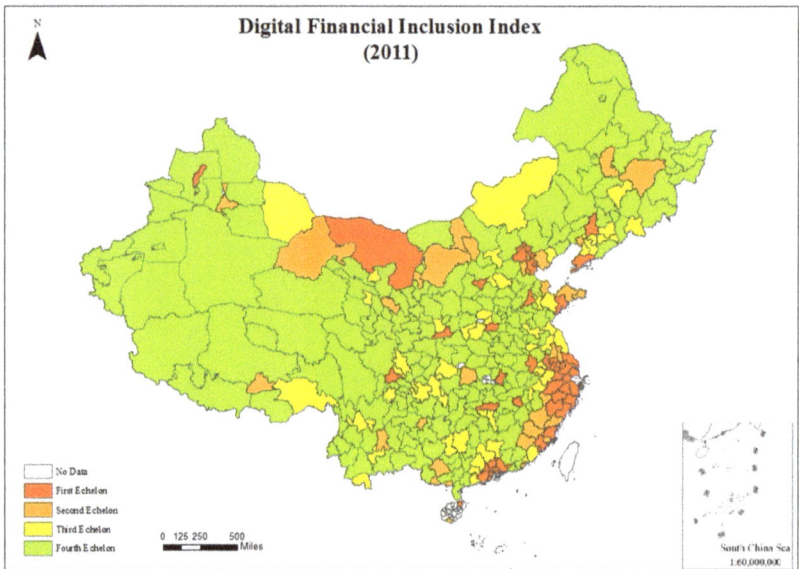

Figure 6.3 Rapid regional convergence of fintech development, 2011

Note: The echelon classification rule is as follows: taking the highest-level index of the year as the benchmark, cities with an index higher than 80 per cent of the benchmark index are classified as the first echelon; 70–80 per cent are the second echelon; 60–70 per cent are the third echelon; and less than 60 per cent are the fourth echelon.

Source: Institute of Digital Finance (2011–18).

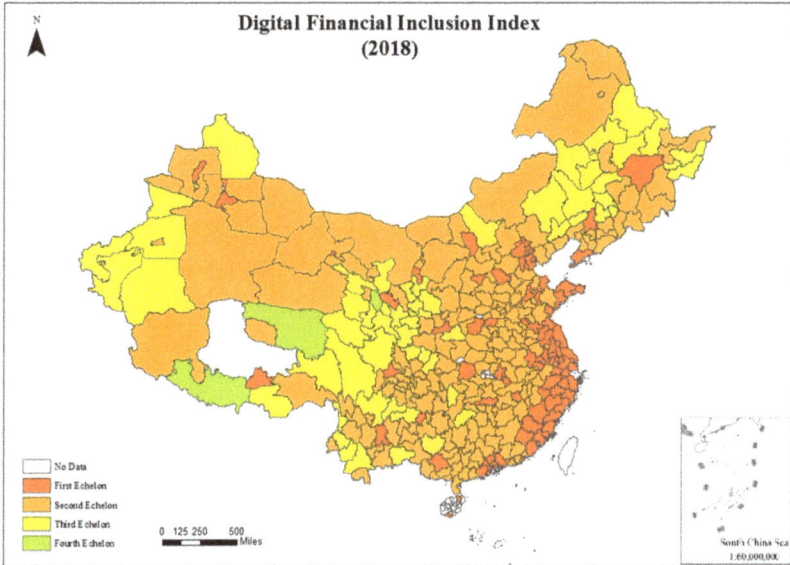

Figure 6.4 Rapid regional convergence of fintech development, 2018

Note: The echelon classification rule is as follows: taking the highest-level index of the year as the benchmark, cities with an index higher than 80 per cent of the benchmark index are classified as the first echelon; 70–80 per cent are the second echelon; 60–70 per cent are the third echelon; and less than 60 per cent are the fourth echelon.

Source: Institute of Digital Finance (2011–18).

The rapid development of digital finance in China is uneven. The growth in the eastern coastal region has been fastest, with central provinces coming in second and the western region third. It is worth noting that the central and western regions have narrowed the gap with the eastern region very significantly. The Peking University Digital Financial Inclusion Index shows rapid regional convergence of fintech development in China, as shown in Figures 6.3 and 6.4 (see more in Guo et al. 2019).

How China's mobile payment system has evolved: The case of Alipay

With the popularity of personal computers increasing after 2000, more and more individuals were able to use them to easily access the internet. Initially lacking a well-developed social credit system, e-commerce in China grew very slowly. The trade volume of online shopping website Taobao in 2003 was only RMB34 million. Users were concerned about the security of their money. So, the biggest problem with online transactions was the lack of trust due to information asymmetry between the buyer and the seller.

Alipay was initially developed to solve Taobao's trust issues by providing secure transactions. The secured transactions work like this: the buyer chooses goods on Taobao and pays via Alipay; Alipay informs the seller to deliver the goods and sends the payment to the seller after the buyer confirms receipt of the goods. During this process, Taobao serves as a trading intermediary that temporarily holds the money for the two parties.

With more and more goods supported by secured transactions, the volume of bank account transfers increased the pressure on banks, so that, for example, the West Lake Branch of the Industrial and Commercial Bank of China once even hoped to stop cooperation with Alipay. Meanwhile, Taobao was required to pay expensive transfer fees to the banks. How to reduce the transfer costs and the pressure on the banks? If every user in the Alipay ecosystem has a virtual account, into which the buyer can deposit their money, and the seller can receive the money automatically after a successful transaction, the efficiency of settlement would be significantly improved and the transfer cost tremendously reduced.

Driven by this innovative idea, Alipay was separated from Taobao in December 2004 and focused mainly on development of a payment system and the promotion of social trust. To promote users' confidence in Alipay, in February 2005, cofounder Jack Ma announced full compensation coverage for payments using the system. At that time, another problem about which users often complained was the success rate of payments, which ranged from a low of 40 per cent to a high of 66 per cent in 2010. That is, bad payment experiences were causing merchant on Taobao to lose roughly half of their customers.

Quick payment was the alternative solution, the basic logic of which was that Alipay would send the bank a deduction order on the user's account on behalf of the user. This was quite hard to arrange in 2010 as this logic contradicted banks' traditional risk management. Traditionally, by methods such as the U-Shield app, banks had to ensure a deduction order was issued by the user. While security was enhanced, the convenience of payment was greatly reduced. To complete a payment, it is necessary to insert a U-Shield and then jump to the payment page provided by the bank. For each additional operation, the probability of payment failure will increase.

Alipay finally persuaded banks by paying risk-loss margins and arranging deposits with the branches, which greatly helped Alipay expand the coverage of online payments. Compared with the one-step quick payment, under traditional online banking services, consumers needed to jump through seven webpages to complete a payment. More importantly, the success rate with quick payments reached 95 per cent, which is 30 percentage points higher than that with the business-to-consumer model of online banking. In this sense, quick payment enhanced the convenience of online payments in the era of the personal computer and also paved the way for mobile payments.

The advent of Apple signalled the coming era of smartphones and mobile internet—the uptake of which accelerated after 2010. One year after the introduction by Tencent of WeChat, which is now the most popular social media platform, mobile internet users exceeded desktop users for the first time, in 2012. In 2013, Alipay launched its 'All-In' strategy and shifted its business focus to the area of wireless networks.

Since restructuring in 2013, Alipay's wallet is no longer just a simple payment tool, but also has been positioned as a mobile life assistant and financial platform. Yu'e Bao, which functions as a money market fund in the new version of Alipay, rapidly occupied the dominant share of the mobile wealth management product market due to its double function of allowing deposits and paying interest. As shown in Figure 6.5, the interest rate paid on the balance in Yu'e Bao is, on average, 2 per cent higher than that of term deposits in a bank. Alipay is therefore known as the only wallet that makes money.

The ubiquity of Alipay's payment QR-code, which launched in 2017, enabled the expansion of mobile payment services to small businesses due to the ease of transaction and lower processing fees. Merchants are not required to be online or download the Alipay app. All they need are two numbers: one for the mobile phone and one for the bank card. Alipay can then help the merchants associate with the QR-code for payment. When the consumer scans the code for payment, the money is directly transferred to the merchant's bank account.

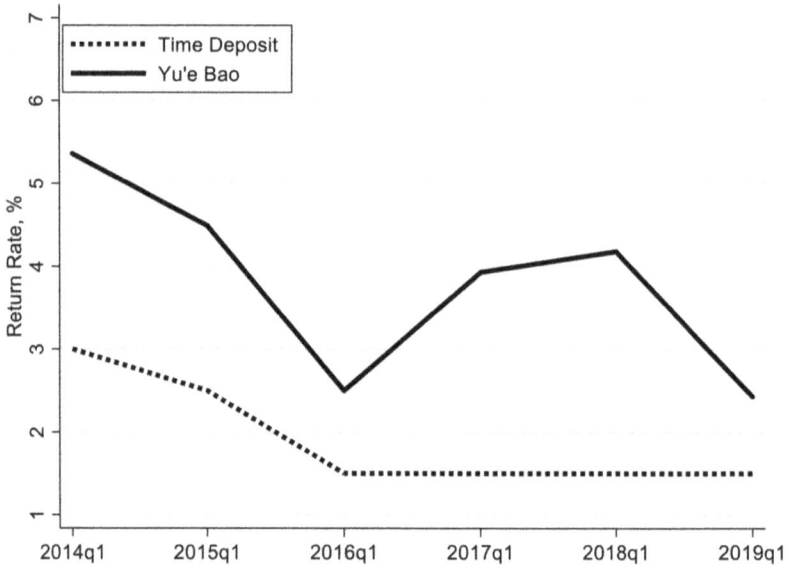

Figure 6.5 Return rates on term deposits and Yu'e Bao (per cent)
Source: Authors' calculations using data from CEIC.

Regulation of mobile payments in China

The relaxed regulations and legal guarantees provide an active institutional environment for China's mobile payment system. China enacted a law relating to electronic signatures in 2004, which established their legal validity for online contracts. Since 2005, the State Council has released a series of policy documents to accelerate e-commerce development. Alipay and WeChat Pay were launched accordingly without legal risks. The PBC did not begin to regulate and licence mobile payments until 2010.

The PBC released its 'Measure for the Administration of Payment Services for Nonfinancial Institutions' in June 2010, recognising the legal status of payment institutions. Since then, the central bank has issued nearly 270 third-party payment licences to Alipay and other payment companies and adopted prudential and inclusive regulations for this industry. These have allowed the rapid growth of mobile payments almost without compliance costs, entry barriers or regulatory constraints. With the rising risks in the peer-to-peer lending market, regulation of digital finance, including mobile payments, has been strengthened since 2015.

Table 6.1 Main policy documents on mobile payments in China

Year	Policy decision	Regulatory organisation
April 2009	Announcement on the registration of nonfinancial institutions engaged in payment and settlement services	PBC
June 2010	Administration of payment services for nonfinancial institutions	PBC
December 2010	Regulations on the administration of payment services for nonfinancial institutions	PBC
February 2011	Guidance on the supervision and management of payment services for nonfinancial institutions	PBC
May 2011	Notice on regulating management of commercial prepaid cards	State Council; PBC
March 2012	Management of anti–money-laundering and antiterrorism financing for payment agencies	PBC
July 2012	Notice on establishing a regulatory reporting system for payment agencies	PBC
September 2012	Management methods on prepaid card business for payment agencies	PBC
June 2013	Deposit methods for the customer provisions for payment agencies	PBC
July 2013	Administrative methods on bank card–acquiring business	PBC
December 2013	Notice on the pilot of foreign exchange payment services for cross-border e-commerce for third-party payment agencies	State Administration of Foreign Exchange
April 2014	Notice on strengthening the management of cooperative business between commercial banks and third-party payment agencies	China Banking Regulatory Commission; PBC
January 2015	Guidance for the pilot of cross-border foreign exchange payment services for payment agencies	State Administration of Foreign Exchange
July 2015	Guidance on promoting the healthy development of internet finance	PBC; Ministry of Finance; China Banking Regulatory Commission; China Security Regulatory Commission; China Insurance Regulatory Commission
December 2015	Management methods for internet payment services of nonbank payment agencies	PBC

Year	Policy decision	Regulatory organisation
April 2016	Implementation plan for special rectification of internet financial risks	State Council
April 2016	Implementation plan for special rectification on financial risks of nonbank payment agencies	PBC; Ministry of Finance; National Development and Reform Commission
August 2016	Specifications for barcode payment services	Payment Clearing Association

Source: PBC (www.pbc.gov.cn/).

Improving individual and household risk-sharing

Informal social networks in China provide an important means by which households and individuals share risk, while the insurance they provide is often incomplete. A number of reasons for this incompleteness have been proposed, including moral hazard and limited commitment, both of which result in positive correlations between consumption and realised income.

Transaction costs—the cost of transferring money or other forms of resources between individuals—are another source of the incompleteness. The rapid development and acceptance of mobile payments are a recent innovation in China, and have allowed individuals to transfer purchasing power within the ecosystems of Alipay or WeChat Pay, dramatically reducing the cost of sending money across large distances and between bank accounts.

Since China's accession to the World Trade Organization (WTO), families and social networks in China have been dispersed over large distances due to internal migration, mainly from the western provinces to the eastern coastal areas. This migration is largely motivated by employment and other opportunities. By the end of 2018, there were 288 million migrant workers in China, of whom more than 60 per cent were intercity migrants, leaving their home city for another to find work. Furthermore, more than 70 per cent of these workers did not bring their family members with them. In this context, lowering transaction costs could have significant impacts on the frequency and size of internal remittances, and hence the ability to smooth risk.

One predominant use of Alipay and WeChat Pay is for person-to-person remittances. Before mobile payment systems were available, most households delivered remittances through China Post or by bank transfer—a relatively costly and time-consuming process. Mobile payments require only several simple steps; not only are the actual costs of the transfers lower, but also the convenience and time saved mean substantial reductions in the total cost of sending and receiving money (see more detailed analysis in Wang et al. 2019).

Promoting entrepreneurship and innovation

Although most Chinese small and medium-sized enterprises (SMEs) are privately owned, they play an important role in supporting innovation, creating jobs and promoting local and national economic growth in China. SMEs are, however, suffering from significant credit constraints. In China's state-owned bank–based financial system, SMEs have to rely heavily on retained earnings to finance investments and operational costs.

Mobile payment systems in China not only facilitate payments and transfers, but also promote entrepreneurship and innovation. Lower-cost transfers and real-time payments motivate the setting up and operation of small business activities. Before mobile payments were available, it was inconvenient for vendors to break up and deposit large amounts of cash in their bank account.

With mobile payment systems, vendors need only post a QR-code on the door of, or somewhere conspicuous in, their premises. The adoption of QR-codes allows merchants who are not connected to the phone or internet to still access the payment system. It is easy for consumers to scan the QR-code and transfer money, with payments directly deposited into the vendors' bank accounts or digital wallets.

Apart from the convenience, the lower fees are a huge incentive for small businesses. A small business is generally charged more than 0.5 per cent of a payment in processing fees in the card-based system (0.5 per cent for debit cards and 0.6 per cent for credit cards). With mobile payments, processing fees vary from 0 per cent to 0.3 per cent. Some empirical studies have shown that the adoption of mobile payments significantly boosts the number of newly registered businesses (Huang et al. 2019).

More specifically, mobile payments promote agricultural households to start informal businesses and existing informal businesses to continue their operations or to transition to formal business (Wang 2019). The impact on entrepreneurial activities is associated with significant increases in income.

China's payment enterprises go global

Chinese payment technology has started to support mobile payment businesses in Asia, Europe and Africa. Unlike the approach to going global taken by the original equipment manufacturer trade and subsequent overseas mergers and acquisitions, Alipay's approach seems to be more popular. Its unique approach is characterised by 'local partnership plus knowhow output', which has greatly facilitated the outbound travel of Chinese tourists and, at the same time, helped to develop the local mobile payment system.

According to Ant Financial, Alipay has established cooperation with more than 250 financial institutions around the world. On the one hand, it provides offline payment services for overseas merchants and users; on the other, Alipay provides Chinese consumers with online payment services in 55 countries and regions around the world, covering catering, supermarkets, department stores, convenience stores, duty-free shops, theme parks, airports, and so on. Alipay offers real-time tax rebates at airports and urban areas in 35 countries and access to public transport systems in more than 20 countries.

Alipay has helped establish local versions in nine economies in Asia: Thailand (TrueMoney), the Philippines (GCash), Indonesia (DANA), India (Paytm), Malaysia (TnGD), Pakistan (easypaisa), Bangladesh (bKash), South Korea and Hong Kong (AlipayHK). In Thailand, TrueMoney's and Alipay's QR-codes are often posted together for Thai people and Chinese tourists, respectively. The number of Paytm users in India has increased from 25 million before 2015 to more than 250 million—making it the fourth-largest digital wallet in the world.

The existing international payment services are slow (with transactions often taking two to three days) and costly (with a processing fee of 7.3 per cent of the total sale, on average). In 2018, cross-border remittances based on blockchain technology became available between AlipayHK and

GCash, which achieved real-time transfers with relatively lower costs. Advanced technology supports this rapid development—for example, Alipay's recognition of risk control now occurs within 100 milliseconds and its asset loss rate is less than 0.5 millionth, which is far lower than the 0.2 per cent of other international third-party payment companies. Alipay and its local partners have now served more than one billion active users worldwide.

Comparative advantage of China's fintech companies

One striking achievement in recent years has been the leapfrogging development of Chinese fintech. According to a report by the Peterson Institute for International Economics, while the United States and other developed countries have advantages in most technological innovations, China has taken a leading position in mobile payments.

China's fintech development currently leads the world, whether in terms of technology or business models. From the perspective of technology, China's big data analysis technology is more advanced than that of other Southeast Asian economies. For example, Thailand's TrueMoney wants to introduce China's risk-assessment model, while China's Alibaba has begun to provide a cross-border payment system based on blockchain for Hong Kong and the Philippine markets.

In terms of their business models, China's fintech companies have expanded from payments to loans (microloans, Ant My Loan), insurance and financial management (Yu'e Bao). In contrast, the business model of Southeast Asia's payment providers is still at an elementary level, focused mainly on payments. Chinese fintech's business model also provides a reference for India and other Southeast Asian economies.

The popularity of smartphones and the internet has driven the transfer from online to mobile payments in China. When the volume of nonbank payments reached RMB9.2 trillion in 2013, Alipay surpassed PayPal to become the world's largest online payment platform. One year later, nonbank online payments grew by nearly 170 per cent and exceeded the payment volume of debit cards soon after.

How have mobile payments in China leapfrogged the card-based system? The simple answer is the low penetration rate of credit cards and the rapid growth of big tech companies, which stimulated the emergence and rapid development of the online payment system in China. After 2000, China's internet companies began to expand. Due to the backward payment infrastructure, low penetration rate of credit cards and low level of e-banking business, e-commerce companies in China were encouraged to develop new payment tools to expand their market. Therefore, internet companies, including Tencent and Alibaba, have successively established payment systems to solve specific problems.

Alipay, launched in 2004, was originally designed to address the issue of a lack of trust between e-commerce participants due to information asymmetry. However, early in the 1990s, credit cards were widely accepted and could be used to initiate a refund, which allowed holders to conveniently pay at home and abroad. In this context, US e-commerce companies such as eBay and Amazon did not need to establish new payment systems to solve the trust problem.

However, one thing that should be kept in mind is the leapfrogging development of mobile payments in China has not been accompanied by the establishment of a sound social credit system. Consequently, in the absence of effective financial supervision, regulatory arbitrage by internet platforms is likely to lead to rapid growth in payment and peer-to-peer markets, damage to the legitimate rights and interests of consumers and even financial risk contagion.

Insufficient supply of inclusive financial services in Asia

Generally, the financial systems in Southeast and South Asia are underdeveloped, except for Singapore's, and there is a severe shortage of formal financial services. In Southeast Asia, 60 per cent of people do not have a bank account. Credit card penetration rates in Indonesia, the Philippines, Vietnam and other countries are less than 2 per cent. In India, 60 per cent of business orders are paid in cash. Although there are 800 million bank accounts in India, only 250–300 million people use them, and the formal financial services in Bangladesh are even more backward. Meanwhile, these regions have large populations and a very young demographic structure (70 per cent of people in Southeast Asia are aged under 40 years), so they have a strong ability to accept new technologies. Therefore, the fintech markets in Southeast and South Asia boast very broad prospects. In fact, the development of fintech can to a large extent help relieve the problem of insufficient coverage of financial services and improve the welfare of local residents.

Compared with China, Southeast Asia's fintech is still in its initial stage and the accompanying infrastructure lags far behind. Therefore, the fintech business model in the region differs greatly from that in China and service provision is still at an elementary level, focusing mainly on payments. On the one hand, new regulatory licences must be acquired before businesses can provide high value-added services such as loans. On the other hand, Southeast Asia has not accumulated sufficient technology and data to expand other fintech services on a large scale. Of course, both ECP and TrueMoney, which promote e-commerce and e-wallets, respectively, have indicated they want to expand into the loans and insurance sectors. Indeed, Paytm has begun to provide financial services such as 'digital gold' for individuals and credit support for small businesses—on a small scale. In the future, Paytm hopes to provide credit assessment services for Indian residents who lack credit reporting services and increase their credit support on this basis. In Bangladesh, bKash has also expressed strong interest in Ant Financial's successful experience of using payment information to grant lines of credit.

Second, poor infrastructure and poor financial literacy in Southeast and South Asia also restrict the development of fintech. When ECP provided e-commerce services, many local banking systems failed to support online transfers and most local residents had poor basic financial knowledge, hindering the promotion of fintech products. In such circumstances, local fintech providers were required to develop new business models. The ability to 'top up' is very important for e-wallet users. In China, most users top up their balance or WeChat wallet via a bank transfer. However, due to the lack of banking services in Southeast Asia and other regions, e-wallets are mainly topped up offline at retail stores and other places, rather than via bank transfer. For instance, TrueMoney signed a partnership agreement with the largest local retail store, 7-Eleven, so that residents can deposit money into their wallets at its stores. TrueMoney also provided its own ATM to allow residents to top up their accounts. Bangladesh faces a similar situation. Due to insufficient coverage of bank outlets, it is difficult to convert money into digital currency. To solve this problem, bKash set up 187,000 agents nationwide. Customers can visit an agent to convert digital currency in the bKash system into cash.

In a word, the business models of fintech companies in Southeast and South Asia are still backward. Most focus on payments. Meanwhile, poor infrastructure restricts fintech's expansion. At present, fintech companies have begun to set out plans to provide more comprehensive services with higher value added and have innovated according to their respective environment, demonstrating great potential for development.

Local examples of payment enterprises in Asia

With the promotion of ECP, which is headquartered in Singapore but serves the whole of Southeast Asia, two major problems with e-commerce have been solved. The first is the high cash-on-delivery rate. In the past, this rate reached 99 per cent of e-commerce payments in the region, but the cost of cash payment is very high, so e-payments can reduce this cost. The second problem is the low success rate of online payments in Southeast Asian countries, which is caused by two main factors. First, due to poor infrastructure, users have to spend more time making online payments through banks, and the success rate is low. Of course, users can transfer money to a bank account offline and make a payment, but this is inconvenient. Second, e-wallets are not widely accepted by users. Many users do not keep money in their e-wallets, so if they need to buy goods, they have to visit a nearby outlet (such as a convenience store) to deposit money into their wallets within 24 hours of a purchase. As a result, the payment success rate is low. ECP enables users time to get accustomed to using an e-wallet, which significantly improves the success rate of payments and helps enterprises expand their business in a more convenient and quick manner.

TrueMoney in Thailand and Paytm in India are mainly designed to operate in a market that has insufficient formal financial services. Bank cards are not widely used in either country and many payments are still made in cash. Using TrueMoney or Paytm to make e-payments can reduce the high cost of using cash. In addition, young people who do not have a credit card cannot buy goods or play games online. TrueMoney can provide young people with these new services, while Paytm offers lower payment rates for businesses, as well as credit support for those small businesses that cannot get a bank loan.

In Bangladesh, bKash was also created against a background of inadequate formal financial services, including an underdeveloped system for online payments. Anyone wanting to buy a mobile phone or computer in Bangladesh must purchase it offline, which is very inconvenient. Second, there is a charge of $0.12 to open a bank account, which is a very high cost for many poor people. More importantly, banks do not provide free access to the internet. Young people from rural areas working in the cities are unable to remit their salaries back home. One of the more common practices is to ask a truck driver to deliver the money, but this practice is inefficient and very risky. To reduce the time and capital costs of transactions, the founder of bKash decided to create a new medium to solve these problems and provide low-cost services for the poor and small businesses.

AlipayHK launched its cross-border e-wallet remittance service based on block chain to solve the pain point of cross-border transfers, which have always been a cumbersome procedure but are very important throughout Southeast Asia. For example, a large number of Filipino maids work in Hong Kong and need to transfer their salaries back to the Philippines. Currently, the methods for cross-border transfers include cash, bank transfers or transfer by a remittance company. These traditional cross-border businesses involve many participants, different laws and regulations in each jurisdiction and exchange rate issues, so the process is very complex and it can take 10 minutes to several days to make a payment. AlipayHK's cross-border e-wallet remittance business can achieve real-time domestic transfers, provides customer service around the clock and is safe and transparent. Bangladesh has a similar demand for such a service. There are 10 million Bangladeshis working abroad and unofficial statistics suggest 15 billion Bangladeshi taka (US$177 million) are remitted through official channels. Overseas remittances are very expensive, so bKash strives to use block chain technology to make such transfers much faster, cheaper and more convenient.

Challenges and competition in Asia's payments market

There is fierce competition in the payments market in Southeast and South Asia, with China's Ant Financial and Tencent and Amazon and Google from the United States all actively expanding their services in the region. So far, however, no company has taken a dominant position. Driven by these multinational corporations, local fintech companies have also seen rapid development.

Ant Financial has established nine e-wallets through cooperation in Southeast Asia and invested in Lazada, the largest e-commerce company in the region. Supported by Tencent, Shopee has also grown rapidly in Southeast Asia. In addition to financial support, Chinese fintech companies send technical teams to local companies to help them develop. Apart from Chinese enterprises, Amazon, Google, WhatsApp and other US companies are actively gaining market share in Southeast and South Asia. In some countries, there is even competition between the QR-code standards adopted by Chinese-funded corporations and those adopted by US-funded firms.

Of course, the regulatory authorities of each country are more prudent about the foreign enterprises that carry out financial business in their jurisdiction and generally do not want them to hold all the market shares. Institutions such as Ant Financial, Tencent and LU.com are very successful in China and have a good reputation in the global market. Local regulatory authorities and fintech companies are willing to cooperate with these Chinese enterprises, but of course, most such companies carry out business in Southeast and South Asia through strategic shareholding, rather than controlling as major shareholders.

Attitudes and practices of financial regulation in Asia

The governments of Thailand, Singapore, India and Hong Kong take an open and inclusive attitude towards the monitoring and regulation of fintech. Of course, different governments have different motives. Thailand and India hope fintech can improve their financial efficiency and support the development of inclusive finance. Hong Kong and

Singapore, as international financial centres, are more concerned with how to maintain their leading edge and pay more attention to cross-border payments and other business. To promote the development of fintech, the Thai and Singaporean governments have formulated development plans and designated special departments and personnel for coordination and implementation. Both countries have also adopted the regulatory sandbox approach to support fintech innovation.

An official development plan provides one of the guarantees for the orderly development of the fintech industry. In August 2015, the Singaporean Government began a six-month study of fintech to investigate key issues such as whether it is helpful to Singapore's financial system and how much risk comes with it, after which it developed a fintech development program. The Government of Thailand organised the Ministry of Finance, its central bank and other departments to implement the multisector 'National Master Plan for E-Payment', promoted the PromptPay payment system and used the unified Thai standard QR-code to guide the development of the country's fintech industry.

To support innovation, Singapore and Thailand have introduced a regulatory sandbox to allow fintech companies to move beyond existing regulatory frameworks and conduct small-scale experiments. A regulatory sandbox can control major financial risks while also effectively supporting innovation. Of course, due to different national conditions, Singapore and Thailand took different approaches when implementing the regulatory sandbox.

Generally speaking, these governments want to create a regulatory environment suitable for fintech innovation, while paying attention to the risks fintech may bring.

Conclusion and prospects for regional digital connectivity

Common demand lays the basic foundation for digital connectivity in Asia and other regions. China has started to take the lead in mobile payments within the past 16 years and has made outstanding achievements in promoting the development of inclusive finance. However, fintech development in China is driven mainly by market demand and technological innovation. One basic fact in China is that the services provided by the traditional financial sector are insufficient, especially for small and microenterprises and low-income groups. And the credit card penetration rate in China is still less than 20 per cent.

A similar situation also exists in other developing Asian countries, where some problems are even more prominent—for example, before the availability of mobile payments, most migrant rural workers delivered remittances home informally though friends or bus drivers, which is an expensive approach and one that is fraught with delay and risk. The development of fintech can serve as an important complement to the traditional financial sector and is one that all developing countries need.

Regulatory authorities and fintech companies in Asia have shown a strong desire to cooperate with Chinese enterprises. The Monetary Authority of Singapore has welcomed China's fintech companies, including Ant Financial and Tencent, which have set up branches in Singapore. In many ways, financial technology and its development path are most suitable for developing countries. The regulatory authorities and fintech companies in countries including Thailand, India, Malaysia and Pakistan are actively exploring the possibility of business cooperation with Chinese companies.

While finance is among the most strictly regulated sectors and financial cooperation remains a sensitive issue for every country, business cooperation initiated by fintech companies seems to be much more successful and sustainable. Alipay has kept a relatively low profile in cooperating with overseas partners, by providing technology support and holding a relatively small share in enterprises.

More importantly, payment technology in China is relatively mature and is still developing rapidly. For example, Alipay's technological capacity has increased from about 200 transactions per second to more than 210,000 transactions per second. Chinese companies aim to work with local partners to provide payment systems that incorporate local technology, culture and policies. Through cooperation with Alipay, the number of users of Paytm in India increased dramatically, to more than 20 million within one year.

Moving forward, we think the following issues should be addressed properly: first, data. Who owns the data—individuals or big tech companies? Data are becoming an important resource, but the significance of consumer privacy should be highlighted as well.

Second is the problem of digital inequality, as many people do not have access to mobile payment services. Perhaps countries should adopt wider coverage of digital finance, education on inclusive finance and measures to create greater financial openness regarding access to mobile payments.

The third issue is financial risk. What are the right strategies for dealing with risk, including cyberattacks and the disintermediation of financial services? Digital finance can raise the risk of financial contagion without effective financial regulation—which brings us to the final issue. As big tech companies expand into financial services, building on mobile payments, how should these companies be regulated? How can we balance efficiency and stability? On the one hand, regulatory authorities should improve efficiency by transforming from an institution-based regulatory framework to functional regulation and adopting more advanced supervision technology. On the other hand, conduct regulation should be emphasised and strengthened to enhance the protection of financial consumers in China, probably by learning from the experience of Australia's 'twin-peak' regulatory framework (a combination of prudential and conduct regulation).

References

Guo, F., Wang, J.Y., Wang, F., Kong, T., Zhang, X. and Cheng, Z.Y. 2019. *Measuring China's digital financial inclusion: Index compilation and spatial characteristics*. Institute of Digital Finance Working Paper. Beijing: Peking University.

Hexun. 2018. '支付宝的15年—使命、泪水与成长？ [15 years of Alipay: Mission, tears and growth?].' *Hexun*, 12 November. Available from: news.hexun.com/2018-11-12/195185325.html.

Huang, Z., Shen, Y., Guo, F. and Huang, Y. 2019. *Digital finance supports high-quality economic development in China*. Institute of Digital Finance Working Paper. Beijing: Peking University.

Institute of Digital Finance. 2011–18. *Peking University Digital Financial Inclusion Index*. Beijing: Institute of Digital Finance, Peking University.

Klein, A. 2019. *Is China's New Payment System the Future?* Brookings Economic Studies. Washington, DC: Brookings Institution.

PBC, 2020. Report on the Overall Operation of the Payment System in China. People's Bank of China.

Wang, X. 2019. Mobile payment facilitates income? A perspective of entrepreneurial activity. Mimeo. Beijing: Institute of Digital Finance, Peking University.

Wang, X., Wang, X., Huang, Y. and Zheng, S. 2019. *Digital finance and risk sharing: Household-level evidence from China*. Institute of Digital Finance Working Paper. Beijing: Peking University.

7

The investment agenda

Christopher Findlay

Introduction

The purpose of this chapter is to examine the role of the international investment policy regime in facilitating foreign investment in Asia-Pacific countries, with attention to the delivery of connectivity services. It is argued there is a substantial agenda of work at the economy level but, in addition, there is a rich menu of additional options for regional cooperation to support these efforts.

The chapter proceeds as follows. The next section discusses key aspects of connectivity and its various dimensions. The origins of the demand for connectivity and some aspects of performance in the region are reviewed in the Introduction to this volume. The focus of this chapter is the supply side with respect to the provision of infrastructure. Various estimates are made of the difference, or gap, between the quantity demanded and that supplied. Some estimates of the scale of the 'gaps' are presented in the next section. The main interest here is the scope to mobilise private-sector investment to help fill these gaps.

To identify the impediments to private participation, the chapter concentrates on three sets of drivers of these gaps. One is the policy environment in which foreign investment decisions are made and, related to that, the processes of its implementation. The second set of drivers relates to risks in infrastructure projects. The third set are factors that, if attended to, have been demonstrated to raise the rate of return on infrastructure projects.

The first of the drivers of this apparent gap are the policy barriers to investment in infrastructure. This includes the policy regime affecting foreign investment, which is outlined in section three, with attention to its elements, which contribute to connectivity. There is in addition a discussion of the nature of investment facilitation and the contribution it can make, including the priorities for attention in the course of regional cooperation.

There are also substantial risks involved in the relevant projects, which add to the actual cost of finance and help explain the reticence of investors to participate. This, too, contributes to the apparent gap between projected investment demand and current levels of investment. Section four contains some talking points about these risks that are specific to investments related to connectivity, including the cooperation of private and public-sector investors, the treatment of security issues and the political economy of success.

The third set of factors are those that might raise the returns on investment. Topics of attention in this chapter in that respect are the importance of coordinating network designs and the role of complementary services-sector policies.

The conclusion of the chapter discusses the consequences for regional cooperation.

Spending and gaps

Closing the gaps identified in the Introduction chapter concerning connectivity performance in the region translates into large absolute amounts of investment. Elek and Findlay (2019) review the methodologies involved in estimating the scale of these gaps in investment. An example of this work is that of the Asian Development Bank (ADB 2017b), which includes estimates of the demand for infrastructure according to projections of various macroeconomic indicators. The result is a gap between likely demand and current spending levels, across the period 2016–20, of 2.4 per cent of GDP for all members (the value of the gap is US$459 billion per year). This is higher than earlier estimates because of an adjustment for climate change. When China is excluded from the country list, the gap rises to 5 per cent of GDP. The bulk of this relates to transport and telecommunications as well as power (ADB 2017a).[1]

The ADB (2017b) reports that currently 90 per cent of this investment is undertaken by the public sector. It also estimates that, with fiscal reforms, the member economies might close half the estimated gap, but the balance would have to be found by the private sector. Over the period 2016–20, a response by the private sector would involve an increase in spending from $63 billion a year to $250 billion a year.

The Organisation for Economic Co-operation and Development (OECD 2018: Ch. 3) examines the financing of transport infrastructure for connectivity. Its estimate is that, worldwide, US$315 billion a year is spent on this infrastructure in developing countries. Of that, governments finance about 80 per cent, the private sector 15 per cent and overseas development funding (ODF) about 5 per cent. The OECD estimate is that, to meet the United Nations' Sustainable Development Goals, this spending on transport must increase by US$440 billion a year. In 2014–15, most private-sector investment was in roads in upper middle-income countries and in Latin America. The OECD attributes the private sector's interest in roads to the capacity to earn revenue via toll fees. ODF is also spent on roads, but more so in lower-income economies. Airports are popular with private investors and railways and ports less so, so those activities have a higher share in ODF spending (OECD 2018: Fig. 3.2). A relatively small share of private-sector investment occurs in Asia. A small proportion (5 per cent) of ODF is applied directly to mobilise investment from the private sector (this does not include the provision of guarantees) but the amount mobilised is a tiny share of total expenditure.

Governments are already financing a high share of spending on infrastructure assets that support connectivity. The question is how private-sector funds, internally and from the rest of the world,[2] can be mobilised to fund socially valuable projects. There are examples of economies, such as Australia's, where such funds (for example, accumulated for retirement incomes) have been mobilised for long-term investment in infrastructure,

1   A small proportion applies to water and sanitation.
2   These might include funds publicly managed, such as public-sector retirement funds in high-income countries.

such as airports, ports and roads (Bowditch and Noble 2018). There appears to be space for the private sector to make this contribution, since the amount likely to be involved is small relative to the current and prospective volumes of funds under management.[3] There also appears to be an incentive to participate, given the rates of return on alternative investments and the prospective value in connectivity projects, according to the benefits identified earlier in this volume.

Investment policy and facilitation

Barriers to private-sector participation in infrastructure projects include matters of both policy on investment in relevant connectivity projects and the management of those policies. Reform of the former is a matter of the liberalisation of investment policy and the latter refers to investment facilitation. These are now discussed in that order.

Investment liberalisation

Investment in infrastructure, whether from foreign or domestic sources, tends to be regulated because of the concern that investors will accrue a significant degree of monopoly power if their project proceeds. There have also been concerns about access to the services of infrastructure, especially among residents in less densely settled areas or those with lower incomes. These efficiency and equity objectives have driven the forms of intervention, such as public provision. There are new approaches to these problems, which are discussed below.

Meanwhile, there are additional concerns in host economies about foreign investment in these sectors, including the transfer of profits offshore, the security of access to infrastructure at times of national emergency and protection of domestic providers of construction, management and operation services. These concerns have led to the imposition of a variety of specific policy measures related to foreign investors, such as:

- foreign equity limitations
- screening or approval mechanisms

---

3   Berger et al. (2019) quote an estimate of PWC that 'funds under management' will rise from US$100 trillion to US$145 trillion by 2025.

- restrictions on the employment of foreigners as key personnel
- operational restrictions—for example, restrictions on capital repatriation or landownership.

These are the elements of the OECD's Foreign Direct Investment (FDI) Regulatory Restrictiveness Index, and values of this index are reported in Table 7.1 for Asia-Pacific economies in the sectors of transport, communications and electricity. Scores range from zero to one, with higher scores indicating a more restrictive regime. The OECD average score is also shown and cells are shaded when the score exceeds the OECD average. The majority of cells are shaded—that is, these economies operate relatively restrictive regimes in these sectors. The main contributors to these scores are equity limitations and, in some cases, screening or approval systems. The first step in seeking to mobilise private funding— particularly now in communications—is to review these impediments. There is further discussion of this question in later sections.

Table 7.1 OECD FDI Regulatory Restrictiveness Index

Sector	Electricity	Transport	Communications
OECD members			
Australia	0.20	0.27	0.40
Canada	0.10	0.25	0.56
Japan	0.03	0.28	0.27
South Korea	0.42	0.51	0.33
Mexico	0.10	0.51	0.10
New Zealand	0.19	0.27	0.39
United States	0.20	0.55	0.11
OECD average	**0.12**	**0.21**	**0.08**
OECD non-members			
Cambodia	0.01	0.04	0.01
China	0.09	0.41	0.75
India	0.06	0.09	0.18
Indonesia	0.11	0.43	0.26
Lao PDR	0.16	0.23	0.08
Malaysia	0.50	0.30	0.38
Myanmar	0.01	0.01	0.01
Philippines	0.37	0.66	0.65
Vietnam	0.01	0.53	0.58

Source: OECD (n.d.).

Investment facilitation

Hamdani (2018: 1) says investment facilitation

> concerns the application of investment policy. It is not about the right to regulate or to formulate investment law. It is not about investment protection, policy liberalization or even investment promotion. Rather, it is a downstream activity that involves engagement with investors and other stakeholders in the application of policies in practice. Such interaction improves the efficiency and efficacy of the overall investment process. (p. 1)

Novik and de Crombrugghe (2018) explain that the notion of investment facilitation is related to that of trade facilitation, which concerns the design of procedures for trade. They also stress that investment facilitation (making it easier for investors to establish and operate) is a broader notion than investment promotion (which is about marketing an economy as an investment destination). Berger et al. (2019) say investment facilitation should concentrate on practical aspects and technical measures, such as improving transparency and predictability, streamlining procedures and enhancing coordination between agencies. It should not include 'controversial and polarizing areas of market access, investment protection and investor–state dispute settlement'. They say it 'should not be conceived in such a way that it restricts the policy space of national governments'. They also observe that the design of investment facilitation measures can draw on the experience of the development of ideas about and the success in developing agreements with respect to trade facilitation (Berger et al. 2019; see also Wu 2018).

The OECD says investment facilitation provides 'investors with a transparent, predictable and efficient regulatory and administrative framework' (Novik 2017). Examples of measures listed by the OECD include tools, policies and processes.

Tools:

- one-stop shop or single window for incoming investors
- online business registration system
- information portal on legal and administrative procedures to start a business
- client service charters for all authorities dealing with investors
- systematic 'aftercare' services for existing investors.

Policies:

- sound, transparent and consistent legal framework for investment
- regulatory measures to simplify/streamline administrative procedures
- policy measures to ensure investments are responsible and sustainable
- good governance laws and mechanisms.

Processes:

- public–private dialogue
- interagency coordination
- capacity-building for public officials
- monitoring and evaluation of existing tools, mechanisms and policies.

The OECD also points out that investment facilitation can be considered at several levels. First, there are actions that can be implemented by national governments; second, there are measures that can be included in trade and investment agreements; and third, there is scope to develop a multilateral agreement. There is an argument that the application of investment facilitation measures will improve the business environment for domestic investors as well (Berger et al. 2019). Japan is a leader in this respect, both in terms of inward FDI flows to Japan (JETRO 2018b) and in the treatment of the topic in regional trade agreements (METI 2010).

The World Trade Organization (WTO) has been working on investment facilitation in general, following the endorsement of that work program at its ministerial meeting in December 2017 by 70 members. Meetings of the 'Structured Discussions on Investment for Facilitation for Development' followed (from March 2018), to develop a multilateral framework on investment facilitation, involving about 100 members.[4] Berger et al. (2019) argue that middle-income countries are relatively more important in this work than in the overall WTO membership, with

---

4   Brazil has offered a draft of an agreement (accessed from: www.ictsd.org/bridges-news/bridges/news/brazil-circulates-proposal-for-wto-investment-facilitation-deal [page discontinued]). This includes clauses on national focal points, the use of a single electronic window for the submission of documents by foreign investors, establishing criteria and performance indicators for the processing of applications, setting up an appeal process and publishing all documents relevant to FDI projects. The draft reiterates the importance of the most-favoured nation application of the elements of the agreement and the 'right to regulate'.

fewer developing countries participating.[5] Opening a session in March 2019, then WTO director-general Roberto Azevêdo summarised progress to date by reporting that the focus was now on:

1. improving the transparency and predictability of investment measures
2. streamlining and speeding up administrative procedures and requirements
3. enhancing international cooperation, information-sharing and the exchange of best practices
4. exploring technical assistance and capacity-building support
5. looking at how this topic relates to other issues in the global economy— including, for example, the challenges faced by smaller businesses.

Work was to proceed by sharing examples in all these areas.

With respect to the WTO work program, Berger et al. (2019) call for more attention to the scope of investment facilitation and more empirical work on its impact (following the model of the approach to making the case for an agreement on trade facilitation). They suggest mapping domestic policies and procedures affecting facilitation. They also discuss how to engage more WTO members in the discussion (through the provision of capacity-building, adoption of the principle of special and differential treatment and confirmation of the right to regulate and pursue their own public policy goals) and how to make the discussions more transparent (by involving other stakeholders).

Berger et al. (2019) identify several actions that would facilitate investment, including a focus not just on the entry phase but also on the conditions after establishment. They argue that a good facilitation system will anticipate issues and thereby reduce the number of disputes. Other principles they endorse include the adoption of a whole-of-government approach in the host country, the engagement of source countries of FDI flows (noting those governments are beginning to issue guidelines for offshore investment), the application of any systems on a multilateral and most-favoured nation basis and the development of processes of capacity-building.

---

5   The United States is not a signatory, nor are India, Indonesia, the Philippines, Thailand and Vietnam.

The Asia-Pacific Economic Cooperation (APEC) forum also has a program of work related to investment facilitation (originally adopted by leaders in 2008). Its areas of focus are e-transparency, reducing investor risk and simplifying business regulation. Provisions related to investor risk include the opportunity for public comments on proposed changes to laws and regulations and establishing effective formal mechanisms for resolving disputes, while work on business regulation involves the use of single windows for investment matters (Bayhaqi and Crisologo-Hernando 2017).

Though strenuous efforts are made in these sorts of commentaries to separate facilitation and liberalisation, they are in fact connected. The complexities of the policies managing the processes of entry and operation determine the scope of the work on facilitation. Countries with screening processes, for example, will have more facilitation issues than those which do not. Investment liberalisation is a valuable complement to the facilitation of investment flows.

Risks in infrastructure projects

In this section, special features of investments associated with the provision of connectivity services are explored. These features, it will be argued, are linked to the perception of risk by investors in infrastructure projects, and these perceptions help explain the presence of an apparent gap between the expected and the actual investment flows in the sector.

Cooperation of public and private-sector investors

There are various ways in which private-sector[6] engagement can be arranged—one as a source of funding and the other in combinations of project design, building and operations. The latter is also linked to the former. Some forms are simple versions of public procurement—for example, a construction contract. Of more interest here are those that involve investment by the private sector in the larger, longer-lived and more complex projects related to the provision of connectivity services.

---

6   'Private' here means investors other than the government of the host country of the project, which could include sovereign wealth funds.

Infrastructure projects are complex and involve a series of stages (design, construction, ramping-up, operations), each of which entails a different type of risk. No one investor may be prepared to manage all those risks, and the participation of others creates the opportunity to allocate risk more efficiently. Investors may cover some risks related to decision-making outside their control only at a high cost, unless government provides some assurances. In this case, Arezki et al. (2016) suggest, for example, that risks associated with construction would sit with the private sector, risks associated with politics and regulation would sit with governments and demand risks might be shared. Private-sector firms might specialise in managing risks at different stages (for example, design versus construction). This allocation would translate into the forms of funding provided and the guarantees offered (for a discussion of the complexities involved in designing this allocation, see Arezki et al. 2016). The structure of funding would also account for the public good elements of a project. The allocations of responsibilities, financing and risks are the elements of public–private partnerships (P3s).[7]

Gurara et al. (2017) report that P3s in developing countries and emerging markets surged in the early 2010s but have since declined. They amount to about 0.4 per cent of GDP in both low-income developing countries and emerging market economies. Leading participants in Asia are Vietnam, Lao PDR and Bangladesh. In earlier periods, most P3s were in telecommunications, whereas that sector has generally moved to purely private provision. More popular now for P3s are electricity projects, and sometimes roads. Overall, the assessment of Arezki et al. (2016) is that the outcomes in terms of the use of P3s have been disappointing: the cost of capital has proved to be higher than expected relative to public funds, the public sector has borne more risk than expected and service quality expectations have not always been met. As noted earlier, the private sector (in all its forms of investment) contributes a minor share of total investment.

---

7   The World Bank (n.d.) provides information on options for P3s. Provision of funding for maintenance is often reported to be an issue in connectivity-related projects; when the constructor is the operator in the longer term, the P3 approach also helps manage the trade-offs between investment in better construction and later lower costs of maintenance.

The first suggestion by Gurara et al. (2017) to make progress on closing 'the investment gap' is to increase the productivity of public-sector management of infrastructure projects. They report considerable differences in 'investment efficiency' between countries, which they attribute to weaknesses in the institutions that manage public investment. They also report research that says that project productivity falls quickly with the number of projects under management, especially when that number accelerates above historical levels. They suggest, therefore, to not only look at the institutions involved in project management, but also schedule projects carefully. But, overall, Gurara et al. (2017: 18) say that, given its scale, 'tackling the infrastructure challenge [is] inconceivable without a significant increase in private sector participation'.

Gurara et al. (2017) go on to argue that critical to private-sector participation is the development of the regulatory and institutional framework. One measure of the quality of this framework, and of the capacity to deliver infrastructure projects, is the Infrascope Index developed by the Economist Intelligence Unit (EIU).[8] Table 7.2 shows the overall score for this index and those for two components: regulations and institutions. Other elements considered in the construction of the index are the extent of experience in engaging with the private sector, the business climate and the depth of local capital markets. The EIU (2018) concludes:

- Overall conditions are positive in the Asia-Pacific, with a high level of general interest in P3s, and with provisions available on selection criteria, conciliation and arbitration methods, and environmental assessments.

- Many economies have central government agencies for the purpose of engaging with the private sector but some could benefit from support in the design of systems and structures (based on the experience of others) to maintain the independence of those agencies and for the preparation of project proposals.

- There could also be improvements in transparency, arrangements for renegotiations and the treatment of unsolicited proposals, and interagency coordination.

---

8 The index is a 'benchmarking tool that evaluates the capacity of countries to implement sustainable and efficient public–private partnerships … in key infrastructure sectors'. The method involves scoring responses to a series of questions in different policy areas relevant to P3s (EIU 2019).

Table 7.2 Infrascope Index scores, 2018

Rank	Overall score	Score/100	Rank	1) Regulations	Score/100	Rank	2) Institutions	Score/100
1	Thailand	83	1	Thailand	87	1	Thailand	97
2	Philippines	81	2	Philippines	85	2	Sindh Province	95
3	China	80	3	Indonesia	78	=3	China	94
4	India	77	4	India	77	=3	India	94
5	Gujarat State	75	5	Sindh Province	74	=3	Philippines	94
6	Sindh Province	67	=6	China	70	6	Bangladesh	90
=7	Bangladesh	66	=6	Gujarat State	70	7	Pakistan	88
=7	Vietnam	66	8	Bangladesh	65	=8	Gujarat State	86
=9	Indonesia	61	9	Timor-Leste	64	=8	Kazakhstan	86
=9	Kyrgyz Republic	61	10	Kyrgyz Republic	63	10	Vietnam	84
=9	Pakistan	61	11	Vietnam	61	11	Kyrgyz Republic	82
12	Kazakhstan	58	12	Georgia	58	12	Timor-Leste	73
13	Mongolia	54	=13	Kazakhstan	54	13	Mongolia	71
14	Georgia	48	=13	Mongolia	54	14	Indonesia	53
=15	Armenia	45	15	Armenia	51	15	Tajikistan	43
=15	Sri Lanka	45	16	Pakistan	47	16	Sri Lanka	36
17	Timor-Leste	44	17	Tajikistan	43	17	Georgia	8
18	Tajikistan	41	18	Sri Lanka	30	18	Armenia	5
19	Papua New Guinea	28	19	Papua New Guinea	27	19	Papua New Guinea	0

Source: EIU (2019).

The top performers according to this index are Thailand, the Philippines, China and India.[9] Below them, Vietnam and Bangladesh are ranked together, and Indonesia follows that group, ranked equally with Pakistan. Performance by area varies by country, to which the EIU draws attention. The overall score is highly correlated with the national P3 amount (Gurara et al. 2017: Fig. 14) and with a measure of the quality of trade-related and transport-related infrastructure.

The OECD (2015) has produced a checklist for success in the application of P3s that includes:

- An investment regime that is clear and predictable.
- A good process for selecting projects eligible for private participation.
- Access to a wide set of sources of finance.
- Transparency and competition in the procurement regime.
- Better governance of state-owned enterprise partners in projects.
- Unbundling infrastructure systems to carve out those that are competitive and maintaining regulation of those that are not.

Infrastructure projects supporting connectivity could be funded out of current government spending or over time through payments by future taxpayers. They can also be funded by user charges, which are always controversial since there are arguments about whether all consumers will have access to services.[10] Historically, the response to this issue has been to maintain the service provision within the hands of a state-owned monopolist who cross-subsidises services. More efficient, however, is to split out the community service obligations (and other public good elements) as separate contracts, open markets to private providers and deal with any market power issues following unbundling through the operations of a regulator. The OECD (2015) therefore adds to its list:

- establishing an independent regulator
- aligning prices with costs
- identifying dedicated funds to finance universal service requirements.

---

9   See Llanto (2016) for discussion of the development of the P3 framework in the Philippines and the scope to improve by taking actions of the type listed by the EIU and from an OECD report referred to below.
10   As Arezki et al. (2016) point out, toll revenues are not always well accepted and, as the project proceeds, may reinforce the risk of a 'holdup' by government.

There will be challenges in moving towards this model of unbundling and private (including international) provision, even in monopolised components, combined with regulation and community service obligation funding. Political resistance to change in this direction will be one element—for example, based on the concern among citizens about the motivation of the service provider and a perception of their lack of attention to the interests of consumers.

Bowditch and Noble (2018) suggest that a complement to a reform program of this type is to adopt a set of principles related to 'customer stewardship'. This involves a deeper, more structured and continuing interaction with users of services. The outcome, they argue, will be a greater willingness to pay for services because of a better appreciation of the value being created. There should also be greater trust that funds raised in this way are invested in the social interest. This way of thinking also allows providers to 'go beyond the contract' and to design and offer innovative solutions to shifts in user demands, whereas static performance indicators will not produce this outcome. As noted earlier, over the lifespan of assets involved in the provision of connectivity services, the mix of services in demand in the full-cost framework is highly likely to change. The application of 5G technology creates an opportunity to renovate roads to make them 'smarter' (HighwaysIndustry 2019). Bowditch and Noble (2018) argue that infrastructure 'done well should be constantly evolving'.

Bowditch and Noble (2018) offer examples of mechanisms by which a commitment to customer stewardship could be implemented. One takes the form of a price regulator asking the regulated firm in its submission on pricing to explain how it has delivered value to its customers, the answer to which depends on the quality and depth of the interaction the firm has with its clients. Another is an 'app' provided by a toll-road business to allow clients to compare the options of using their services or not using them (via off-tollway roads), and hence the savings in full-cost terms from paying the toll. New reporting systems will be required for other forms of infrastructure that do not involve regular transactions related to their use, and where the value includes providing an option to the consumer or a contribution to a desirable attribute of the community. Bowditch and Noble (2018) propose that customer stewardship involves a commitment to connectedness (across services, discussed further in the next section), providing information to consumers to assist the revelation of their preferences (ideally involving schedules of prices and options of quality mixes), an ability to adapt over time and transparency. Operating in this manner, they reiterate, provides more business opportunities for the service provider than does retaining a fixed list of performance indicators for which boxes are ticked (or not).

Security issues

Given the scale of projects, the extent of their use and their longevity, there has always been a link between the provision of connectivity services and the security of the host economy. These services are critical to the continued operation of the economy when there is a conflict. They will also be elements of delivering support for the operations of defence forces around any conflict. Access to those services is therefore regarded as critical. This translates into a discussion about hosting relevant capacity— for example, cases in various economies have been made for the presence of an international airline ideally based in the home country, which at least can be commandeered if not also owned and operated by its citizens (Findlay 1985). Systems of protection of a 'national carrier' during normal circumstances were then justified to achieve that purpose.

The more modern version of this issue arises in the digital sector (Findlay 2019). For example, Chinese firm Huawei has high market shares in components of 5G telecommunications networks. While the firm is well regarded in its sector for its management and innovation, policy views differ, since Huawei has been involved in intellectual property disputes, allegations of breaking sanctions and of military associations, and of benefiting from government support. There is also concern about China's National Intelligence Law, which says: 'Any organisation and citizen shall, in accordance with the law, support, provide assistance, and cooperate in national intelligence work, and guard the secrecy of any national intelligence work that they are aware of.'

Many have therefore questioned the prudence of allowing Huawei to be involved in building 5G infrastructure. These commentators see risks of disruption, the consequences of which would be high given the likely ubiquity of the technology, or costs of abuse, such as siphoning off data. The United States has responded with bans related to imports of technology, which block the use of equipment from an adversary government. It also has added Huawei to its 'Entity List', which has the effect of banning exports to it and its affiliates.

At the time of writing, the outcome is not clear. This response could be a tactic by the United States to drive other outcomes, in which case the main consequence is the impact of uncertainty on the shape of supply chains. These will be chains linked to equipment, devices and services that are critical to connectivity. In a worst-case outcome, the world would divide into spheres of influence associated with different telecommunications standards. Connectivity would be high within but not between these spheres.

The most efficient solution, on the other hand, is to identify the risks and to cooperate on the design of regulatory or business responses to those risks. At the same time, it will be important to align those responses across economies to facilitate investment and trade (including data) flows. This is a matter for at least regional cooperation, the outcome of which can feed into global strategy.

Political economy of success

Large-scale provision of connectivity services is significant in the economy and, because of their scale, they can have important effects on its structure and on the location of activities. One effect is the diffusion of economic activity—that is, in the presence of 'fixed factor endowments, the increased access to markets and ideas should benefit all regions' (Banerjee et al. 2012). But, as Banerjee et al. (2012: 2) also explain, the fall in trade costs can have consequences in the opposite direction:

> [T]ransportation infrastructure increases the access of rural regions to cities, and the well-known agglomeration effects of cities may cause productive capital and skilled labor to move from rural regions to cities over time, with the result that those who remain in rural areas receive very limited benefits from urbanization or even become impoverished. Along similar lines, it has been argued that the expansion of motor road networks in the United States promoted large-scale suburbanization and left many cities without a viable economic model. (p. 2)

The importance of these effects has been examined in a series of papers about the impact of high-speed rail in China (which is mainly applied to the movement of people). Ke et al. (2017) find that the gains are concentrated in existing transport hubs that are connected to the new network. Yu et al. (2019) find that high-speed rail connections to metropolitan centres lead to reductions in GDP in peripheral but also connected prefectures, compared with unconnected prefectures, as a result of reductions in both productivity and capital inputs. This result is interesting in the context of neighbouring prefectures 'fighting one another for a station along the HSR [high-speed rail] line' in the design phase (Yu et al. 2019: 18). Other studies, in Japan, find different effects of high-speed rail by sector, with the service sector concentrated in urban areas and manufacturing moved to nearby areas (within 150 kilometres) where employment increased, while those areas further out declined in terms of employment (Li and Xu 2018).

Connectivity projects, given their scale, also face constraints on their location. For example, in China, most high-speed rail stations are built in suburbs, given the costs of land and of disruption in downtown areas. The consequences of their establishment on local economies and therefore the value of local fixed inputs like land can be significant. These effects then offer opportunities for the financing of the provision of these services, since their value is capitalised into the value of land in the vicinity of the major nodes in the network. When the service provider can capture that increment in value, they can finance the project (raise and repay debt, for example, or earn a return on their own equity) and do so much sooner than via a long stream of ticket revenue. Arezki et al. (2016) point to the example of the Hong Kong Mass Transit Railway (MTR), which is run by the MTR Corporation and is partly publicly owned. The corporation is also a landowner and the value of its landholdings appreciates as the network extends. The change in value that is captured by the corporation helps fund the extension of the system (Kembrey 2015).[11] Success here, however, depends on the competitiveness of the corporation as a land developer and access to land at the 'pre-rail' price.

Yet, as explained, the completion of connectivity projects also has the effect of shifting economic activity and most likely diminishing the value of assets held elsewhere and/or imposing costs of adjustment on members of the peripheral community who relocate. The response could be a political one, anticipating and resisting change in the first place or demanding other forms of compensation later.

---

11 The value increment can be captured in other ways. See City of Chicago (2010–21) for a discussion of tax increment financing, based on increases in property values.

Raising the returns on infrastructure investment

Some activities can be undertaken that, when successful, will add to the returns on infrastructure investment, thereby increasing the interest of private investors in such projects.

Coordinating network design

Connectivity involves a bundle of services. Consider the output of a factory moving goods to a customer at some distance. Mostly likely this will involve a road journey at each end as well as a longer journey by another mode in between. The physical movement will also be complemented by flows of data and finance, and possibly also by the movement of people (either during the setup of the transactions or in servicing them). As Bowditch and Noble (2018: 52) say:

> Infrastructure is part of a system, and should be managed to give maximum efficacy to that system. Having a great airport or even a very fast rail corridor means little if the adjacent road and rail systems fail to connect with and work coherently with it. To have quality infrastructure, its connectedness is much more than just being physical, but also coordinated and integrated in its functions and values.

Those involved in managing connectivity will certainly take this multipart view: they will examine the full cost of the movement. They will not look at the road segment separately from others. They will also consider the coordination of the data flow with the movement of goods; indeed, they will expect to be able to monitor the good and its condition as it moves within the physical infrastructure. The adoption of standards that facilitate interoperability (from data devices to container sizes) is also important. In the private sector, the boundaries of the connectivity services business (or the alliances it creates), and what packages to put together to provide a perspective that the consumer values, will have to be considered.

The value of connectivity across systems has implications for the public and private sectors. A considerable amount of planning is valuable to produce the right project portfolio. No one person will be able to imagine all these options and there is value in using a market process in this context. This would involve a mechanism to accept unsolicited proposals from the market, not just as a result of tenders or requests for proposals.

Arezki et al. (2016) observe that the ability to raise finance for any one project depends on a whole network and the connectivity between its elements, as well as its density. They also argue that it would be valuable to bring in private investors who have a bundle of infrastructure assets at an early stage in the planning process. This is because they have a better idea of what a whole infrastructure network should look like. Furthermore, they argue that most P3s are now conceived at the national level, which does not take account of the externalities involved across borders. They argue that a role for the development banks is to facilitate the cooperation across governments and the participation of private investors in this way. An example is the work of the ADB in the Greater Mekong Subregion (ADB 2018).

The Belt and Road Initiative (BRI) illustrates the orders of magnitude involved. De Soyres et al. (2018) report that, within the BRI, trade costs will fall by an average of 3.5 per cent across bilateral pairs among the 71 members. But costs will also fall by 2.8 per cent, on average, in their trade with the rest of the world. Third parties also benefit from access to BRI infrastructure in their own bilateral transactions not involving BRI members. The average decrease worldwide (191 countries) in trade costs is 2.2 per cent. These are significant impacts, which is not unexpected given the number of members of the BRI and its geographic coverage. But de Soyres et al. (2018) also make the point of the significance of the spillovers involved in connectivity projects and the value of working to internalise them.

Complementary services

As is already evident, the successful operation of a network of providers of connectivity services will depend on access to such services. The performance of both public (for example, movements across borders) and private (for example, competition in the transport sector) providers matters. Several papers observe that not only the physical infrastructure, but also the quality of institutions matter. An example is the result of Francois and Manchin (2007)—who measure institutional quality by various characteristics of governance—that these variables affect both the levels of exports and the participation in exporting. Brooks (2016) stresses the importance of access to world-class logistics services, especially as the composition of trade changes.

The World Bank makes this point in relation to the BRI. De Soyres et al. (2018) argue that the benefits in terms of transit times and trade costs will only be captured if policy issues are also tackled—for example, border crossing and trade facilitation, logistics services ('weak links') as well as FDI regimes.[12] Baniya et al. (2019) examine the effects of a series of interventions proposed in the BRI on 71 participating economies. They find that these projects reduce trade times by up to 4.4 per cent. When in addition there are improvements in trade facilitation, trade times fall by up to 10.9 per cent. The positive effects of the BRI projects, they say, are magnified by the trade facilitation reforms. The effect on trade is growth of more than 7 per cent, which rises to 13 per cent when these changes are complemented by trade agreements that improve market access.

The provision of competitive complementary services therefore leverages the benefits created by good connectivity projects. Another way of saying this is to observe the fact that failure to liberalise these complementary services would allow the benefits created to be captured by service providers or wasted by inefficient government processes.

Conclusion

Projects designed to deliver connectivity services are highly prospective, since they offer significant reductions in the costs of the movement of goods, people and data, with subsequent benefits in terms of the costs of movements, trade flows, investment flows, productivity, growth and equity. Governments have been the major providers of funds for connectivity investment (of the order of 85 per cent); however, they face financial and human resource constraints on making further investments. Instead, the question is asked: what greater role can the private sector play in connectivity projects in the economies of the Asia-Pacific, including investors from offshore? If at least some part of the likely significant benefits can be captured, the projects become more 'bankable' and of more interest to the private sector. However, these sorts of projects are not easy to implement because of three sets of factors identified here: 1) policy barriers to investment, 2) risks associated with infrastructure projects because they are big, specific and long lived, and 3) loss of the opportunity to capture extra benefits through the management of networks or the

---

12   For further commentary on these policy issues, see the discussion in World Bank (2018).

provision of complementary policy change. Barriers to investment flows in general are an important element to consider, along with action to facilitate those flows. But of more interest here are the special conditions related to investment projects in infrastructure that facilitate connectivity.

With respect to the risks involved, the interest is not just in the scale of investment likely to be involved in providing connectivity services, but also in the lumpiness of these projects (such as a highway, a port, an airport). This situation incurs the risk of the abuse of monopoly power, which also draws the attention of governments and their regulators. Projects will in that case involve the interaction of investors with regulators, whose decisions have a significant effect on profitability. Technological change can, however, shift the significance of this aspect, as has occurred in the case of telecommunications.

There are also concerns about the consequences of connectivity projects for various user groups. The traditional concern was the provision of services to low-income or isolated areas. In addition, since these projects are large in scale, they can shift the location of economic activity and change values of assets such as land in participating locations, which offer financing opportunities. They also have significant redistributive effects within economies, which can trigger political reactions in anticipation of (thereby retarding), or because of, projects. The latter becomes of source of risk from the investor's point of view, depending on the government response to that reaction, including the scope to renege on previous commitments related to pricing, for example.

The scale of connectivity projects offers access to significant benefits, but it also exposes the host community to new risks. The impact of a disruption of a facility once constructed would have significant impacts on the economy. This is the security risk. This concern was always present, especially when the provision of services involved cross-border operations (as in aviation). With technological change and access to digital technology, it is becoming more evident in relation to modern telecommunications infrastructure. The concern is that foreign governments not only can 'cut off' services, but also can now 'reach in' to disrupt or capture them.

These projects are specific, since a facility built in one location need not be suitable for another. Consequently, implementation involves upfront work, conceiving of the project and then developing details, even before the case for execution can be made clear and finance is arranged. This early stage demands significant human capital but also involves significant risks, which crystallise when a project does not proceed. Private-sector firms may have the capacity for project planning and access to international providers will offer a wider range of experiences, but the allocation of the risks involved will have to be clear if they are to participate.

Connectivity projects are long lived and, across the course of their lives, many conditions may change. Technology may change, shifting the way an existing facility might be managed (for example, the application of the Internet of Things to roads). Technological change can also shift the demand for connectivity services (for example, the growth of air freight relative to road or sea). The distribution of the costs and benefits of adjustment will affect the initial willingness of various parties to invest or, in other words, the efficiency of the distribution of risks associated with these changes should be considered upfront. A long-lived project is open to the risk of a government 'holdup' (driven perhaps by the consequences of projects for different interest groups), the risk of which will also deter private investors.

Finally, greater benefits are achieved when the complementarity between projects is recognised (such as data flow alongside goods movements) and the value of networking within and across countries is appreciated. Projects created in isolation of these considerations are likely to incur later add-on costs to capture the opportunities from better networking that become clear in hindsight. Failure to introduce reforms that facilitate the use of the infrastructure also involves lost opportunities and lesser returns than others to investment.

This is a significant bundle of issues for any national government to resolve to attract private investment. It is not surprising, then, that assessments by bodies like the OECD, the ADB and the International Monetary Fund indicate a big gap between the number of projects in the region that are likely to be socially valuable and those that are implemented. This draws attention to the ways in which investment flows might be facilitated.

There is a substantial conversation in progress about international investment facilitation in general. That conversation, including efforts in the WTO and APEC, as well as coverage of these issues in trade agreements, is relevant to projects related to connectivity. These include efforts to add to the transparency and consistency of policymaking in relation to international investment. But the characteristics just listed demand an additional layer of effort to deal with the issues that arise in connectivity projects. The issues to be managed include the following, which comprise the 'investment facilitation plus' agenda for connectivity projects—that is:

- Organising the funding of work on and access to human capital for the development phase of projects, including attention to the productivity of government agencies involved in this work and the scope to engage the private sector.

- Paying strict attention to the economic benefits of projects and thereby the ability to repay borrowed or invested funds, and to good practice in procurement that produces projects at least cost.

- Building consensus on the value of projects to user communities (for example, adopting the 'customer stewardship' model), enhancing their willingness to pay for projects and hence their 'bankability'.

- Achieving consistency over time in the operations of regulatory systems and giving attention to efforts to unbundle elements of the services chain that are competitive, especially as technology changes.

- Meeting obligations for universal services but also funding them directly and transparently.

- Recognising the risks of government holdup on long-lived projects and making commitments to manage that risk.

- Anticipating a distribution of the costs and benefits of adjusting to technological change, not only with respect to the facility itself, but also to its users, and how that changes their demands for services.

- Realising an efficient (least trade-distorting) approach to the treatment of security issues and the participation of foreign input providers.

- Maintaining a diverse set of sources of finance for projects, being clear about risks borne by the holders of different securities and checking the efficiency of the distribution of those risks among the parties.

- Paying attention to policy applying to complementary service providers, ensuring that restrictions in those policy regimes are not limiting the benefits created from connectivity projects or diverting those benefits to specific service providers.

Cooperation across borders is valuable in this context. In the first instance, there is value in learning from the experience of others in responding to these issues,[13] but there are aspects in which additional and more specific

---

13   APEC (2018) has produced a guidebook on infrastructure investment that is an example of this level of capacity-building.

cooperation is useful. For example, cooperation—between agencies with economies and across borders—that introduces the perspective of global and regional networks in project design and selection, and which drives an outcome to capture its benefits, will be valuable. The ADB provides examples of this form of cooperation.

New models of cooperation have been suggested. For example, Arezki et al. (2016) discuss the role of an international platform that would facilitate private-sector investment. The managers of this platform are acting as an intermediary (or 'making the market') between governments and investors. A third party in the form of a development bank could play that key role in this platform.[14] The services provided might be project design. Development banks can also contribute to the enforcement of contracts—for example, using their leverage to 'tame opportunistic' governments. Governments could also bring to the table their interest in greenfield projects; according to recent history, there has been a lack of interest by private investors in these compared with already operating projects, yet they are the projects 'at the margin' where significant benefits are to be captured. Allowing many projects to compete on a single platform reduces the risk that governments will 'pick winners' and make the wrong selection.[15] Private investors would bring to the market a requirement for projects to be economically sound, access to funds and their various forms of expertise. The key feature of these platforms is the engagement of the private sector at their foundation.

A further development on these platforms might be greater consistency among or standardisation of projects, which would aid the application of securitisation methods to raise funding. Arezki et al. (2016) argue that progress in this respect provides advantages of diversification for investors, a lower cost of capital and higher liquidity.

This is an interesting suggestion for a mode of cooperation and the chapter concludes with observations about a number of questions that it prompts.

---

14   Arezki et al. (2016) observe that an advantage of the Asia Infrastructure Investment Bank (AIIB) is that it is a specialist infrastructure bank that could play the role of a development bank on the sort of platform they envisage. This includes the ability to fund larger projects and to coordinate across networks, adding to the 'bankability' of individual projects. It is a topic for further work of how much the AIIB is contributing or could contribute to the other items on the checklist of the 'investment facilitation plus' agenda.

15   An often-cited example is the government-promoted investment in railroads in the United States and the assessment by Fogel (1962) of the small increment in GDP compared with an extension of the canal system that might otherwise have occurred.

The first set concerns its direction and management. First, what is the ultimate goal—or vision of the outcome—of this cooperation? Some guidance might be, for example, taken from the goals of the ASEAN Master Plan on Connectivity (see Box 1 in the Introduction to this volume) to achieve a 'seamlessly and comprehensively connected and integrated region'. Were this platform to be built in the East Asian region, its success is more likely when it has a clear set of 'owners'—that is, those creating the expectations of outcomes, setting targets, receiving reports of progress and then responding. An obvious set of owners meeting these capacities are ministers from regional economies, involving ASEAN at least, with relevant responsibilities.

Second, further work would also be required on how this platform interacted with other forms of cooperation. There would be interaction with the BRI (see Chapter 2 in this volume) to consider, as well as the work in ASEAN on connectivity, as already mentioned. Other forms include the work by China and Japan to promote their cooperation in third countries, according to the principles of openness, transparency, economic viability and fiscal sustainability.[16] The United States and partners Japan and Australia, building on cooperation among development banks including those of Singapore, Canada and the European Union, have formed the Blue Dot Network (US Department of State 2019: 16). Its purpose appears to be to facilitate investment via the certification that best practices have been adopted in particular infrastructure projects.[17]

Third, there is a concern that the platform model may be difficult to scale up, which is important given the orders of magnitude involved in the investment 'gap'. Access to human capital is one issue, and Arezki et al. (2016) discuss how the private sector might also contribute to resolving that constraint. Compensation for inputs to the design of projects that do not proceed has to be considered; Elek (2018) points to a private-sector organisation that provides these services.[18]

---

16   See, for example, JETRO (2018a) and MOFCOM (2018).
17   McCawley (2019) provides a commentary on this initiative, including questions about the manner of its operation.
18   See InfraCo Asia's website at: infracoasia.com.

References

Arezki, M.R., Bolton, P., Peters, S., Samama, F. and Stiglitz, J. 2016. *From global savings glut to financing infrastructure: The advent of investment platforms*. IMF Working Paper 16/18. Washington, DC: International Monetary Fund. doi.org/10.5089/9781475591835.001.

Asian Development Bank (ADB). 2017a. 'How much should Asia spend on infrastructure?' *News*, 28 February. Manila: ADB. Available from: www.adb.org/news/features/how-much-should-asia-spend-infrastructure.

Asian Development Bank (ADB). 2017b. *Meeting Asia's Infrastructure Needs*. Manila: ADB.

Asian Development Bank (ADB). 2018. *The Ha Noi Action Plan 2018–2022*. Manila: ADB. Available from: www.adb.org/sites/default/files/institutional-document/409086/ha-noi-action-plan-2018-2022.pdf.

Asia-Pacific Economic Cooperation (APEC). 2018. *APEC Guidebook on Quality of Infrastructure Development and Investment (Revision)*. Committee on Trade and Investment. Singapore: APEC Secretariat. Available from: mddb.apec.org/Documents/2018/SOM/CSOM/18_csom_014app11.pdf.

Banerjee, A., Duflo, E. and Qian, N. 2012. 'On the road: Access to transportation infrastructure and economic growth in China.' *Journal of Development Economics* 145: 102442. doi.org/10.1016/j.jdeveco.2020.102442.

Baniya, S., Gaffurri, R., Patrizia, N. and Ruta, M. 2019. *Trade effects of the New Silk Road: A gravity analysis*. Policy Research Working Paper No. WPS8694. Washington, DC: World Bank Group. doi.org/10.1596/1813-9450-8694.

Bayhaqi, A. and Crisologo-Hernando, R. 2017. 'Investment facilitation in APEC.' *News*. Melbourne: RMIT. Available from: www.rmit.edu.au/news/all-news/2017/local-news/investment-facilitation-in-apec.

Berger, A., Gsell, S. and Olekseyuk, Z. 2019. *Investment facilitation for development: A new route to global investment governance*. Briefing Paper 5/2019. Bonn: German Development Institute. Available from: www.die-gdi.de/briefing-paper/article/investment-facilitation-for-development-a-new-route-to-global-investment-governance.

Berger, A., Ghouri, A., Ishikawa, T., Sauvant, K. and Stephenson, M. 2019. *Towards G20 guiding principles on investment facilitation for sustainable development*. Policy Brief. Tokyo: T-20 Secretariat. doi.org/10.2139/ssrn.3352630.

Bowditch, G. and Noble, G. 2018. *Customer stewardship: Infrastructure's missing link*. Policy Outlook Paper No. 5. Sydney: John Grill Centre for Project Leadership, University of Sydney.

Brooks, D.H. 2016. 'Connectivity in East Asia.' *Asian Economic Policy Review* 11(2): 176–94. doi.org/10.1111/aepr.12132.

City of Chicago. 2010–21. *Tax Increment Financing Program*. Chicago: City of Chicago. Available from: www.chicago.gov/city/en/depts/dcd/supp_info/tax_increment_financingprogram.html.

de Soyres, F.M.M.R., Mulabdic, A., Murray, S., Gaffurri, R., Patrizia, N. and Ruta, M. 2018. *How much will the Belt and Road Initiative reduce trade costs? (English)*. Policy Research Working Paper No. WPS8614. Washington, DC: World Bank Group. doi.org/10.1596/1813-9450-8614.

Economist Intelligence Unit (EIU). 2018. *Evaluating the Environment for Public–Private Partnerships in Asia: The 2018 Infrascope*. London: The Economist Group.

Economist Intelligence Unit (EIU). 2019. *Infrascope Index*. London: The Economist Group. Available from: infrascope.eiu.com.

Elek, A. 2018. 'Gaps in Asia's economic infrastructure.' *East Asia Forum*, 13 February.

Elek, A. and Findlay, C.C. 2019. 'Investment in connectivity.' In F. Kimura, M. Pangestu, S. Thangavelu and C. Findlay (eds), *Handbook of East Asian Integration*. Cheltenham, UK: Edward Elgar.

Findlay, C.C. 1985. *The Flying Kangaroo, An Endangered Species? An economic perspective of Australian international civil aviation policy*. Sydney: Allen & Unwin.

Findlay, C.C. 2019. 'Can cooperation prevent the descent of a digital Iron Curtain?' *East Asia Forum*, 27 October. Available from: www.eastasiaforum.org/2019/10/27/can-cooperation-prevent-the-descent-of-a-digital-iron-curtain.

Fogel, R. 1962. 'A quantitative approach to the study of railroads in American economic growth: A report of some preliminary findings.' *Journal of Economic History* 22(2): 163–97. doi.org/10.1017/S0022050700062719.

Francois, J. and Manchin, M. 2007. *Institutions, infrastructure, and trade*. Policy Research Working Paper No. 4152, March. Washington, DC: World Bank Group. doi.org/10.1596/1813-9450-4152.

Fugazza, M. and Hoffmann, J. 2017. 'Liner shipping connectivity as determinant of trade.' *Journal of Shipping and Trade* 2(1): 1. doi.org/10.1186/s41072-017-0019-5.

Gurara, D., Klyuev, M.V., Mwase, M., Presbitero, A., Xu, X.C. and Bannister, M.G.J. 2017. *Trends and challenges in infrastructure investment in low-income developing countries.* IMF Working Paper 17/233. Washington, DC: International Monetary Fund. doi.org/10.5089/9781484324837.001.

Hamdani, K. 2018. 'Investment facilitation at the WTO is not investment redux.' *Columbia FDI Perspectives* (226)(May).

HighwaysIndustry. 2019. 'Why 5G smart roads are the future of transport.' *HighwaysIndustry.com*, 18 June. Available from: www.highwaysindustry.com/why-5g-smart-roads-are-the-future-of-transport.

Japan External Trade Organization (JETRO). 2018a. 1st Japan–China Third Country Market Cooperation Forum. October, Tokyo. Available from: www.jetro.go.jp/en/jetro/topics/2018/1810_topics11.

Japan External Trade Organization (JETRO). 2018b. *JETRO Invest Japan Report 2018.* Tokyo: JETRO. Available from: www.jetro.go.jp/ext_images/invest/ijre/report2018/pdf/jetro_invest_japan_report_2018en_rev.pdf.

Ke, X., Chen, H., Hong, Y. and Hsiao, C. 2017. 'Do China's high-speed-rail projects promote local economy? New evidence from a panel data approach.' *China Economic Review* 44: 203–26. doi.org/10.1016/j.chieco.2017.02.008.

Kembrey, M. 2015. 'Hong Kong metro system operators MTR spread "value capture" message to Australia.' *Sydney Morning Herald*, 18 December. Available from: www.smh.com.au/national/hong-kong-metro-system-operators-mtr-spread-value-capture-message-to-australia-20151215-glo0wq.html.

Li, Z. and Xu, H. 2018. 'High-speed railroads and economic geography: Evidence from Japan.' *Journal of Regional Science* 58(4): 705–27. doi.org/10.1111/jors.12384.

Llanto, G.M. 2016. 'Philippine infrastructure and connectivity: Challenges and reforms.' *Asian Economic Policy Review* 11(2): 243–61. doi.org/10.1111/aepr.12141.

McCawley, P. 2019. 'Connecting the dots on the Blue Dot Network.' *The Interpreter*, 12 November. Available from: www.lowyinstitute.org/the-interpreter/connecting-dots-blue-dot-network.

Ministry of Commerce (MOFCOM). 2018. 'The First China–Japan Third-Party Market Cooperation Forum held in Beijing.' Press release, 28 October. Beijing: MOFCOM. Available from: english.mofcom.gov.cn/article/news release/significantnews/201810/20181002801052.shtml.

Ministry of Economy, Trade and Industry (METI). 2010. 'Part III Chapter 8: Settlement of disputes between states, improvement of business environment.' In *2010 Report on Compliance by Major Trading Partners with Trade Agreements: WTO, FTAs/EPAs, BITs*. Tokyo: METI. Available from: www.meti.go.jp/english/report/data/gCT2010coe.html.

Novik, A. 2017. Investment facilitation: National or international? Presentation, 20 March, Geneva. Available from: www.wto.org/english/forums_e/business _e/ana_novik_oecd.pdf.

Novik, A. and de Crombrugghe, A. 2018. 'Towards an international framework for investment facilitation.' *Investment Insights*, April. Paris: OECD Publishing. Available from: www.oecd.org/investment/Towards-an-international-framework-for-investment-facilitation.pdf.

Organisation for Economic Co-operation and Development (OECD). n.d. *FDI Regulatory Restrictiveness Index*. Paris: OECD. Available from: www.oecd.org/investment/fdiindex.htm.

Organisation for Economic Co-operation and Development (OECD). 2015. *Fostering Investment in Infrastructure: Lessons learned from OECD investment policy reviews*. Paris: OECD Publishing.

Organisation for Economic Co-operation and Development (OECD). 2018. *Enhancing Connectivity through Transport Infrastructure: The role of official development finance and private investment*. The Development Dimension series. Paris: OECD Publishing. doi.org/10.1787/9789264304505-en.

United States Department of State. 2019. *A Free and Open Indo-Pacific: Advancing a shared vision*. 4 November. Washington, DC: Department of State. Available from: www.state.gov/wp-content/uploads/2019/11/Free-and-Open-Indo-Pacific-4Nov2019.pdf.

World Bank. n.d. 'About public–private partnerships.' *Public–Private-Partnership Legal Resource Center*. Washington, DC: World Bank Group. Available from: ppp.worldbank.org/public-private-partnership/about-public-private-partnerships.

World Bank. 2018. *Belt and Road Initiative*. Brief, 29 March. Washington, DC: World Bank Group. Available from: www.worldbank.org/en/topic/regional-integration/brief/belt-and-road-initiative.

Wu, H. 2018. *Trade Facilitation in the Multilateral Trading System: Genesis, course and accord.* London: Routledge. doi.org/10.4324/9780429468148.

Yu, F., Lin, F., Tang, Y. and Zhong, C. 2019. 'High-speed railway to success? The effects of high-speed rail connection on regional economic development in China.' *Journal of Regional Science* 59(4): 723–42. doi.org/10.1111/jors.12420.

www.ingramcontent.com/pod-product-compliance
Lightning Source LLC
Chambersburg PA
CBHW042319210326
41599CB00048B/7160